# Bible Studies
## Daniel
## Revelation

**Third Edition**

James Malm

**ISBN: 978-1-989208-09-0**
Copyright © 2018 James David Malm
All Rights Reserved

All Scriptures Quoted
Are from the King James Version

# Dedication

*This work is dedicated to the Great God whose house is eternity; the Father and Sovereign of all that exists and the sum of all Truth, Wisdom, Love, Justice and Mercy.*
*May God's house be filled with children whose chief joy is to be like Him!*

## Table of Contents

### Daniel ... 7

- Introduction ... 8
- Daniel 1 ... 11
- Daniel 2 ... 14
- Daniel 3 ... 22
- Daniel 4 ... 29
- Daniel 7 ... 36
- Daniel 8: The 2,300 Day Prophecy ... 44
- Daniel 5 ... 56
- Daniel 10 ... 63
- Daniel 11 ... 68
- Daniel 12 ... 87
- Daniel 9: Dating the Ministry of Jesus Christ! ... 97
- Daniel 9: The 70th Week ... 113
- Daniel 6 ... 125

### Revelation ... 135

- Revelation 1 ... 136
- Revelation 2 ... 144
- Revelation 3 ... 159
- Matthew 23 ... 171
- Revelation 4 ... 182
- Revelation 5 ... 186
- Revelation 6 ... 190
- Revelation 7 and 14; The 144,000 ... 197
- Revelation 8 ... 206
- Revelation 9 ... 210
- Revelation 10 ... 216
- Revelation 11; God's Two Witnesses ... 224
- Revelation 12 ... 235
- Revelation 13 ... 248
- Revelation 15 ... 258
- Revelation 16 ... 262

Revelation 17..........................................................................................268
Revelation 18..........................................................................................280
Revelation 19..........................................................................................286
Revelation 20..........................................................................................289
Revelation 21..........................................................................................293
Revelation 22..........................................................................................298

# Daniel

## Introduction

The people who organized the book of Daniel have placed the various prophecies in the wrong order.

Daniel himself tells us this when he dates his prophecies by the reigns of various kings. For example, we know that Belshazzar was the son [descendant] of Nebuchadnezzar, actually his grandson; and we know that Cyrus the Persian became ruler of the Persian Empire after Belshazzar; and Darius the Mede became ruler of the Persian Empire after Cyrus' son Cambyses 2.

Daniel specifically dates his writings by the regnal years of the various kings. In spite of that the organizers of chapters and verses have mixed up the prophecies given to Daniel from their proper sequence. It may be helpful in the understanding by reading them in the proper order in which they were given to Daniel.

I will provide the various prophecies in their proper order as recorded by Daniel, while maintaining the given chapter identifications for easier reference, which order is the chapters given during the reigns of: Nebuchadnezzar (Dan 1, 2, 3, 4: Belshazzar Dan 7, 8, 5: Cyrus Dan 10, 11, 12) and Darius Dan 9, 6.

wiki **Daniel** (Hebrew: דָּנִיֵּאל, Modern *Daniyyel* Tiberian *Dāniyyêl* ; Arabic: دانيال, Meaning "God is my Judge")

In the third year of the reign of Jehoiakim (c. 605 BC), Daniel and his friends Hananiah, Mishael, and Azariah were among the young Jewish nobility sent to Babylon. The four were chosen for their intellect and beauty to be trained as advisers to the Babylonian court (Daniel 1). Daniel was given the name Belteshazzar, i.e. prince of Bel or Bel protect the king, not to be confused with the neo-Babylonian king Belshazzar. Hananiah, Mishael, and Azariah were given the Babylonian names Shadrach, Meshach, and Abednego respectively.

One might initially think that these men were being taken captive because of some sin when quite the contrary, they were sent to Babylon to be set up in high authority as men of considerable administrative skill.

It would appear that God was removing these faithful men from that wicked city, Jerusalem, BEFORE the terrible war, siege and famine which a few years later destroyed so many of the wicked.

**A brief history of the Babylonian sieges of Jerusalem**

Daniel was taken to Babylon with a small number of the elite from Jerusalem in c 605-604 BC.

In 605 BC Nebuchadnezzar II, king of Babylon defeated Pharaoh Necho at the Battle of Carchemish, and subsequently invaded Judah. To avoid the destruction of Jerusalem, King Jehoiakim of Jerusalem, in his third year, changed allegiances from Egypt to Babylon.

Judah then made an alliance with Babylon and paid tribute from the treasury in Jerusalem, giving Babylon some temple artifacts, and sent some of the royal family and nobility [inculding Daniel] to Babylon.

The King of Babylon sought out skilled and wise men to teach them the language of Babylon, so that they might provide wise advice in running the kingdom and help the Chaldeans in their massive building projects in Babylon.

Nebuchadnezzar took Daniel, Hananiah, Mishael, and Azariah and other prominent citizens and craftsmen, along with about 10,000 Master Craftsmen of many nations for the great Babylonian construction projects.

Some years later king Jehoiachim died and the regents of the new young king Jeconiah (about eight years old) rebelled against Babylon.

Nebuchadnezzar captured Jerusalem the first time on 2 Adar (16 March) 597 B.C. and took Ezekiel and the new young king Jeconiah to Babylon. Dates in the book of Ezekiel are given according to the year of captivity of Jeconiah (i.e. the first fall of Jerusalem, 597 B.C.).

Following the siege of 597 B.C., Nebuchadnezzar installed Zedekiah as tributary king of Judah at the age of twenty-one. However, Zedekiah also revolted against Babylon, and entered into an alliance with Pharaoh Hophra, king of Egypt.

Nebuchadnezzar responded by invading Judah and began a siege of Jerusalem in January 589 BC. During this siege, which lasted about eighteen months, "every worst woe befell the city, which drank the cup of God's fury to the dregs."

In 587 BC, the eleventh year of Zedekiah's reign, Nebuchadnezzar broke through Jerusalem's walls, conquering the city. Zedekiah and his followers attempted to escape, but were captured on the plains of Jericho and taken to Riblah. There, after seeing his sons killed, Zedekiah was blinded, bound, and taken captive to Babylon, where he remained a prisoner until his death.

After the fall of Jerusalem, the Babylonian general Nebuzaraddan was sent to complete its destruction. Jerusalem was plundered and Solomon's Temple was destroyed. Most of the elite were taken into captivity in Babylon. The city was razed to the ground in 586 B.C.

Only a small number of people were permitted to remain to tend to the land. Gedaliah was made governor of the remnant of Judah, which became the Yehud Province of Babylon with a Chaldean guard stationed at Mizpah. On hearing this news, the Jews who were in Moab, Ammon, Edom, and in other countries returned to Judah.

Gedaliah was assassinated two months later by agents of the king of Ammon, and the population that had remained and those who had returned from the surrounding nations, then fled to Egypt for safety. In Egypt, they settled in Migdol, Tahpanhes, Noph, and Pathros where they were later destroyed by a Babylonian invasion of Egypt.

## Daniel 1

**Daniel 1:1** In the third year of the reign of Jehoiakim king of Judah came Nebuchadnezzar king of Babylon unto Jerusalem, and besieged it.

**1:2** And the Lord gave Jehoiakim king of Judah into his hand, with part of the vessels of the house of God: which he carried into the land of Shinar to the house of his god; and he brought the vessels into the treasure house of his god.

**1:3** And the king spake unto Ashpenaz the master of his eunuchs, that he should bring certain of the children of Israel [Judah], and of the king's seed, and of the princes;

**1:4** Children in whom was no blemish, but well favoured, and **skilful in all wisdom, and cunning in knowledge, and understanding science,** and such as had ability in them to stand in the king's palace, and whom they might teach the learning and the tongue of the Chaldeans.

People were chosen from among all the conquered nations including the Jews, and taught the language of Babylon and the king's court procedures over three years.

**1:5** And the king appointed them a daily provision of the king's meat, and of the wine which he drank: so nourishing them three years **[during which**

they were trained], that at the end thereof they might stand before [serve] the king.

**1:6** Now among these were of the children of Judah, **Daniel, Hananiah, Mishael, and Azariah:**

**1:7** Unto whom the prince of the eunuchs gave names: for he gave unto **Daniel the name of Belteshazzar; and to Hananiah, of Shadrach; and to Mishael, of Meshach; and to Azariah, of Abednego.**

Daniel requested that he not be forced to partake of wine [that might befuddle him] or any unclean meat.

**1:8** But Daniel purposed in his heart that he would not defile himself with the portion of the king's meat, nor with the wine which he drank: therefore he requested of the prince of the eunuchs that he might not defile himself.

Daniel made the best of his opportunity to learn and wisely advise Nebuchadnezzar and served the Chaldean's well.

**1:9** Now God had brought Daniel into favour and tender love with the prince of the eunuchs.

Daniel's overseer feared the king lest Daniel's request would make Daniel become weak and sickly.

**1:10** And the prince of the eunuchs said unto Daniel, I fear my lord the king, who hath appointed your meat and your drink: for why should he see your faces worse liking than the children which are of your sort? then shall ye make me endanger my head to the king.

Then Daniel asked Melzar to test them for only ten days and Malzar agreed. Notice that Daniel uses the plural servants and us, which was a strong indication that Hananiah, Mishael, and Azariah [and possibly unnamed others] were making this same request together with Daniel. We see that these people were determined to avoid any unclean thing and yet used wisdom in how they made their request, proving themselves among the wise men of Judah.

**1:11** Then said Daniel to **Melzar,** whom the prince of the eunuchs had set over Daniel, Hananiah, Mishael, and Azariah,

**1:12** Prove thy servants, I beseech thee, ten days; and let them give us pulse [grain or bread made of grain only and water] to eat, and water to drink.

Daniel asked that after ten days they be examined and their health and appearance be compared to those who ate the unclean things.

**1:13** Then let our countenances be looked upon before thee, and the countenance of the children that eat of the portion of the king's meat: and as thou seest, deal with thy servants.

**1:14** So he consented to them in this matter, and proved them ten days.

**1:15** And at the end of ten days their countenances appeared fairer and fatter in flesh than all the children which did eat the portion of the king's meat.

**1:16** Thus Melzar took away the portion of their meat, and the wine that they should drink; and gave them pulse.

These four were blessed by God for their zeal for his Word even in Babylon.

**1:17 As for these four children, God gave them knowledge and skill in all learning and wisdom: and Daniel had understanding in all visions and dreams.**

**1:18** Now at the end of the days [the end of the three years that was given them to learn the language and customs] that the king had said he should bring them in, then the prince of the eunuchs brought them in before Nebuchadnezzar.

Because of their faithfulness to the Word of God under extremely adverse conditions, God gave them understanding and wisdom above their fellows; and they were chosen to advise and serve the king at his side. By the grace and gift of God, they were wiser than all the wise men of Judah or the wise men of the Chaldean's.

**1:19** And the king communed with them; and among them all was found none like Daniel, Hananiah, Mishael, and Azariah: **therefore stood they before the king**.

**1:20** And in all matters of wisdom and understanding, that the king enquired of them, he found them ten times better than all the magicians and astrologers that were in all his realm.

**1:21** And Daniel continued even unto the first year of king Cyrus.

This is a lesson for today's spiritually called out; that if we partake of the unclean things of worldliness, then we shall fall by the wayside; yet if we hunger and thirst for the meat of God's Word, to learn it and to do it; God will give his faithful spiritual wisdom and we shall stand with the King of kings in that day!

## Daniel 2

**Daniel 2:1** And in **the second year of the reign of Nebuchadnezzar** [c. 605 BC – 562 BC. the 2nd year would have been about 603 B.C.] Nebuchadnezzar dreamed dreams, wherewith his spirit was troubled, and his sleep brake from him.

The king seeks an answer from the wise men, the spiritualists and false religions of Babylon, and Daniel was not among them.

**2:2** Then the king commanded to call the magicians, and the astrologers, and the sorcerers, and the Chaldeans, for to shew the king his dreams. So they came and stood before the king.

The king demands that they not only interpret his dream but that they describe to him the dream which he had dreamed.

**2:3** And the king said unto them, I have dreamed a dream, and my spirit was troubled to know the dream. **2:4** Then spake the Chaldeans to the king in Syriack, O king, live for ever: tell thy servants the dream, and we will shew the interpretation.

The king demands they tell him what he had dreamed and its meaning on pain of death.

**2:5** The king answered and said to the Chaldeans, The thing is gone from me: if ye will not make known unto me the dream, with the interpretation thereof, ye shall be cut in pieces, and your houses shall be made a dunghill. **2:6** But if ye shew the dream, and the interpretation thereof, ye shall receive of me gifts and rewards and great honour: therefore shew me the dream, and the interpretation thereof.

They ask the king his dream again, in fear of their lives.

**2:7** They answered again and said, Let the king tell his servants the dream, and we will shew the interpretation of it.

**2:8** The king answered and said, I know of certainty that ye would gain the time, because ye see the thing is gone from me. **2:9** But if ye will not make known unto me the dream, there is but one decree for you: for ye have prepared lying and corrupt words to speak before me, till the time be changed: therefore tell me the dream, and I shall know that ye can shew me the interpretation thereof.

These spiritualists [Satanists] give their defense, that they simply cannot know such a thing.

**2:10** The Chaldeans answered before the king, and said, There is not a man upon the earth that can shew the king's matter: therefore there is no king, lord, nor ruler, that asked such things at any magician, or astrologer, or Chaldean. **2:11** And it is a rare thing that the king requireth, and there is none other that can shew it before the king, except the gods, whose dwelling is not with flesh.

Then the king decrees that all the wise men be killed, and the word comes to Daniel for although worshipers of God and not the magicians of Babylon; Daniel and his friends are also considered wise men and therefore among those to be killed.

**2:12** For this cause the king was angry and very furious, and commanded to destroy all the wise men of Babylon. **2:13** And the decree went forth that the wise men should be slain; and **they sought Daniel and his fellows to be slain**.

Daniel asks why he must die and is told the reason.

**2:14** Then Daniel answered with counsel and wisdom to Arioch the captain of the king's guard, which was gone forth to slay the wise men of Babylon: **2:15** He answered and said to Arioch the king's captain, Why is the decree so hasty from the king? Then Arioch made the thing known to Daniel.

Then Daniel informs the king that he will inquire of God and ask him the dream and its interpretation so he may tell the king. We can see that this was set up by God to reveal to Nebuchadnezzar that the God of Daniel is God indeed, and that the gods of the Babylonian mysteries were not gods at all.

It is the Eternal who is God above all gods and it is wickedness to inquire of any false god.

**2:16** Then Daniel went in, and desired of the king that he would give him time, and that he would shew the king the interpretation.

Then Daniel and his friends inquired of the Eternal.

**2:17** Then Daniel went to his house, and made the thing known to Hananiah, Mishael, and Azariah, his companions: **2:18** That they would desire mercies of the God of heaven concerning this secret; that Daniel and his fellows should not perish with the rest of the wise men of Babylon.

Then the Eternal God revealed the dream to Daniel. This situation shows that a person need not be godly to have an inspired dream from God, but that God will only reveal the meaning to a godly person

It is the Eternal to whom we should go for understanding, and anyone who seeks support for his own false suppositions from the writings of false religions will fall into the same ditch of ignorance that such false teachers are in; and they will reap severe correction for the wickedness of seeking understanding of spiritual things from demons.

**2:19** Then was the secret revealed unto Daniel in a night vision. Then Daniel blessed the God of heaven.

Daniel gave all praise and glory to the Eternal alone; for the Eternal alone is the source of all wisdom and truth; not Satan and his ministers!

Daniel's prayer of thanksgiving; that the Eternal by giving him an understanding of the dream has saved the lives of all God's faithful in the king's service.

**2:20** Daniel answered and said, Blessed be the name of God for ever and ever: for wisdom and might are his:

**2:21** And he changeth the times and the seasons: he removeth kings, and setteth up kings: he giveth wisdom unto the wise, and knowledge to them that know understanding:

**2:22** He revealeth the deep and secret things: he knoweth what is in the darkness, and the light dwelleth with him.

**2:23** I thank thee, and praise thee, O thou God of my fathers, who hast given me wisdom and might, and hast made known unto me now what we desired of thee: for thou hast now made known unto us the king's matter.

Daniel went to Arioch who seems to have been very reluctant to carry out the king's orders and desirous to save the lives of the wise men.

**2:24** Therefore Daniel went in unto Arioch, whom the king had ordained to destroy the wise men of Babylon: he went and said thus unto him; Destroy not the wise men of Babylon: bring me in before the king, and I will shew unto the king the interpretation.

**2:25** Then **Arioch brought in Daniel before the king in haste**, and said thus unto him, I have found a man of the captives of Judah, that will make known unto the king the interpretation.

The king asked Daniel if he can reveal the dream.

**2:26** The king answered and said to Daniel, whose name was Belteshazzar, Art thou able to make known unto me the dream which I have seen, and the interpretation thereof?

Daniel answered the king.

**2:27** Daniel answered in the presence of the king, and said, The secret which the king hath demanded cannot the wise men, the astrologers, the magicians, the soothsayers, shew unto the king;

**2:28** But **there is a God in heaven that revealeth secrets,** and maketh known to the king Nebuchadnezzar **what shall be in the latter days.**

God alone gives understanding of the things of God including the Word of God and the dreams and visions sent by God: Not the ignorant followers of Satan.

Anyone who imagines his own interpretations and then seeks out support for them from the writings of the unconverted, is spiritually blind and no prophet of God.

Daniel then tells the king his dream and the interpretation. The dream is a prophecy of the future of the kingdom of Babylon.

. . . Thy dream, and the visions of thy head upon thy bed, are these;

**2:29** As for thee, O king, thy thoughts came into thy mind upon thy bed, what should come to pass hereafter: and he that revealeth secrets maketh known to thee what shall come to pass.

Daniel declared that the understanding was given to him from God and does not come from any wisdom of his own.

Like Daniel I say, if I have been right in any thing it is from God and not from any wisdom of mine. I am no better than any other; indeed I am less than nothing. Give ALL glory to the Eternal who reveals his wisdom unto worldly babes who put their complete trust in him!

**2:30 But as for me, this secret is not revealed to me for any wisdom that I have more than any living**, but for their sakes that shall make known the interpretation to the king, and that thou mightest know the thoughts of thy heart.

The dream

**2:31** Thou, O king, sawest, and behold a great image. This great image, whose brightness was excellent, stood before thee; and the form thereof was terrible.

**2:32** This image's head was of fine gold, his breast and his arms of silver, his belly and his thighs of brass,

**2:33** His legs of iron, his feet part of iron and part of clay.

**2:34** Thou sawest till that a stone was cut out without hands, which smote the image upon his feet that were of iron and clay, and brake them to pieces.

**2:35** Then was the iron, the clay, the brass, the silver, and the gold, broken to pieces together, and became like the chaff of the summer threshingfloors; and the wind carried them away, that no place was found for them: and the stone that smote the image became a great mountain, and filled the whole earth.

Later, king Nebuchadnezzar was to make a replica of this dream image and demand that all people worship it.

The interpretation

**2:36** This is the dream; and we will tell the interpretation thereof before the king.

God gave the kingdom of Babylon to Nebuchadnezzar; He and the kingdom that he built in Babylon are the head of gold.

**2:37** Thou, O king, art a king of kings: for **the God of heaven hath given thee a kingdom, power, and strength, and glory. 2:38** And wheresoever the children of men dwell, the beasts of the field and the fowls of the heaven hath he given into thine hand, and hath made thee ruler over them all. **Thou art this head of gold.**

The breast of silver was the empire of the Medes and Persians which was dominated by the Persians for a time and then by the Medes with the advent of king Darius.

The Medes and Persians took over the Babylonian empire (539 B.C.) but maintained the same Babylonian church state governance system intact. The people changed, and the system remained the same; therefore the different kingdoms were each still a part of the same Babylonian system like the different metals were still a past of the same statue.

The third kingdom of brass was the same Babylonian system now taken over from the Medes and Persians by the Greeks

**2:39** And after thee shall arise another kingdom inferior to thee, and another third kingdom of brass, which shall bear rule over all the earth.

The fourth part of the image was of iron, but still the same statue; the Babylonian Mysteries church state system. The iron represents Rome and its powerful military.

**2:40** And the fourth kingdom shall be strong as iron: forasmuch as iron breaketh in pieces and subdueth all things: and as iron that breaketh all these, shall it break in pieces and bruise.

The feet and toes of the statue of Babylon, picture the church state Holy Roman Empire with its own seven revivals (Rev 17), the final revival consisting of ten nations working together like the ten toes of the statue.

The whole statue was of the Babylonian system and each succeeding empire although led by a different people, maintained the same Babylonian Mysteries church state system.

This system is called Babylon the Great, and a final revival of the church state Holy Roman Empire [regardless of what it is named] will be a New European federal system including ten nations which will soon rise up and come back to life for the final time only to be destroyed and replaced by the coming Messiah the Christ.

**2:41** And whereas thou sawest the feet and toes, part of potters' clay, and part of iron, the kingdom shall be divided; but there shall be in it of the strength of the iron, forasmuch as thou sawest the iron mixed with miry clay.

**2:42** And as the toes of the feet were part of iron, and part of clay, so the kingdom shall be partly strong, and partly broken [weak].

The strength of some nations will be mingled with weaker peoples in the coming final revival. This federal system of ten European nations will feature several strong nations and several weaker nations in its makeup.

**2:43** And whereas thou sawest iron mixed with miry clay, they shall mingle themselves with the seed of men: but they shall not cleave one to another, even as iron is not mixed with clay.

The ten toes represent ten rulers who will form this final Babylonian system by giving their authority to one leader. Messiah the Christ will come to destroy the Babylonian Mysteries System that the statue represents; and he will set up the kingdom of God.

> **Revelation 17:12** And the ten horns which thou sawest are ten kings [rulers], which have received no kingdom as yet; but receive power as kings one hour [a short time, 42 months, Rev 11] with the beast. **17:13** These have one mind, and shall give their power and strength unto the beast. **17:14** These shall make war with the Lamb, and the Lamb shall overcome them: for he is Lord of lords, and King of kings: and they that are with him are called, and chosen, and faithful.

**Daniel 2:44 And in the days of these kings shall the God of heaven set up a kingdom, which shall never be destroyed**: and the kingdom shall not be left to other people, but it shall break in pieces and consume all these kingdoms, and it shall stand for ever.

The Chief Corner Stone [Messiah the Christ] will come down from the mountain of the government of God the Father in heaven.

**2:45** Forasmuch as thou sawest that the stone was cut out of the mountain without hands , and that it brake in pieces the iron, the brass, the clay, the silver, and the gold; the great God hath made known to the king what shall come to pass hereafter: and the dream is certain, and the interpretation thereof sure.

**2:46** Then the king Nebuchadnezzar fell upon his face, and worshipped Daniel, and commanded that they should offer an oblation and sweet odours unto him.

This whole process and prophecy revealed to Nebuchadnezzar that the Eternal is God indeed and that the other god's and their servants and priests were as nothing and totally without godly wisdom.

In our day, when Christ comes and this final revival of the Babylonian system is destroyed; all people will sincerely repent and turn to worship God. Then people who had been deceived by this system will understand and reject it.

> **Revelation 17:16** And the ten horns which thou sawest upon the beast, these shall hate the whore [the false religion which has deceived and dominated them], and shall make her desolate and naked, and shall eat her flesh, and burn her with fire. **17:17 For God hath put in their hearts to fulfil his will, and to agree, and give their kingdom unto the beast, until the words of God shall be fulfilled.**

**Daniel 2:47** The king answered unto Daniel, and said, Of a truth it is, that your God is a God of gods, and a Lord of kings, and a revealer of secrets, seeing thou couldest reveal this secret.

**2:48** Then the king made Daniel a great man, and gave him many great gifts, and made him ruler over the whole province of Babylon, and chief of the governors over all the wise men of Babylon.

**2:49** Then Daniel requested of the king, and he set Shadrach, Meshach, and Abednego, over the affairs of the province of Babylon: but Daniel sat in the gate of the king.

## Daniel 3

After his dream was revealed and explained by God through Daniel; Nebuchadnezzar instead of worshiping God, worshiped Daniel as the servant of God.

Brethren, we are to obey the message and he who sent it; We are NOT to worship the messenger who merely brings the message!

Then the king was driven by his great pride to set himself and his kingdom up as a god, building a replica of the dream statue representing himself and his kingdom, and commanding all people to worship it.

This statue represented Nebuchadnezzar and it represents the entire historical empire of the Babylonian system including the rising final New Federal Europe that the world will worship in the sense of fearing it, for a short time.

> **Revelation 13:3** And I saw one of his heads as it were wounded to death; and his deadly wound was healed: and all the world wondered after the beast.
>
> **13:4** And they worshipped the dragon which gave power unto the beast: and they worshipped [feared] the beast, saying, Who is like unto the beast? who is able to make war with him?

**13:5** And there was given unto him a mouth speaking great things and blasphemies; and **power was given unto him to continue** [Margin, to make war for the 1,260 day tribulation period.] **forty and two months.**

**13:6** And he opened his mouth in blasphemy against God, to blaspheme his name, and his tabernacle, and them that dwell in heaven.

**Daniel 3:1** Nebuchadnezzar the king made an image of gold, whose height was threescore cubits [about 30 meters or 90 feet], and the breadth thereof six cubits [3 meters or about 9 feet]: he set it up in the plain of Dura, in the province of Babylon.

This image represented the Babylonian church state system; and is also representative of the idolatry of exalting men, churches and governments, whether national or corporate entities, above the Word of God.

**3:2** Then Nebuchadnezzar the king sent to gather together the princes, the governors, and the captains, the judges, the treasurers, the counsellors, the sheriffs, and all the rulers of the provinces, to come to the dedication of the image which Nebuchadnezzar the king had set up.

The chief of the people came as commanded

**3:3** Then **the princes, the governors, and captains, the judges, the treasurers, the counsellors, the sheriffs, and all the rulers of the provinces**, were gathered together unto the dedication of the image that Nebuchadnezzar the king had set up; and they stood before the image that Nebuchadnezzar had set up.

Then the command to bow done before this representation of the king and his kingdom was proclaimed. As we read this, we wonder at this command to worship a statue, but they were really worshiping [worship means to obey] what the statue represented, which was Babylon the great and by extension all false religions and idols.

This people bowing down and worshiping this statue will soon be repeated in our day when all people within the influence of the soon coming New Europe will worship [fear] the same system; which this statue represents.

Brethren, it is no different today when we bow down before our idols of men and obey their false traditions contrary to the Word of God. If we bow down and make idols of men to blindly obey them contrary to the Word of God, we are NO DIFFERENT than these ancients!

To obey men and pollute God's holy Sabbath by cooking or buying on God's weekly or annual Sabbath Holy Day's is exactly the same as bowing before a huge statue on the plain of Dura.

By bowing to ANY man and exalting him above the Word of God: We are IDOLATERS and brethren of the Babylonian Mysteries in rebellion against the Word of God!

**3:4** Then an herald cried aloud, To you it is commanded, O people, nations, and languages,

**3:5** That at what time ye hear the sound of the cornet, flute, harp, sackbut, psaltery, dulcimer, and all kinds of musick, ye fall down and worship the golden image that Nebuchadnezzar the king hath set up:

**3:6** And whoso falleth not down and worshippeth shall the same hour be cast into the midst of a burning fiery furnace.

All the people then submitted to the Babylonian Mysteries by bowing before the idol. Just as almost all of today's Ekklesia submits to the Babylonian Mysteries, by bowing before their idols of men, false traditions and corporate entities!

**3:7** Therefore at that time, when all the people heard the sound of the cornet, flute, harp, sackbut, psaltery, and all kinds of musick, all the people, the nations, and the languages, fell down and worshipped the golden image that Nebuchadnezzar the king had set up.

Then the people rightly accused the Jews of not bowing to the idol.

This a type of today's accusations against those who are faithful to God who bow to the Eternal alone, exalting and zealously keeping the whole Word of God: refusing to bow before and make idols of men and refusing to exalt men above the Word of God!

**3:8** Wherefore at that time certain Chaldeans came near, and accused the Jews. **3:9** They spake and said to the king Nebuchadnezzar, O king, live for ever.

**3:10** Thou, O king, hast made a decree, that every man that shall hear the sound of the cornet, flute, harp, sackbut, psaltery, and dulcimer, and all kinds of musick, shall fall down and worship the golden image: **3:11** And whoso falleth not down and worshippeth, that he should be cast into the midst of a burning fiery furnace.

**3:12** There are certain Jews whom thou hast set over the affairs of the province of Babylon, Shadrach, Meshach, and Abednego; these men, O king, have not regarded thee: they serve not thy gods, nor worship the golden image which thou hast set up.

Then Nebuchadnezzar became enraged not because the idol represented HIM; and these people, by not bowing to the idol, were rejecting HIM as their god king!

So it is today, that many church leaders and elders filled with arrogant pride and seeking to exalt themselves, feel threatened by any zeal for God. They are enraged at those who are zealous for God; because they see that as a rejection of themselves.

**3:13** Then Nebuchadnezzar in his rage and fury commanded to bring Shadrach, Meshach, and Abednego [the leaders of the Jews]. Then they brought these men before the king.

Then Nebuchadnezzar tried to reason with these faithful men of God, and he gave them a chance to recant and worship his idol and himself, or be cast into a furnace heated seven times hotter than normal. This was not a home heating furnace, but most likely a large brick kiln or metal refining furnace.

Today many religious leaders also give ultimatum's to the brethren to stop following the Word of God and to follow themselves and their false teachings or they will be rejected and cast out of the congregation for being faithful to God.

Today's professing Christian leaders and elders LIE to the brethren, promising that those who are faithful to God and will not exalt men will be cast into the lake of fire for not idolizing men!

**3:14** Nebuchadnezzar spake and said unto them, Is it true, O Shadrach, Meshach, and Abednego, do not ye serve my gods, nor worship the golden image which I have set up?

**3:15** Now if ye be ready that at what time ye hear the sound of the cornet, flute, harp, sackbut, psaltery, and dulcimer, and all kinds of musick, ye fall down and worship the image which I have made; well: but if ye worship not, ye shall be cast the same hour into the midst of a burning fiery furnace; and who is that God that shall deliver you out of my hands?

Then these three men, as the leaders of the Jews, plainly answered the king.

**3:16** Shadrach, Meshach, and Abednego, answered and said to the king, O Nebuchadnezzar, we are not careful [**not afraid**] to answer thee in this matter.

Then the three men declared that whether they live or whether they die; they will do so serving the Eternal God!

Do we have this kind of faith and courage today, to refuse to bow to idols of men and false traditions? Will we, like these three, exalt the Eternal God the Father with all our being; over every man and every authority that exists in heaven and earth?

**3:17** If it be so, our God whom we serve is able to deliver us from the burning fiery furnace, and he will deliver us out of thine hand, O king.

**3:18** But if not, be it known unto thee, O king, that we will not serve thy gods, nor worship the golden image which thou hast set up.

Then the king was enraged that these three rejected his command to worship this idol representing himself and his empire as their chief god.

This was more than just emotional rage at rejection; because these three men were the leaders of all the Jews in Babylon and he could not permit the example of the Jews being loyal to their God to infect the other nationalities, lest they all prefer their own gods above him.

So it is with the false leaders in today's Spiritual Ekklesia; they are enraged by those who are faithful to Almighty God because they greatly fear that the example of true godliness will infect others and spread.

They reject godliness for their own ways and they want the brethren to follow themselves; therefore they also reject those that are zealous for God!

**3:19** Then was Nebuchadnezzar full of fury, and the form of his visage was changed against Shadrach, Meshach, and Abednego: therefore he spake, and commanded that they should heat the furnace one seven times more than it was wont to be heated.

The king could not allow this open public denial of his ultimate authority over the people and commanded that these upstarts who were passionately courageously faithful to God, be thrown into the seven times hottest furnace.

Neither will today's church leaders allow any open public denial of their supposed ultimate moral authority over the people, and they command that upstarts who are passionately courageously faithful to God be ejected from the congregations.

**3:20** And he commanded the most mighty [strongest, fittest] men that were in his army to bind Shadrach, Meshach, and Abednego, and to cast them into the burning fiery furnace.

**3:21** Then these men were bound in their coats, their hosen, and their hats, and their other garments, and were cast into the midst of the burning fiery furnace.

Then those who rejected God for the king's word and attacked the LORD's beloved were killed, while the faithful pillars were saved alive. Jesus standing with them in the fire to demonstrate for us that it is Jesus Christ the Lamb of God who CAN and WILL save his faithful from the second death in the lake of fire!

**3:22** Therefore because the king's commandment was urgent, and the furnace exceeding hot, the flames of the fire **slew those men that took up** Shadrach, Meshach, and Abednego.

**3:23** And these three men, Shadrach, Meshach, and Abednego, fell down bound into the midst of the burning fiery furnace.

**3:24** Then Nebuchadnezzar the king was astonied, and rose up in haste, and spake, and said unto his counsellors, Did not we cast three men bound into the midst of the fire? They answered and said unto the king, True, O king.

**3:25** He answered and said, Lo, I see four men loose, walking in the midst of the fire, and they have no hurt; and the form of **the fourth is like the Son of God**.

Then the king called them to come out of the furnace

**3:26** Then Nebuchadnezzar came near to the mouth of the burning fiery furnace, and spake, and said, Shadrach, Meshach, and Abednego, ye servants of the most high God, come forth, and come hither. Then Shadrach, Meshach, and Abednego, came forth of the midst of the fire.

The power of the God who later gave up his God-hood to become flesh as Jesus Christ was so overwhelming against the fire and the command of the king, that the faithful to God were not as much as singed or smelling of smoke. The power of God the Father and Jesus Christ is far greater than ANY human being or corporate church today, far greater than even the power of death itself!

**3:27** And the princes, governors, and captains, and the king's counsellors, being gathered together, saw these men, **upon whose bodies the fire had no power, nor was an hair of their head singed, neither were their coats changed, nor the smell of fire had passed on them.**

Then God was praised by the king before all the nations that were gathered together, just as the faithful to God will be resurrected to spiritual life at the coming of Christ; and all nations will praise God and turn to live by every Word of God.

**3:28** Then Nebuchadnezzar spake, and said, Blessed be the God of Shadrach, Meshach, and Abednego, who hath sent his angel, and delivered his servants that trusted in him, and have changed the king's word, and yielded their bodies, that they might not serve nor worship any god, except their own God.

When Messiah the Christ comes to resurrect God's chosen out of the grave, and after the wedding feast in heaven; Messiah the Christ will return with his resurrected chosen to save humanity; then all nations will understand and turn to God in sincere repentance to begin a millennium of peace!

**3:29** Therefore I make a decree, That every people, nation, and language, which speak any thing amiss against the God of Shadrach, Meshach, and Abednego, shall be cut in pieces, and their houses shall be made a dunghill: because there is no other God that can deliver after this sort.

Then Jesus Christ, the King of kings, will resurrect those who have been faithful to live by every Word of God and they will rule with him in God's kingdom; while their brethren who persecuted them shall be greatly ashamed.

**3:30** Then the king promoted Shadrach, Meshach, and Abednego, in the province of Babylon.

## Daniel 4

Daniel 4 is a royal proclamation by Nebuchadnezzar to all the nations concerning his seven years madness.

Babylon had brought the wisest and most skilled people to Babylon where they assisted in massive building projects and formed a "college" of wise men to advise the government on all matters.

Each of these groups worshiped the gods of their native lands, and brought with them the mysteries of their own gods. Daniel and his friends worshiped the Eternal, but Nebuchadnezzar would have regarded the God of Abraham as just one god among many other gods.

Daniel and his friends were lumped together with the magicians and wise men of the nations by the king; and it was the purpose of the Eternal to separate himself in the minds of people primarily as a lesson for us in the last days just before Messiah comes: Separating himself from all the other gods and to teach us that the Eternal is God alone.

Therefore the king proclaimed to all the people his conclusion that the Eternal was the God above all gods

**Daniel 4:1** Nebuchadnezzar the king, unto all people, nations, and languages, that dwell in all the earth; Peace be multiplied unto you.

**4:2** I thought it good to shew the signs and wonders that the high God hath wrought toward me.

**4:3** How great are his signs! and how mighty are his wonders! his kingdom is an everlasting kingdom, and his dominion is from generation to generation.

Nebuchadnezzar relates that he had a troubling dream and that he had called all the wise men from across the empire, seeking their interpretation of his dream through their wisdom and magical spiritual powers.

**4:4** I Nebuchadnezzar was at rest in mine house, and flourishing in my palace:

**4:5** I saw a dream which made me afraid, and the thoughts upon my bed and the visions of my head troubled me. **4:6** Therefore made I a decree to bring in all the wise men of Babylon before me, that they might make known unto me the interpretation of the dream.

**4:7** Then came in the magicians, the astrologers, the Chaldeans, and the soothsayers: and I told the dream before them; but they did not make known unto me the interpretation thereof.

At the last Daniel came before the king. Note that the king knows that Daniel has the Spirit of God, but thought of that as the same spirit of ALL the gods. The Eternal wanted this lesson to teach all of the people then and now; that HE ALONE is God and beside him there is NO OTHER!

This lesson is one that the spiritually called out should know today; yet it is a lesson that needs to be relearned by us today.

Today's Ekklesia has fallen into the spiritual idolatry of exalting of men; and the false traditions of men have become the false gods of today. Each group exalting its leaders, boards and elders as idols above the Word of God! We have made many men our idols, just as these ancients and modern people worshiped their many false gods.

**4:8** But at the last Daniel came in before me, whose name was Belteshazzar, according to the name of my God, and in whom is the spirit of the holy gods: and before him I told the dream, saying,

Nebuchadnezzar sought understanding from God through Daniel after the many false gods have failed.

It is time right now for the leaders and elders of today's called out to the spiritual New Covenant to turn back to the Husband of our espousal; and to stop trying to insert men between the brethren and God; making idols of them and their false traditions. It is time for the church of God brethren to sincerely repent of their idols of men, and to turn away from their idols of men and false traditions, and to seek understanding from the Word of God alone!

It is because we exalt idols of men and false traditions and have no zeal to live by every Word of God preferring our own imaginations instead of what God has said; that there is no understanding of spiritual things in today's Spiritual Ekklesia!

**4:9** O Belteshazzar [Daniel], master [chief in wisdom, the king not understanding the difference between the God of Daniel and the other gods.] of the magicians, because I know that the spirit of the holy gods is in thee, and no secret troubleth thee, tell me the visions of my dream that I have seen, and the interpretation thereof.

**Nebuchadnezzar tells the dream to Daniel**

**4:10** Thus were the visions of mine head in my bed;

I saw, and behold a tree in the midst of the earth, and the height thereof was great.

**4:11** The tree grew, and was strong, and the height thereof reached unto heaven, and the sight thereof to the end of all the earth: **4:12** The leaves thereof were fair, and the fruit thereof much, and in it was meat for all: the beasts of the field had shadow under it, and the fowls of the heaven dwelt in the boughs thereof, and all flesh was fed of it.

**4:13** I saw in the visions of my head upon my bed, and, behold, a watcher and an holy one came down from heaven; **4:14** He cried aloud, and said thus, Hew down the tree, and cut off his branches, shake off his leaves, and scatter his fruit: let the beasts get away from under it, and the fowls from his branches:

**4:15** Nevertheless leave the stump of his roots in the earth, even with a band of iron and brass, in the tender grass of the field; and let it be wet with the dew of heaven, and let his portion be with the beasts in the grass of the earth: **4:16** Let his heart be changed from man's, and let a beast's heart be given unto him; and let seven times pass over him.

**4:17** This matter is by the decree of the watchers, and the demand by the word of the holy ones: to the intent that the living may know that the most High ruleth in the kingdom of men, and giveth it to whomsoever he will, and setteth up over it the basest of men.

Nebuchadnezzar, remembering that only Daniel could explain the statue dream of Daniel two, commanded Daniel to explain the tree dream that no one else and no other god could interpret. This separates Daniel and his friends from the other wise men [of the other gods] and separates the Eternal from all other gods.

**4:18** This dream I king Nebuchadnezzar have seen. Now thou, O Belteshazzar, declare the interpretation thereof, forasmuch as all the wise men of my kingdom are not able to make known unto me the interpretation: but thou art able; for the spirit of the holy gods is in thee.

Then immediately when he had heard the king's dream God gave Daniel the understanding, and Daniel was deeply troubled over this prophetic dream.

**4:19** Then Daniel, whose name was Belteshazzar, was astonied for one hour, and his thoughts troubled him. The king spake, and said, Belteshazzar, let not the dream, or the interpretation thereof, trouble thee. Belteshazzar [Daniel] answered and said, My lord, the dream be to them that hate thee, and the interpretation thereof to thine enemies.

**The interpretation that the Eternal gave to Daniel.**

**4:20** The tree that thou sawest, which grew, and was strong, whose height reached unto the heaven, and the sight thereof to all the earth; **4:21** Whose leaves were fair, and the fruit thereof much, and in it was meat for all; under which the beasts of the field dwelt, and upon whose branches the fowls of the heaven had their habitation:

**4:22** It is thou, O king, that art grown and become strong: for thy greatness is grown, and reacheth unto heaven, and thy dominion to the end of the [known] earth.

The Eternal has his angels watching the affairs of men and watching over the affairs of the called out. Jesus Christ knows our affairs and that is why he says that he is going to reject us in this latter day (Rev 3:16), just as he rejected Nebuchadnezzar; because we are full of the very same sins of enormous pride and gross idolatry.

**4:23** And whereas the king saw a watcher and an holy one coming down from heaven, and saying, Hew the tree down, and destroy it; yet leave the stump of the roots thereof in the earth, even with a band of iron and brass, in the tender grass of the field; and let it be wet with the dew of heaven, and let his portion be with the beasts of the field, till **seven times** pass over him;

**4:24** This is the interpretation, O king, and this is the decree of the most High, which is come upon my lord the king:

**4:25** That they shall drive thee from men, and thy dwelling shall be with the beasts of the field, and they shall make thee to eat grass as oxen, and they shall wet thee with the dew of heaven, and seven times shall pass over thee, till thou know that the most High ruleth in the kingdom of men, and giveth it to whomsoever he will.

Brethren, in this latter day most of the church of God organizations and people are going to be rejected by God into great correction (Rev 3:15-22); until we learn that the Eternal is God and beside HIM there is NO OTHER (Deu 4:35)! Then when each individual learns this lesson and sincerely repents, he will find Christ at the door ready to receive him with open arms and many tender mercies.

**4:26** And whereas they commanded to leave the stump of the tree roots; thy kingdom shall be sure unto thee, after that thou shalt have known that the heavens do rule.

Here is the advice of Daniel to the king; and it is also God's advice to today's idolatrous Ekklesia and to all those who make idols of men, and follow men, paying lip service to God while teaching for doctrine the words of men.

Let us break off from our many idols and sins; and turn to learn and keep the righteousness of the whole Word of God.

> **Mark 7:7** Howbeit in vain do they worship me, teaching for doctrines the commandments of men.

**Daniel 4:27** Wherefore, O king, **let my counsel be acceptable unto thee, and break off thy sins by righteousness, and thine iniquities** by shewing mercy to the poor; if it may be a lengthening of thy tranquility.

The king in his pride would not repent of his idolatry and sins; as quite honestly, most of today's Spiritual Ekklesia will not repent until our pride has been crushed to contrition like Nebuchadnezzar's was.

**4:28** All this came upon the king Nebuchadnezzar.

### The prophetic warning from God is fulfilled

**4:29** At the end of twelve months he walked in the palace of the kingdom of Babylon.

The king is lifted up with pride and will not repent! Just as most of us in our great pride will not repent until we have been taught a lesson by God.

**4:30** The king spake, and said, **Is not this great Babylon, that I have built for the house of the kingdom by the might of my power, and for the honour of my majesty?**

When the final false prophet is set up in the Vatican doing miracles he will go to the Holy Mount within 75 days and the tribulation of our correction will begin.

**4:31** While the word was in the king's mouth, there fell a voice from heaven, saying, O king Nebuchadnezzar, to thee it is spoken; The kingdom is departed from thee.

**4:32** And they shall drive thee from men, and thy dwelling shall be with the beasts of the field: they shall make thee to eat grass as oxen, and **seven times** shall pass over thee, **until thou know that the most High ruleth in the kingdom of men, and giveth it to whomsoever he will.**

**4:33** The same hour was the thing fulfilled upon Nebuchadnezzar: and he was driven from men, and did eat grass as oxen, and his body was wet with the dew of heaven, till his hairs were grown like eagles' feathers, and his nails like birds' claws.

When we have learned our lesson in the furnace of affliction and when we have sincerely repented with a whole heart, when our great pride has been crushed and our idolatries forsaken; then those who have learned the lesson and have sincerely repentant will turn to exalt the Eternal God just like Nebuchadnezzar did.

**4:34** And at the end of the days I Nebuchadnezzar lifted up mine eyes unto heaven, and mine understanding returned unto me, and I blessed the most High, and I praised and honoured him that liveth for ever, whose dominion is an everlasting dominion, and his kingdom is from generation to generation:

**4:35** And all the inhabitants of the earth are reputed as nothing: and he doeth according to his will in the army of heaven, and among the inhabitants of the earth: and none can stay his hand, or say unto him, What doest thou?

**4:36** At the same time my reason returned unto me; and for the glory of my kingdom, mine honour and brightness returned unto me; and my counsellors and my lords sought unto me; and I was established in my kingdom, and excellent majesty was added unto me.

All humanity including today's faithless Spiritual Ekklesia must be humbled and learn that God requires obedience and not lip-service. When we KNOW that the Eternal reigns, and we wholeheartedly follow him to live by EVERY WORD of God; then we shall be accepted by HIM into eternal life!

**4:37** Now I Nebuchadnezzar praise and extol and honour the King of heaven, all whose works are truth, and his ways judgment: and those that walk in pride he is able to abase.

# Daniel 7

## Introduction

Nebuchadnezzar having died the kingdom was passed to his son Nabonidus who in due time elevated his own son Belshazzar as co-ruler and second ruler of Babylon after himself.

Belshazzar was a co-ruler with his father Nabonidus for several years before the fall of Babylon and because Nabonidus was often away on military campaigns Belshazzar was often left in full charge in Babylon itself.

The end of Belshazzar (Dan 5); must be understood in light of the dreams and experiences of his grandfather Nebuchadnezzar, which Belshazzar would have been well aware of.

Daniel 7 is dated in the first year of the co regency of Belshazzar and so should be placed before Daniel 5 which deals with the end of Belshazzar..

**Daniel 7:1 In the first year of Belshazzar** king of Babylon **Daniel had a dream** and visions of his head upon his bed: then he wrote the dream, and told the sum of the matters.

**Daniel's had a dream during the first year of Belshazzar's co rulership of Babylon.**

**7:2** Daniel spake and said, I saw in my vision by night, and, behold, the four winds of the heaven strove upon the great sea.

The great sea is the people and the winds are the empires of the statue of Daniel 2; the image was of the complete Babylonian system and the various empires that would constitute Babylon.

The four winds are then likened to four beasts that came up out of the sea of people. This shows that these beasts that are a part of the Babylonian system are humanly [spiritually blinded and inspired by Satan] devised.

**7:3** And four great beasts came up from the sea, diverse one from another.

### The first beast

The first beast corresponded to the head of gold of the statue of Daniel 2; the first manifestation of the Babylonian system.

**7:4** The first was like a lion, and had eagle's wings [the winged lion was the symbol of Nebuchadnezzar's Babylon]: I beheld till the wings thereof were plucked, and it was lifted up from the earth, and made stand upon the feet as a man, and a man's heart was given to it.

### The second beast

The bear represents the ancient Persians; the bear is the animal figure of the silver breast that replaced the gold head in the Babylonian mystery system.

The Persians rose up to conquer the Medes, the Babylonians and Egypt; the three empires typified by the three ribs [the Medes, Egyptians and Babylon in the mouth (in the power of) of the Persians] in its mouth and the power to conquer many nations [devour much flesh].

The Empire of the Medes had allied with the Babylonians in 612 B.C. overthrowing Assyria and leading to the rise of Babylon and Nebuchadnezzar about 604 B.C.

In 553 B.C. (a second report puts the event in 550 BCE) the Medes were defeated by "Cyrus, king of Anshan" the Persian and separated from their Babylonian alliance. The Medes then joined with the Persians, beginning the rapid rise of the Persian Empire.

Cyrus the Persian was the first king of the Persian dominated Achaemenid Empire followed by his son Cambyses 2. This Darius a Mede became the ruler of the Persian empire about 522 B.C.

This Darius the Mede also called Gobryas by the Greeks, was the Mede general who had captured the city of Babylon for the Persian Emperor Cyrus in 539 B.C.

> **Note:** There was no such person as Darius the Persian, Darius was a Mede; this misunderstanding that there was a Persian Darius comes from the fact that Darius [the Mede] later became the ruler of the Persian Empire.

**7:5** And behold another beast, a second, like to a bear, and it **raised up itself on one side**, and it had **three ribs in the mouth of it** between the teeth of it: and they said thus unto it, Arise, devour much flesh [conquer many nations].

### The third beast

Now comes the leopard the symbol of Greece, which replaced the Persian part of the great statue of Babylon. The third beast had the agility and strength of the leopard and was very fast in actions as if it had wings, picturing Greece and the lightening conquests of Alexander.

The leopard of Greece typified by the brass in Daniel 2, had four heads picturing the dividing of the successors of Alexander into four kingdoms.

**7:6** After this I beheld, and lo another, like a leopard, which had upon the back of it four wings of a fowl; the beast had also four heads; and dominion was given to it.

A fourth part of the Babylonian system is then revealed as having teeth of iron. This is the fourth part of the statue of Daniel 2 which was the legs of iron of Rome.

This Roman Empire was to be stronger than the other beasts; and its final rise as the soon coming New Europe will include ten kings under one emperor or president leader.

### The fourth beast

**7:7** After this I saw in the night visions, and behold a fourth beast, dreadful and terrible, and strong exceedingly; and it had great iron teeth: it devoured and brake in pieces, and stamped the residue with the feet of it: and it was diverse from all the beasts that were before it; and **it had ten horns**.

The fourth beast is the Roman Empire, the two legs of the Daniel 2 statue, which took over the Babylonian Mysteries governance form and religion from the Greeks.

In today's latter days the two legs are to be completed by the ten toes of the last revival of the Holy Roman Empire which is now rising in Europe, by whatever name it will be called.

**The seat of the Babylonian Mysteries transferred to Rome**

The Greeks had moved the center of the Babylonian Mystery religion to Pergamos

> **Revelation 2:12** And to the angel of the church in Pergamos write; These things saith he which hath the sharp sword with two edges; **2:13** I know thy works, and **where thou dwellest, even where Satan's seat is**:

Attalus III Philometor Euergetes, king of Pergamum from 138 to 133 B.C. died in 133 B.C. bequeathing his domains to Rome ended the history of Pergamum as the last Greek King of the North; and Babylon/Syria the King of the North and the Babylonian Mysteries, were absorbed by Rome.

Later during the collapse of the Roman Empire in the West and the wars of Justinian; the Papacy and emperor were set up as the Holy Roman Empire by The Decree of Justinian.

**The ten horns on the Roman fourth beast**

**7:8** I considered the [the explanation begins in 7:20] horns, and, behold, there came up among them **another** little horn [an eleventh horn, the **papacy**], before whom there were three of the first horns plucked up by the roots: and, behold, in this horn were eyes like the eyes of man, and a mouth speaking great things.

> **Daniel 7:24** And the ten horns out of this kingdom are ten kings that shall arise and **another shall rise after them**; and he shall be diverse from the first [ten], and he shall subdue three kings.

The 10 horns on the fourth beast in Daniel represent ten successive kingdoms or dynasties that would arise out of imperial Rome.

After it's collapse the Roman empire was for a time ruled by Gothic tribes. The Visigoths took Rome in 410, the Vandals in 455 and the Ostrogoths in 493. Not only did the kings of these tribes rule over Rome in their time but they also set up kingdoms in areas that had formerly been part of the empire; the Visigoths in southern Gaul and Spain, the Vandals in North Africa and the Ostrogoths Italy, Sardinia and Sicily. These three Gothic kingdoms are represented by three of the ten horns.

The arrangement of Justinian with the bishop of Rome also resulted in the birth of the papacy as dominating the emperor; which is represented by the little horn that came up among the ten horns.

When emperor Justinian now accepting papal authority resolved to restore the Western Roman Empire his armies conquered these three Gothic kingdoms and with his arrangement with the bishop of Rome he established the first of seven empires that would later become known as the Holy Roman Empire.

The three Gothic tribes had brought their laws, culture, traditions and religions to Rome and to the lands where they established their kingdoms. Many Goths had been converted to Arian Christianity before their conquests of Rome and this belief became widespread in Rome and in their kingdoms. Arianism was a heresy in Roman Catholicism as it contradicted the Nicene creed so the bishop of Rome, set up by Justinian as pope, set about removing all traces of Gothic culture and beliefs from the empire. This is what the little horn [the Papacy] plucking up three of the horns before him represents.

We are also told that the little horn would speak great words against the Eternal [by teaching people to obey the traditions of men instead of living by every Word of God] and seek to change times and laws and wear out the saints. The popes through the ages have done all these things and the coming false prophet will be the culmination.

The end of the entire system will come at the coming of Messiah the Christ; who will crush this Babylonian Mysteries system and totally destroy it (Daniel 2).

**Daniel 7:9** I beheld till the thrones were cast down, and the Ancient of days did sit [in judgment], whose garment was white as snow, and the hair of his head like the pure wool: his throne was like the fiery flame, and his wheels as burning fire.

**7:10** A fiery stream issued and came forth from before him: thousand thousands ministered unto him, and ten thousand times ten thousand stood before him: the judgment was set, and the books were opened.

Jesus Christ will cast the final political leader of the New Europe and the final miracle working false prophet who deceives humanity into rebellion against God, together into the lake of fire.

**Daniel 7:11** I beheld then because of the voice of the great words which the horn [the little horn, the papacy] spake: I beheld even till the beast [the whole Babylonian Mysteries system, including the political leader and the final false religious leader] was slain [destroyed], and his body destroyed, and given to the burning flame.

> **Revelation 19:20** And the beast was taken, and with him the false prophet that wrought miracles before him, with which he deceived them that had received the mark of the beast, and them that worshipped his image. **These both were cast alive into a lake of fire burning with brimstone.**

**Daniel 7:12** As concerning the rest of the beasts [the other three beasts, not the fourth Roman beast of ten successive dynastic horns], they had their dominion taken away: yet their lives were prolonged for a season and time.

### A prophecy of dominion being given to Jesus Christ

**7:13** I saw in the night visions, and, behold, **one like the Son of man came with the clouds of heaven, and came to the Ancient of days, and they brought him near before him.**

The everlasting kingdom of God will be given to Jesus Christ and it will replace the Babylonian Mystery church state system [replacing Satan and his followers and ways] of Daniel 2, Christ smiting the last revival of Babylon and smashing it.

**7:14** And there was given him dominion, and glory, and a kingdom, that all people, nations, and languages, should serve him: his dominion is an everlasting dominion, which shall not pass away, and his kingdom that which shall not be destroyed.

### Then Daniel was upset and longed to understand the prophecy

**7:15** I Daniel was grieved in my spirit in the midst of my body, and the visions of my head troubled me. **7:16** I came near unto one of them that stood by [an angel still in the vision], and asked him the truth of all this. . .

The explanation from God

. . . So he told me, and made me know the interpretation of the things.

**7:17** These great beasts, which are four, **are four kings** [or national empires; Babylon, Persia, Greece and Rome], which shall arise out of the earth.

These four are each a part of the Babylonian system represented by the whole statue of Daniel 2.

The system of Satan, the Babylonian Mysteries, which will climax in the Holy Roman Empire; will be destroyed by Christ at his coming with his chosen resurrected elect; and those faithful to God in this life will receive an eternal kingdom.

**7:18** But **the saints of the most High shall take the kingdom, and possess the kingdom for ever, even for ever and ever.**

**The explanation of Rome the fourth beast**

**7:19** Then I would know **the truth of the fourth beast**, which was diverse from all the others, exceeding dreadful, whose teeth were of iron, and his nails of brass; which devoured, brake in pieces, and stamped the residue with his feet;

**7:20 And of the ten horns** [which are ten successive Roman dynastic systems] that were in his head, and of the other [the little horn, the papacy] which came up, and before whom three fell; even of that horn that had eyes, and a mouth that spake very great things, whose look was more stout than his fellows.

**7:21** I beheld, and the same **horn** [little horn, the papacy] **made war with the saints, and prevailed against them; 7:22** Until the Ancient of days [Jesus Christ in this context] came, and judgment was given to the saints of the most High [that the chosen should be resurrected to spirit and receive their inheritance]; and **the time came that the saints possessed the kingdom.**

Rome is the fourth beast, the legs and feet of iron of the statue of Babylon.

**7:23** Thus he said, The fourth beast shall be the fourth kingdom [Rome] upon earth, which shall be diverse from all kingdoms, and shall devour the whole [the known earth at that time] earth, and shall tread it down, and break it in pieces.

**7:24** And **the ten horns out of this kingdom** [the ten successive kingdoms which come out of Imperial Rome] **are ten kings**[doms] that shall arise and another [little horn, the papacy] shall rise after them; and he shall be diverse from the first [ten], and he shall subdue three kings [the three Gothic kingdoms].

**7:25** And he [the little horn, the papacy] shall speak great words against the most High [saying that we must obey them in place of obeying the Word of God as our moral authority, just like the leaders of today's Ekklesia falsely teach], and shall wear out the saints of the most High, and think to change times and laws: and they [today's apostate called out] shall be given into his hand until a time and times and the dividing of time.

This entire Roman [Babylonian] system of ten successive dynastic systems and its final political ruler and the final false prophet will be destroyed by the coming of the Eternal Messiah with his chosen!

**7:26** But the judgment shall sit [is sure], and they shall take away his [Christ will destroy the dominion of the revived Holy Roman Empire Babylonian Mysteries] dominion, to consume and to destroy it unto the end.

**7:27** And **the kingdom** [God shall establish God's kingdom over all the earth, after this abomination is destroyed] **and dominion, and the greatness of the kingdom under the whole heaven, shall be given to the people of the saints of the most High, whose kingdom is an everlasting kingdom, and all dominions shall serve and obey him.**

**7:28** Hitherto is the end of the matter. As for me Daniel, my cogitations much troubled me, and my countenance changed in me: but I kept the matter in my heart.

## Daniel 8: The 2,300 Day Prophecy

This vision of Daniel is dated in the third year of Belshazzar, while the dream of Daniel 7 was dated in the first year if Belshazzar. The events of the Belshazzar period conclude with Daniel 5 and the fall of Babylon.

**Daniel 8:1 In the third year of the reign of king Belshazzar** a vision appeared unto me, even unto me Daniel, after that which appeared unto me at the first.

**8:2** And I saw in a vision; and it came to pass, when I saw, that **I was at Shushan in the palace, which is in the province of Elam; and I saw in a vision, and I was by the river of Ulai.**

A vision is very much like watching a short extremely vivid picture or movie while awake, which remains sharply imprinted on one's mind for many years. One sees the vision which is as clear and sharp as the very best film right before one's eyes, while wide awake.

**The vision begins with the fall of Babylon to the Persians**

First the vision is given and later in the chapter an explanation is provided. In the hope that it will be helpful I am adding the explanation to the presentation of the vision.

## The Ram

**8:3** Then I lifted up mine eyes, and saw, and, behold, there stood before the river **a ram** which had **two horns**: and the **two horns were high; but one was higher than the other, and the higher came up last**.

After Babylon fell it was first ruled by king Cyrus the Persian the first horn, later after Cyrus' son Cambyses, Darius the Mede the second horn, became king of the Persian Empire.

> **Explanation: Daniel 8:20** The **ram which thou sawest having two horns are the kings of Media and Persia.**

**Daniel 8:4** I saw the **ram pushing westward, and northward, and southward**; so that no beasts [no other nation] might stand before him, neither was there any that could deliver out of his hand; but he did according to his will, and became great.

## The He Goat

**8:5** And as I was considering, behold, **an he goat came from the west on the face of the whole earth, and touched not the ground: and the goat had a notable horn between his eyes.**

> **Explanation: Daniel 8:21** And **the rough goat is the king of Grecia**: and the **great horn that is between his eyes is the first king**.

Alexander carried out the plans of his father king Philip of Macedonia, and united the Greeks becoming the first king of a united Greece; after which he conquered Persia.

## Alexander Conquers Persia.

**8:6** And **he came to the ram that had two horns** [the Medes and Persians], which I had seen standing before the river, and ran unto him in the fury of his power.

**8:7** And I saw him [the he goat; Alexander's Greek empire] come close unto the ram [The Persian empire], and he was moved with choler [fury] against him, and **smote the ram, and brake his two horns**: and there was no power in the ram to stand before him, but he cast him down to the ground, and stamped upon him: and there was none that could deliver the ram out of his hand.

**8:8** Therefore the **he** [Greece, Alexander] **goat waxed very great: and when he was strong, the great horn was broken** [Alexander died suddenly at Babylon June 323 B.C.]; **and for it** [the Greek empire] **came**

**up four notable ones** [after infighting by many contenders Alexander's empire was divided into four parts somewhere near 280 B.C.] **toward the four winds** [four directions; north, east, south and west] **of heaven.**

> **Explanation:** **Daniel 8:22** Now that being broken, whereas four stood up for it, [After Alexander died his empire was ultimately divided into four kingdoms somewhere around 277 B.C.] **four kingdoms shall stand up out of the nation,** but not in his power.

The prophecy tells us that Alexander's empire would be divided into four parts, and then immediately skips to the end time and the final end time fierce king of the North.

Out of one of these four divisions came the king of the north, which carried on as Babylon; historically called Seleucid Syria.

**8:9** And **out of one of them** [one of the four, Seleucid Syria called Babylon at that time] **came forth a little horn** [henceforth called the the king [ruler] of the north, became very powerful], **which waxed exceeding great, toward the south, and toward the east, and toward the pleasant land.**

> **Explanation:** One of these four; the king of the north called Babylon, or Seleucid Syria became very powerful across Syria. Daniel 11 is a history of the competition between this king of the north Seleucid Syria and the king of the south Egypt, over control of Judea Palestine.
>
> Seleucid Syria became a part of the Roman empire in 133 B.C. when the king of Pergamos, Attalus 3, died and willed that kingdom to Rome. At that time Rome assumed the mantel of king of the king of the north continuation of the Babylonian Mysteries System, the iron legs of Daniel 2.
>
> At the final end time "the latter time" of the king of the north; Babylon the Great, the final [seventh] revival of the Holy Roman Empire [by whatever name it is called] will take place and this same system will once again make war against the king of the South [Egypt and Judea and their allies].
>
> **Daniel 8:23** And in the **latter time** [the end time] **of their kingdom, when the transgressors are come to the full, a king of fierce countenance** [intimidating appearance], **and understanding dark sentences** [secret things including complicated technology and evil spiritual powers], **shall stand up** [become ruler of the North, the

New European Holy Roman Empire (by whatever name it takes) revival].

**8:24** And his power shall be mighty, but not by his own power [he will be supported by Satan's power]: and he shall destroy [take much spoil by peaceful devious means] wonderfully, and shall prosper, and practise, and shall destroy the mighty and the holy people.

This final revival of the Holy Roman Empire Babylonian church state system in a New Federal Europe will overcome many, beginning in a time of peace and shall be very rich for about two years before attacking Asia in the third year; and later he will attempt to fight the arriving Christ.

**8:25** And through his policy also he shall cause craft to prosper in his hand; and he shall magnify himself in his heart, and **by peace** shall destroy [take much spoil by peaceful devious means] many: **he shall also stand up against the Prince of princes; but he shall be broken without hand.**

The prophecy now insets to Satan, of whom this political system and its ruler are a servant and a type. Satan being the one who led one third of the angels in rebellion against God and ascended to try to make war on God.

**Daniel 8:10** And **it waxed great, even to the host of heaven; and it cast down some of the host and of the stars to the ground, and stamped upon them.**

Here this final political [beast] ruler of the last revival of Babylon, the now rising New Federal Europe; is used as an allegory of Satan who fought against the host of heaven and cast some of the stars [angels] to the ground. This kind of allegory is consistent with the Isaiah and Ezekiel verses using men as a type of Lucifer / Satan.

This man will persecute the called out Spiritual Ekklesia on the earth and he will fight Christ at his coming, but this man is only a tool of [and a type of] the real Adversary, Satan.

This king of the North, is clearly identified as the system of the dragon, the scarlet beast, Satan (Rev 17); and as the final ruler of the Babylonian system of Daniel 2.

**Revelation 12:3** And there appeared another wonder in heaven; and behold a **great red dragon** [Satan], **having seven heads** [picturing the seven revivals of the Holy Roman Empire system] **and ten horns** [the final seventh revival consisting of ten rulers (nations) with a different man leading the whole system], **and seven crowns** [one crown on each of its seven heads, representing the seven revivals of the Holy Roman Empire system] **upon his heads.**

**12:4** And his tail **drew the third part of the stars** [angels] **of heaven, and did cast them to the earth** [the true dragon is Satan the devil, and the earthly Holy Roman Empire dragon system is of Satan the devil] : and the dragon stood before the woman which was ready to be delivered, for to devour her child as soon as it was born.

This final ruler called the king of the north [and the whole Babylonian Mysteries Holy Roman Empire system], now rising in Europe will be destroyed by Jesus Christ at his coming, and Satan will also ultimately be destroyed by Christ as well.

**Daniel 8:11** Yea, **he magnified himself even to** [against] **the prince of the host** [the high priest], **and by him the daily sacrifice was taken away,**

This came by Antiochus Epiphanes and again later in C 70 A.D. when the Roman Prince Titus destroyed the temple at Jerusalem ending the sacrifices; which are not to resume until Christ comes and builds the Ezekiel Temple.

**. . . and the place of the sanctuary was cast down** [this happened in c 70 A.D. and the city and people will again be taken in this latter day for the second half of the 70th week (Dan 9) or 42 months].

As Satan fights against God and tries to exalt himself above God; so this physical leader of the latter day kingdom of the north will also seek to fight against the Word of God throughout his reign and at the coming of Christ. The physical end time ruler [a Euopean king of the North] will occupy Jerusalem and the place of the sanctuary for 42 months (Rev 11:2).

This physical ruler is given an army to fight and overcome the people of God on the earth. Because of the great transgressions of today's Spiritual Ekklesia and the physical nations of Israel against the Word of God.

Power to make war for 42 months will be given to this king of the North to overcome the called out, because of their many sins against the Eternal.

**8:12** And **an host was given him against the daily sacrifice** [in c 70 A.D. Titus destroyed the Temple and stopped the Daily, and in this latter day the king of the North receives power for another 42 months, against physical and spiritual Israel, because of the multitude of our transgressions.] **by**

**reason of transgression** [of the Ekklesia and the nations of Israel], **and it cast down the truth to the ground; and it practised, and prospered.**

**8:13** Then I heard one saint speaking, and another saint said unto that certain saint which spake, How long shall be the vision concerning [about when the daily will be cleansed] the daily sacrifice, and [when the abomination completes trampling the daily?] the transgression of desolation, to give both the sanctuary and the host to be trodden under foot?

The question here is about **how long the entire vision** of the king of the north is: NOT about how long the stopping of the daily will be!

The whole vision about the 2300 days, concerns the time from the fourth division of Alexander's empire being established and the first king of the North being set up, until Christ comes.

The 2,300 days is not about the daily sacrifice being stopped which was done by the Roman Prince Titus in c 70 A.D.; the 2,300 days is about the King of the North which began about 277 B.C, when Alexander's empire was finally divided into four parts.

The whole prophecy of the King of the North will last for 2,300 days [years]! Until the final king of the north is destroyed by Christ and the sanctuary is cleansed!

**8:14** And he said unto me, **Unto two thousand and three hundred days; then shall the sanctuary be cleansed.**

Who comes to cleanse the sanctuary? Jesus Christ! Because Daniel 9 tells us that the sanctuary will lay desolate [will NOT be cleansed] until the consummation [completion] of the final 42 months of the second half of the full seven years.

**Gabriel gives the interpretation of the vision.**

**8:15** And it came to pass, when I, even I Daniel, had seen the vision, and sought for the meaning, then, behold, there stood before me as the appearance of a man.

**8:16** And I heard a man's voice between the banks of Ulai, which called, and said, Gabriel, make this man to understand the vision.

**8:17** So he came near where I stood: and when he came, I was afraid, and fell upon my face: but he said unto me, Understand, O son of man: **for at the time of the end shall be the vision** [the cleansing of the sanctuary by the coming of Christ!].

**8:18** Now as he was speaking with me, I was in a deep sleep [Daniel fainted and fell on his face] on my face toward the ground: but he touched me, and set me upright.

The vision covers the history of the King of the North from the division of Alexander's empire into four parts, up to the coming of Messiah the Christ; and Messiah's cleansing of the temple sanctuary!

**8:19** And he said, Behold, I will make thee know what shall be in the last end of the indignation: for **at the time appointed** [at the end of the 2,300 days of the kingdom of the North.] **the end shall be**.

**8:20** The ram which thou sawest having two horns are the kings of Media and Persia.

**8:21** And the rough goat is the king of Grecia: and the great horn that is between his eyes is the first king.

**8:22** Now that being broken, whereas four stood up for it, four kingdoms shall stand up out of the nation, but not in his power.

**8:23** And **in the latter time of their kingdom**, when the transgressors are come to the full, a king of fierce countenance, and understanding dark sentences [the last king of the north will understand secret things], shall stand up.

**8:24** And his power shall be mighty, but not by his own power [by Satan's power]: and he shall destroy wonderfully [awesomely], and shall prosper, and practise, and shall destroy the mighty and the holy people.

He will have power to occupy Jerusalem and Judea for 42 months and to rise above the other nations of Israel.

**8:25** And through his policy also he shall cause craft to prosper in his hand; and he shall magnify himself in his heart [become very proud], and by peace shall destroy many: he shall also stand up against the Prince of princes; but he shall be broken without [this man and the entire system will be destroyed by Jesus Christ at his coming, without any human help] hand.

**The vision that the sanctuary will be cleansed 2,300 days after the empire of Alexander is divided into four parts is true.**

**8:26 And the vision of the evening and the morning which was told is true: wherefore shut thou up the vision; for it shall be for many days.**

**8:27** And I Daniel fainted, and was sick certain days; afterward I rose up, and did the king's business; and I was astonished at the vision, but none understood it.

**History**

The sanctuary will be cleansed at the coming of Christ; therefore to have a good idea of when Christ will come, we must date when Alexander's empire was divided into four parts and then count forward 2,300 years; a day for a year.

The history of the successors of Alexander is very complex and extremely difficult, yet as we get closer and closer to the time; God is keeping his promise to Daniel and increasing knowledge and understanding day by day.

Historically, the first king of a united Greece was Alexander, who died in 323 B.C. after conquering the Persian Empire.

After his death, many men tried to assume his mantle as ruler of the lands that he had conquered.

In 304 B.C. Antigonus declared himself king and demanded that all the others submit to him. They did not agree and also declared themselves to be kings over their own lands.

In 301 B.C. Antigonus 1 was defeated and killed. Meanwhile, the son of Antigonus, Demetrius, was able to flee the field and continued as king of various areas in his father's place, thus keeping six kings.

In 297 B.C. Cassander died and was succeeded by his eldest son Philip, who in turn died the next year (296 B.C.). In 295 B.C., the widow of Cassander, Thessalonice; divided the kingdom of Macedonia between her two remaining sons, Antipater and Alexander. They took to quarreling and Antipater murdered his mother and attacked his brother Alexander. Alexander called for help from Demetrius, who came and murdered the young man, seizing his kingdom.

Demetrius then attacked Alexander's brother, Antipater, who fled to his uncle Lysimachis. Lysimachis had the lad executed for the murder of his sister, the boy's mother, in 294 B.C. These events brought to an end the family of Cassander. Extinguishing Cassander, his wife and his three sons.

To further complicate things a number of the possessions of Demetrius declared their independence while these struggles were going on.

After Demetrius took the necessary time to secure Macedonia he proceeded to retake Thessaly and Boeotia in 291 B.C., completing the job in 290 BC.

Then in 288 B.C. Pyrrhus, Lysmachis and Ptolemy united against Demetrius and defeated him, making joint war against him and forcing him to abandon his kingdom of Macedonia.

Demetrius, left with only his possessions outside of Macedonia; tried to attack Seleucus and move into Asia with his army, but was finally taken prisoner in 285 BC after his army fell apart. His kingdom was then taken over by his son Antigonus 2 Gonatas

"In 285 B.C., Demetrius, worn down by his fruitless campaign, surrendered to Seleucus." In 283 B.C., at the age of 55, Demetrius died in captivity in Syria and was succeeded by his son Antigonus 2 Gonatas who continued to rule the kingdom of his father Demetrius.

Soon Lysimachus made the fatal mistake of having his son Agathocles murdered at the say-so of his second wife, Arsinoe (282 B.C.) who wanted her own son to become king.

The murdered Agathocles's widow, Lysandra, fled to Seleucus, who now made war upon Lysimachus.

Seleucus, after appointing his son Antiochus ruler of his Asian territories, defeated and killed Lysimachus at the Battle of Corupedium in Lydia in 281 B.C. Then in 281 B.C. Seleucus was assassinated as he tried to invade Macedonia and Thrace.

Then certain Syrian officers of Seleucus rejected Antiochus from becoming their king in 280 B.C.; seeking to take over the kingdom for themselves. Antiochus then invaded Syria from his own possessions to put down the pretenders to his father's throne, and became sole ruler of all his father's possessions in spring 280 B.C. However taking advantage of the troubles of Antiochus, Nicomedes murdered his brothers and sought to become an independent king of Bythnia.

Antiochus then proceeded to advance on Nicomedes I king of Bythnia and the army of Gauls he had called to help him and Nicomedes of Bythnia bowed to Antiochus without a serious fight in 278 B.C. Nicomedes then continued to rule Bythnia but accepted the dominance of Antiochus king of Babylon [Seleucid Syria] in 277 B.C.

In 277 B.C. the remnants of the empire of Alexander were reduced to four parts fulfilling the prophecy that finally there would be only four divisions of Alexander's empire. Which four parts were established in c 277 B.C. with Babylon, Greece, Asia Minor and Egypt Palestine.

I do want to caution that even though this looks and may be correct; we must still be alert to watch events and WAIT FOR THE SIGNS. This history is incredibly complex and there is the matter of the ancient Greek city state calendars as related to our common calendar today. **This could possibly be out by a few years.**

**Nevertheless these things would be meaningless if we were to die tonight; it is imperative that we seek to be as close to God as possible. None of us is secure from sudden tragedy; therefore let us always put our trust in the only one who can save!**

> **Ecclesiastes 12:13** Let us hear the conclusion of the whole matter: **Fear God, and keep his commandments: for this is the whole duty of man.**

### The Vision is for The End Time

> **Daniel 8:17** For at the TIME of the END the VISION [The vision is about the end of the 2,300 days of years.] shall be
>
> **Daniel 8:19** Behold, I will make thee know what shall be in the LAST END of the indignation: for at the TIME APPOINTED the END SHALL BE.
>
> **Daniel 8:23** And in the LATTER TIME of their kingdom, when the transgressors are COME TO THE FULL,

This VISION, this prophecy, is for the END TIMES. This prophecy was not and could not, have been fulfilled by Antiochus Epiphanes over two thousand years ago!

### The prophecy is for our day, NOW!

How long shall be the VISION?

**Daniel 8:14** Unto 2300 days, then shall the sanctuary be cleansed.

Margin 2300 evenings and mornings. What is an evening and morning?

The evening and morning were the first day (Gen 1:5). The evening and morning were the second day (Gen 1:8). The evening and morning were the third day (Gen 1:13). One evening and one morning together are one day. Two evenings and mornings are two days. Three evenings and mornings are three days. One hundred evenings and mornings are one hundred days. **And, twenty-three hundred evenings and mornings are twenty-three hundred days!**

Suddenly from the four divisions of Alexander's kingdom and the founding of the king of the North in Daniel 8:8, the prophecy leaps forward to the last days and the cleansing of the sanctuary (Dan 8:9). Shown in the explanation; are the four divisions in verse twenty-two and then leaping forward to the LATTER TIME and the cleansing of the sanctuary in verse twenty-three.

In the LATTER TIME a king will appear over a New Federal Europe consisting of ten nations. He will understand secret [occult and highly technical matters] things and he will prosper be devious sneaky policies and means (Dan 8:23-24).

He will gain advantage over many while they are AT PEACE (Dan 8:25, 1 Thes 5:3).

He shall stand up against the Prince of Princes, Jesus Christ, at his coming (Dan 8:25), but he shall be broken (Dan 2:35) and thrown into the fire (Rev 19:20 and Dan 7:11).

This final fierce appearing king of the Babylonian system today rising up to be centered in Europe, and at its later end moving to Jerusalem; shall have power to make war, and to occupy Jerusalem; for forty two months or 1260 days (Rev 13:5); after which he and the false prophet will be destroyed and the sanctuary will be CLEANSED by the coming of Messiah the Christ who will build the Ezekiel Temple!

The whole vision about this competition between Babylon [the North] and Egypt/Judea [the South] is covered in Daniel 11.

The vision about Alexander's empire being divided into four parts, would last for **a total of 2300 days from the partition of Alexander's empire into four parts in c 277 BC**, and then [at the end of the 2,300 years] shall the sanctuary be cleansed (Dan 8:13-14).

**The explanation is this:**

From the time that Alexander's empire is divided into four parts [277 B.C.], there will be 2300 days [years] until the sanctuary is cleansed and the destruction of the final seventh resurrection of the Holy Roman Empire of Babylon as described in Daniel 2 and Daniel 7.

At a day for a year this 2300 days is 2300 years in fulfillment. c spring 277 B.C., 2300 years later would be 2023 A.D., now add one for no year zero which is c spring 2024 A.D.

Now subtracting 42 months (1260 days) we arrive in the winter of 2020 A.D. for the start of the tribulation; **If the date beginning the count is correct.**

Given the historical difficulties of the Greek struggles **it is possible that this date might be in error by a few years,** but one thing is certain; IT IS VERY CLOSE INDEED!

These are indications of the nearness of the times only; they are not dates certain until proved by the appearance of ALL of the Biblical signs.

This man of sin will then go to the Holy Place [Temple Mount] 75 days after being set up in the Vatican and the great tribulation of Matthew 24:15 will begin.

## Daniel 5

The last Babylonian king was Nabonidus (*Nabu-na'id*, 556 - 539 BC). While absent from Babylon to put down a rebellion to the south, the Persian army invaded from the north and overcame the regent of Babylon, Nabonidus' son Belshazzar (Jer 27:6-7).

History records that Babylon was under siege for some time until Cyrus' general Darius the Mede [aka Gobryus] arrived and launched its final attack by diverting the river and entering the city via the river bed.

After God gave Daniel the understanding of the writing on the wall and the Persians entered the city the army of Babylon was so disheartened that it gave up without a fight. God had decreed his judgment and it was God who disheartened and confused the defenders.

This should be a lesson for those who claim that we are too strong and that we cannot fall at this time. Instead of proudly trusting in our own strength we should be asking: If God is against us and has rejected us for the overspreading of our idolatries, pride and sins: Who can save us?

After the Persian army surrounded Babylon, thinking the city impregnable Belshazzar held a great feast for his commanders and officials, which was undoubtedly a worship feast in honor of and appealing to their gods to defend the city and was also intended to rally the commanders and people for the battle.

**Daniel 5:1** Belshazzar the king made a great feast to a thousand of his lords, and drank wine before the thousand.

At this feast Belshazzar disrespected the Eternal God by bringing out the vessels of the temple in Jerusalem to drink to other false gods from them; thereby attempting to boast and encourage the people that the Babylonian empire which had conquered Jerusalem was invincible before any army or even against God himself.

Jeremiah makes it clear that Belshazzar was the grandson of Nebuchadnezzar.

> **Jeremiah 27:6** And now have I given all these lands into the hand of Nebuchadnezzar the king of Babylon, my servant; and the beasts of the field have I given him also to serve him. **27:7** And all nations **shall serve him, and his son, and his son's son**, until the very time of his land come:

**Daniel 5:2** Belshazzar, whiles he tasted the wine, commanded to bring the golden and silver vessels which his father [ancestor, i.e. grandfather] Nebuchadnezzar had taken out of the temple which was in Jerusalem; that the king, and his princes, his wives, and his concubines, might drink therein.

**5:3** Then they brought the golden vessels that were taken out of the temple of the house of God which was at Jerusalem; and the king, and his princes, his wives, and his concubines, drank in them.

They drank toasts to their idols and false gods out of the holy vessels from the temple of the Eternal; which was boasting against the Eternal and exalting their idols above the Creator who had made the things they idolized. Just as today's Ekklesia boasts itself in following idols of men.

**5:4 They drank wine, and praised the gods of gold, and of silver, of brass, of iron, of wood, and of stone.**

As they boasted in their idols to defend them against the approaching army and rejected the Eternal to deliver them; judgment was passed on them.

Why was this written, and why was so much recorded about the events of Nebuchadnezzar? This was recorded as an example for us, and for our learning and benefit.

**1 Corinthians 10:11** Now all these things happened unto them for examples: and **they are written for our admonition, upon whom the ends of the world are come.**

**2 Timothy 3:16** **All scripture is given by inspiration of God, and is profitable for doctrine, for reproof, for correction, for instruction in righteousness: 3:17 That the man of God may be perfect, thoroughly furnished unto all good works.**

The lessons that should be drawn from this event is that if we commit the same sins of idolatry and relying on the idols of men instead of being zealous to follow and exalt the Eternal; we shall all likewise be judged as wanting and rejected by our LORD (Rev 3:14-22) into the furnace of affliction so that the spirit might be saved by afflicting the flesh.

Brethren, we have exalted men as idols above our God and his Word; and our correction is now at the door.

**Daniel 5:5** In the same hour came forth fingers of a man's hand, and wrote over against the candlestick upon the plaister of the wall of the king's palace: and the king saw the part of the hand that wrote.

Then Belshazzar was terrified. He who had boasted of his idols against the Eternal became terrified at the appearance of a hand and a short writing. His knees shook and he soiled his pants in terror.

**5:6** Then the king's countenance was changed, and his thoughts troubled him, so that the joints of his loins [bowels] were loosed, and his knees smote one against another.

The king cried out to the priests and the wise men of his gods to reveal the meaning of this thing.

**5:7** The king cried aloud to bring in the astrologers, the Chaldeans, and the soothsayers. And the king spake, and said to the wise men of Babylon, Whosoever shall read this writing, and shew me the interpretation thereof, shall be clothed with scarlet, and have a chain of gold about his neck, and **shall be the third ruler in the kingdom.**

Belshazzar himself being the second ruler, with the first ruler being his father Nabonidus who was away putting down a rebellion in a distant province.

These idolaters could not reveal the matter unto the king, just as today's idolatrous Ekklesia has almost no spiritual understanding and is rapidly losing what understanding they did have.

**5:8** Then came in all the king's wise men: but **they could not read the writing, nor make known to the king the interpretation thereof.**

**5:9** Then was king Belshazzar greatly troubled, and his countenance was changed in him, and his lords were astonied [troubled].

Then the Queen who could have been the wife of Nabonidus and possibly the mother of Belshazzar] who was not present at this feast, heard what had happened and informed the king that a true man of God was in the city and bid the king send for him.

**5:10** Now the queen by reason of the words of the king and his lords came into the banquet house: and the queen spake and said, O king, live for ever: let not thy thoughts trouble thee, nor let thy countenance be changed:

**5:11** There is a man in thy kingdom, in whom is the spirit of the holy gods; and in the days of thy father light and understanding and wisdom, like the wisdom of the gods, was found in him; whom the king Nebuchadnezzar thy father, the king, I say, thy [grand father Nebuchadnezzar] father [ancestor], made master [the chief of] of the magicians, astrologers, Chaldeans, and soothsayers;

**5:12** Forasmuch as an excellent spirit, and knowledge, and understanding, interpreting of dreams, and shewing of hard sentences, and dissolving of doubts, were found in the same Daniel, whom the king named Belteshazzar: now let Daniel be called, and he will shew the interpretation.

### Daniel is summoned and appeared before the king

**5:13** Then was Daniel brought in before the king. And the king spake and said unto Daniel, Art thou that Daniel, which art of the children of the captivity of Judah, whom the king my father brought out of Jewry?

**5:14** I have even heard of thee, that the spirit of the gods is in thee, and that light and understanding and excellent wisdom is found in thee.

Then God exalted himself through Daniel, above all the gods being worshiped by these rulers.

**5:15** And now the wise men, the astrologers, have been brought in before me, that they should read this writing, and make known unto me the interpretation thereof: but they could not shew the interpretation of the thing:

**5:16** And I have heard of thee, that thou canst make interpretations, and dissolve doubts: now if thou canst read the writing, and make known to me the interpretation thereof, thou shalt be clothed with scarlet, and have a chain of gold about thy neck, and shalt be the third ruler in the kingdom.

Daniel rejected the gifts of the king, and revealed the meaning of the writing from God.

**5:17** Then Daniel answered and said before the king, Let thy gifts be to thyself, and give thy rewards to another; yet I will read the writing unto the king, and make known to him the interpretation.

Daniel explained the words

**5:18** O thou king, the most high God gave Nebuchadnezzar thy [grand] father a kingdom, and majesty, and glory, and honour:

**5:19** And for the majesty that he gave him, all people, nations, and languages, trembled and feared before him: whom he would he slew; and whom he would he kept alive; and whom he would he set up; and whom he would he put down.

**5:20** But **when his heart was lifted up, and his mind hardened in pride**, he was deposed from his kingly throne, and they took his glory from him:

**5:21** And he was driven from the sons of men; and his heart was made like the beasts, and his dwelling was with the wild asses: they fed him with grass like oxen, and his body was wet with the dew of heaven; till he knew that the most high God ruled in the kingdom of men, and that he appointeth over it whomsoever he will.

Daniel's preamble goes to the point that Belshazzar was full of pride and knowing all these things which had happened to his grandfather, still exalted his idols above the Almighty Creator God of Eternity.

I tell the truth; today's Ekklesia have the scriptures and we know that the whole Word of God from cover to cover is about following the Eternal above any idol or any man, principality or power, either physical or spiritual! The brethren know this and yet they have chosen to follow idols of men above following the Eternal and living by every Word of God!

Yes, we trust in our idols of men and we reject any zeal for the Word of God to follow the false traditions of men just like Belshazzar did; and if we do not sincerely wholeheartedly repent: then like Belshazzar we shall be found wanting and given over to severe correction by the Almighty Eternal One!

Today's Spiritual Ekklesia is full of pride in our own ways, leaders and traditions and we thumb our noses at the Almighty, rejecting any zeal for keeping his Word in favor of being zealous for our idols; and we shall pay the price!

**5:22** And thou his son [descendant], O Belshazzar, **hast not humbled thine heart, though thou knewest all this;**

Today's Spiritual Ekklesia knows these things and yet we are still lifted up with pride against the LORD of our baptismal commitment, to follow our idols of men and corporations.

**5:23** But hast lifted up thyself against the Lord of heaven; and they have brought the vessels of his house before thee, and thou, and thy lords, thy wives, and thy concubines, have drunk wine in them; and thou hast praised the gods of silver, and gold, of brass, iron, wood, and stone, which see not, nor hear, nor know: and the God in whose hand thy breath is, and whose are all thy ways, hast thou not glorified:

**5:24** Then was the part of the hand sent from him; and this writing was written.

## The meaning of the writing

**5:25** And this is the writing that was written, MENE, MENE, TEKEL, UPHARSIN.

Brethren the writing is on the wall for the Ekklesia today: Jesus Christ has found us wanting and has numbered our days and is about to reject us for our idolatry, pride and wickedness.

**5:26** This is the interpretation of the thing: MENE; God hath numbered thy kingdom, and finished it.

We have been weighed in the balance of God, and have been found proud and righteous in our own eyes, and wicked in the eyes of God (Rev 3:15-22).

**5:27** TEKEL; Thou art weighed in the balances, and art found wanting.

We have been divided many times as God seeks to find any faithful among his called out.

**5:28** PERES; Thy kingdom is divided, and given to the Medes and Persians.

If we will not sincerely and wholeheartedly repent, our potential eternal life and kingdom shall be taken from us and given to others.

**5:29** Then commanded Belshazzar, and they clothed Daniel with scarlet, and put a chain of gold about his neck, and made a proclamation concerning him, that he should be the third ruler in the kingdom.

In that very night the unrepentant idolaters were slain and the kingdom was given to others. We will also face affliction in the furnace of correction; and if we do not sincerely repent, we will lose our birthright of eternal life and the promise of a kingdom.

**5:30** In that night was Belshazzar the king of the Chaldeans slain.

**5:31** And Darius the Median [aka Gobryus, a general of Cyrus, took the city for Cyrus the king of Persia] took the kingdom, being about threescore and two years old.

# Daniel 10

### Daniel 10 is an introduction to Daniel 11-12

Daniel 10 also reveals the awesome appearance of the Cherubs of God and the humility of Daniel who sought the Eternal with all his heart.

### Daniel 5 background History

In 539 B.C. there was a revolt in Southern Babylonia, and the Babylonian king, Nabonidus the son of Nebuchadnezzar, went south with his army to put down the rebellion; leaving his own son Belshazzar ]Nebuchadnezzar's grandson] in charge of Babylon.

Taking advantage of this occupation of the Babylonian army with the southern rebellion at Uruk; the army of Cyrus invaded Babylon from the north.

In June the Babylonian army was completely defeated at Opis, and immediately afterwards Sippara opened its gates to the conqueror. Gobryas (The Mede General Gobryas, who took the regnal name Darius upon ascending the throne of the Persians], was then sent to Babylon, which surrendered "without fighting," and the daily services in the temples continued without a break.

In October, Cyrus himself arrived, and proclaimed a general amnesty, which was communicated by Gobryas [Darius the Mede] to "all the province of Babylon," of which he had been made governor by Cyrus.

Meanwhile, Nabonidus, who had concealed himself, was killed; and when his wife died, Cambyses II, the son of Cyrus, conducted the funeral.

Cyrus the Great (576 – 530 BC king of Persia) now assumed the title of "king of Babylon," (336 B.C.) claiming to be the descendant of the ancient kings, and made rich offerings to the temples.

Babylon fell in 539 BC but Cyrus was not made king of Babylon until 536 BC.

**Daniel 10**

**Daniel 10:1** In **the third year of Cyrus king of Persia** a thing was revealed unto Daniel, whose name was called Belteshazzar; and the thing was true, but the time appointed was long: and he understood the thing, and had understanding of the vision.

Daniel fasted for three whole weeks; yet we are not to assume this was a total fast but rather an abstention from all desirable things to take only bread and water.

**10:2** In those days I Daniel was mourning [fasting and mourning over sin] three full weeks.

**10:3** I ate no pleasant bread [desirable things], neither came flesh [no flesh or wine, only coarse bread and water] nor wine in my mouth, neither did I anoint [no washing or perfuming] myself at all, till three whole weeks were fulfilled.

**10:4** And in the four and twentieth day of the first month, as I was by the side of the great river, which is Hiddekel;

Daniel saw an angel clothed in fine white linen long shirt with a skirt of gold, who's appearance was as a bright shining; and a voice like thunder.

**10:5** Then I lifted up mine eyes, and looked, and behold a certain man clothed in linen, whose loins were girded with fine gold of Uphaz:

**10:6** His body also was like the beryl, and his face as the appearance of lightning, and his eyes as lamps of fire, and his arms and his feet like in colour to polished brass, and the voice of his words like the voice of a multitude.

Daniel saw this being and fainted, while those with him fled away as a great fear overcame them even though they saw nothing.

**10:7** And I Daniel alone saw the vision: for the men that were with me saw not the vision; but a great quaking [a terror made them to shake with fear and flee away] fell upon them, so that they fled to hide themselves.

**10:8** Therefore I was left alone, and saw this great vision, and **there remained no strength in me:** for my comeliness was turned in me into corruption, and I retained no strength.

Daniel fainted and when prostrate he heard the words of Gabriel who lifted Daniel up to his feet. Consider the awesomeness of this being that Daniel would faint in his presence.

**10:9** Yet heard I the voice of his words: and when I heard the voice of his words, then was I in a deep sleep [faint] on my face, and my face toward the ground.

**10:10** And, behold, an hand touched me, which set me upon my knees and upon the palms of my hands.

Daniel is lifted up to his knees and the angel spoke with him.

**10:11** And he said unto me, O Daniel, a man greatly beloved, understand the words that I speak unto thee, and stand upright: for unto thee am I now sent.

Daniel stood trembling in awe before Gabriel

And when he had spoken this word unto me, I stood trembling.

Then the angel Gabriel spoke with Daniel explaining his mission and how Satan had tried to prevent him, and how Michael helped him against Satan. These things reveal that God is running things and that Satan is trying to prevent the fulfillment of God's will on a hidden spiritual level.

In our time as written in Daniel 12 God will proclaim that Satan can go no further in his own plans and Satan will rise up to try to attack God in heaven; Satan will be defeated and cast down and he will be forced to fulfill the prophets regarding the final days.

**10:12** Then said he unto me, Fear not, Daniel: for from the first day that thou didst set thine heart to understand, and to chasten thyself before thy God, thy words were heard, and I am come for thy words.

The spirit head of the Babylonian system then manifested by Persia, possibly Satan himself, withstood Gabriel desiring to prevent the prophecy of Daniel 10-12, and the angel Michael came to aid Gabriel.

**10:13** But the [spirit ruler] prince of the kingdom of Persia [Satan] withstood me one and twenty days: but, lo, Michael, one of the chief princes [Cherubs of God], came to help me; and I remained there with the kings of Persia.

Gabriel and Michael remained for a time with the kings of Persia. The vision is about the history future to Daniel, right up to and including the latter days

**10:14** Now I am come to make thee understand **what shall befall thy people in the latter days: for yet the vision is for many days** [the vision is about many days [years] future to Daniel].

Daniel was speechless before Gabriel

**10:15** And when he had spoken such words unto me, I set my face toward the ground, and I became dumb.

Daniel's mouth is opened and he protests that he is too lowly - even though he is president of the empire under the king - to speak with one such as Gabriel.

**10:16** And, behold, one like the similitude of the sons of men touched my lips: then I opened my mouth, and spake, and said unto him that stood before me, O my lord, by the vision my sorrows are turned upon me, and I have retained no strength.

**10:17** For how can the servant of this my lord talk with this my lord? for as for me, straightway there remained no strength in me, neither is there breath left in me.

Then Daniel was strengthened by an angel and Daniel bid Gabriel to speak on

**10:18** Then there came again and touched me one like the appearance of a man, and he strengthened me,

**10:19** And said, O man greatly beloved, fear not: peace be unto thee, be strong, yea, be strong. And when he had spoken unto me, I was strengthened, and said, Let my lord speak; for thou hast strengthened me.

Gabriel told Daniel that in the future he will go and fight against the evil spiritual forces upholding the Persians and trying to prevent the prophecy of the Greek victory from being fulfilled.

Gabriel was speaking to Daniel in 533 BC. It would not be until 334 BC that Alexander began his campaign against the Persians and in 331 BC the Greeks defeated Persia and took over the Babylonian Mysteries system. New people; same system.

**10:20** Then said he, Knowest thou wherefore I come unto thee? and now [in future] will I return to fight with the prince of Persia: and when I am gone forth, lo, the prince of Grecia shall come [334-331 BC].

**10:21** But I will shew thee that which is noted in the scripture of truth: and there is none that holdeth with me in these things, but **Michael your prince** [Michael is the angel in charge of Judah].

## Daniel 11

I will be quoting Scripture, Rawlinson's History and a few quotes from "The Middle East in Prophecy." All other comments are my own.

Daniel 11 gives us the history from the four divisions of Alexander's empire, particularly the history of the two main divisions of Syria-Babylon and Egypt, until Antiochus Epiphanes a type of the final king of the north; and then jumps from Antiochus to the end time kings of the North and South.

God confirms the rule of Darius the Mede through his angel Gabriel.

This makes it clear that there are spiritual forces working behind the scenes in the nations. God allowing Satan general rule, but within the limits set by God; and when God wants something, Satan always opposes God and God's will is forced on Satan by God's agents.

**Daniel 11:1** Also I [Gabriel Daniel 10] in the first year of Darius the Mede [became king of the Persians in 522 B.C.], even I, [I will stand to help Darius] stood to confirm and to strengthen him.

After he became king of Babylon, Cyrus issued a decree to rebuild the temple at Jerusalem; and after the work was interrupted Darius issued a new decree to resume the work.

The last or fourth strong king over the Persian empire was Xerxes, who was the richest of all and stirred up war with Greece.

**11:2** And now will I shew thee the truth. Behold, there shall stand up yet three kings in Persia; and the fourth [Darius the Mede became king of Persia in 522 B.C. and was followed by three more rulers after him; making four altogether] shall be far richer than they all: and by his strength through his riches he shall stir up all against the realm of Grecia.

King Philip of Macedon made plans to unite the Greek kingdoms under himself and then to attack the Medo-Persian empire. Philip died suddenly and his son **Alexander** carried out his father's plans of conquest, becoming the first king of a united Greece and defeating the Persian empire; taking over the Babylonian system as the brass of Daniel 2 and the leopard of Daniel 7.

**11:3** And a mighty king [Alexander the Great] shall stand up, that shall rule with great dominion, and do according to his will.

Alexander himself died suddenly in 323 BC and after many years of infighting the kingdom was finally divided into four parts in about 277 B.C.

The prophecy is now concerned with the kings of Egypt / Judea the king of the south and Babylon / Syria the kings of the north; beginning with Antiochus the son of Seleucus Nicator [who became king about 280 or 279 B.C. and secured the throne in 277 B.C.] as king of Babylon-Syria [king of the north] and Ptolemy as king of Egypt-Palestine [king of the south].

**11:4** And when he [Alexander] shall stand up, his kingdom shall be broken, and shall be divided toward the four winds [after much fighting was divided into four parts] of heaven; and not to his posterity, nor according to his dominion which he ruled: for his kingdom shall be plucked up, even for others beside those.

Ptolemy I, called Soter, king of Egypt-Palestine became strong and powerful, sending one of his generals Seleucus Nicator to seize control over the northern kingdom of Syria-Babylon.

After successfully seizing Babylon Seleucus fell out with Ptolemy and declared himself the king of an independent Syria-Babylon often called Seleucid Syria by historians.

**11:5** And the king of the south [Egypt/Palestine] shall be strong, and **one of his princes** [Seleucus Nicator would rise in power above the king of the south]; **and he shall be strong above him, and have [a] dominion; his dominion** [Seleucid Syria the kingdom of the north] **shall be a great dominion.**

After some 50 years Antiochus II of Syria-Babylon, called Theos. His wife was named Laodice. Rawlinson's Ancient History, page 251, "Her influence ... engaged him in a war with Ptolemy Philadelphus [king of the south; Egypt/Judea], B.C. 260, which is terminated, B.C. 252, by a marriage between Antiochus and Bernice, Ptolemy's daughter."

The prophecy says "he that begat her" shall be given up. Also that she shall not retain the power of the arm, neither shall the king of the north, whom she married, stand. All three are to come to their end. This came to pass.

Rawlinson's History, pages 251 and 252: "On the death of Philadelphus II of Egypt [he that begat her], B.C. 247, Antiochus [Syria] repudiated Bernice, and took back his former wife, Laodice, who, however, doubtful of his constancy, murdered him to secure the throne for her son Seleucus (II) B.C. 246 ... Bernice ... had been put to death by Laodice."

**11:6** And in the end of years they shall join themselves together; for the king's daughter of the south shall come to the king of the north to make an agreement: but she shall not retain the power of the arm; neither shall he stand, nor his arm: but she shall be given up, and they that brought her, and he that begat her, and he that strengthened her in these times.

"Out of a branch," or "shoot," of her roots. Her parents were her roots. Hence, this must be her brother, who next should occupy the throne of king of the south and fulfill this prophecy. Now listen to this accurate fulfillment, quoted word for word from the same page of Rawlinson's work (p. 252):

"Ptolemy Euergetes [the III, eldest son of Philadelphus (p. 272) and therefore Bernice's brother, Seleucus II; a branch of her roots] invaded Syria, B.C. 245, to avenge the murder of his sister, Bernice ... . In the war which followed, he carried everything before him."

**11:7** But out of a branch of her roots shall one stand up in his estate, which shall come with an army, and shall enter into the fortress of the king of the north, and shall deal against them, and shall prevail:

After a time Egypt would rise up against the king of the north

**11:8** And shall also carry captives into Egypt [the king of the South] their gods, with their princes, and with their precious vessels of silver and of gold; and he shall continue more years than the king of the north.

Ptolemy III did seize the fortress of Syria, Seleucia, the port of Antioch, capital of the kingdom. Then he carried back to Egypt immense booty and 2,500 molten images and idolatrous vessels which, in 526 B.C. Cambyses had carried away from Egypt. He continued to rule until 222 B.C., while the king of the north, Seleucus II, died in 226 B.C.

**11:9** So the king of the south [Egypt-Palestine] shall come into his kingdom, and shall return into his own land.

When Seleucus II died, his two sons took over the kingdom of the north; first Seleucus III, 226-223 B.C., who ruled only three years, and then his brother Antiochus III, called "the Great," 223-187 B.C. Both of these two sons of Seleucus II assembled immense forces to war against Egypt, avenge their father, and recover their port and fortress, Seleucia.

**11:10** But his sons shall be stirred up, and shall assemble a multitude of great forces: and one shall certainly come, and overflow, and pass through: then shall he return, and be stirred up, even to his fortress.

Antiochus the Great, after 27 years, recovered his fortress, Seleucia, and he also conquered the territory of Syria, as far as Gaza, including Judea. But the young Egyptian king, now Ptolemy IV (Philopater), was roused, and with an army of 20,000 inflicted severe defeat on Antiochus the Great; and fulfilling verse 12, he killed tens of thousands and again annexed Judea to Egypt. But he was not strengthened, for he made a rash and speedy peace with Antiochus, and returned to dissipation [drunkenness and chambering], throwing away the fruits of victory.

**11:11** And the king of the south [Egypt-Palestine] shall be moved with choler, and shall come forth and fight with him, even with the king of the north [Syria-Babylon]: and he shall set forth a great multitude; but the multitude shall be given into his hand.

**11:12** And when he hath taken away the multitude, his heart shall be lifted up; and he shall cast down many ten thousands: but he shall not be strengthened by it.

12 years later, in 205 B.C., Ptolemy Philopator the king of the south [Egypt-Palestine] died, leaving his throne to an infant son, Ptolemy Epiphanes. Then Antiochus king of the north assembled a greater army, and won great victories.

He then made a treaty allying Philip of Macedonia with him, and others, against Egypt, and they wrested Phoenicia and southern Syria from the king of the south. In this they were assisted by some of the Jews.

The Hellenized Jews sought to aid the king of the north in order to take over from the Mosaic Jews ruling Palestine and after Ezra there was a continual rivalry between the Mosaic Jews and the Hellenized Jews who originated with the spread of Greek influence by Alexander.

**11:13** For the king of the north shall return, and shall set forth a multitude greater than the former, and shall certainly come after certain years with a great army and with much riches.

**11:14** And in those times there shall many stand up against the king of the south: also the robbers of thy people [the Hellenized branch of Judaism, who were the roots of present day Rabbinic Judaism; tried to establish an independent kingdom at that time and failed] shall exalt themselves to establish the vision; but they shall fall.

**11:15** So the king of the north [Syria-Babylon] shall come, and cast up a mount, and take the most fenced cities: and the arms of the south [Egypt-Palestine] shall not withstand, neither his chosen people, neither shall there be any strength to withstand.

Those who fought against this king of the north would be defeated and forced to do the will of the king of the north. "the glorious land," of course, refers to Judea, the Holy Land.

Antiochus the Great [king of the north] besieged and took Sidon [Lebanon] from Egypt, ruined the interests of Egypt in Judea at the Battle of Mount Panium, 198 B.C., and then Antiochus took possession of Judea.

**11:16** But he that cometh against him shall do according to his own will, and none shall stand before him: and he shall stand in the glorious land, which by his hand shall be consumed.

The one he marries will not stand on his side. In 198 B.C., Antiochus arranged a marriage between his daughter, Cleopatra (not the Cleopatra of 31 B.C. in Egypt) and young Ptolemy Epiphanes, king of the south, by which he hoped subtly to gain complete possession of Egypt; but the plan failed.

Rawlinson, page 254, "Coele-Syria and Palestine promised as a dowry, but not delivered." Cleopatra did not truly stand on the side of Antiochus, for it was only a trick to gain possession of Egypt.

**11:17** He shall also set his face to enter with the strength of his whole kingdom, and upright ones with him; thus shall he do: and he [the king of the south shall give] shall give him the daughter of women, corrupting her: but she shall not stand on his side, neither be for him.

Antiochus then turned his attention in another direction and tried to conquer, 197 to 196 B.C., the islands and coasts of Asia Minor. But the Roman general, Lucius Cornelius Scipio Asiaticus, utterly defeated him at the Battle of Magnesia, 190 B.C.

**11:18** After this shall he turn his face unto the isles, and shall take many: but a prince for his own behalf shall cause the reproach offered by him to cease; without his own reproach he shall cause it to turn upon him.

Antiochus next turned his attention to his own land, Seleucid Syria, But, attempting to plunder the temple of Belus, in Elymais, he was killed, 187 B.C.

**11:19** Then he shall turn his face toward the fort of his own land: but he shall stumble and fall, and not be found.

Seleucus IV Philopator (187-176), his son, in an effort to raise money, sent a tax collector, Heliodorus, through Judea. But he reigned only 11 years, when Heliodorus poisoned him.

**11:20** Then shall stand up in his estate a raiser of taxes in the glory of the kingdom: but within few days he shall be destroyed, neither in anger, nor in battle.

The king of the north left no heir. But his brother, a younger son of Antiochus the Great, named Epiphanes (Antiochus IV), a contemptible reprobate, came by surprise and through flattery took the kingdom. To his aid came his assistant, Eumenes. Rawlinson says, page 255, "Antiochus [Epiphanes], assisted by Eumenes, drives out Heliodorus, and obtains the throne, B.C. 176. He astonished his subjects by an affectation of Roman manners" and "good-natured profuseness [flattery]."

**11:21** And in his estate shall stand up a vile person, to whom they shall not give the honour of the kingdom: but he shall come in peaceably, and obtain the kingdom by flatteries.

Although only a few were with Antiochus Epiphanes at first, by deceit and flattery he crept into power and prospered. He invaded Palestine and Egypt.

Rawlinson, pages 255-256, says, "Threatened with war by the ministers of Ptolemy Philometor [now king of the south (Egypt-Palestine)], who claimed Coele-Syria and Palestine as the dowry of Cleopatra, the late queen-mother, the king of Syria-Babylon Antiochus marches against Egypt ... B.C. 171" (pp. 277-278). But he was met by his nephew, Ptolemy Philometor, king of the south, with another immense army. But the

Egyptian king was defeated through the treachery of his own officers and was outwitted by Antiochus. Verses 26-27 — continuing in Rawlinson, page 278: "After his victory at Pelusium, Antiochus advanced to Memphis, and having obtained possession of the young king's person [Ptolemy Philometor, king of the south], endeavored to use him as a tool for effecting the entire reduction of the country." In 174 B.C., the uncle of the king of the south sat at a banquet. Antiochus pretended to ally himself with the young Ptolemy, against his brother, Euergetes II, but each was trying to deceive the other.

Wherever the conquering Alexander went, the Greeks brought with them Greek culture which rapidly caught on and heavily influenced the world of that day. Greek became the lingua franca of the Mediterranean region and Greek logic, reasoning style and culture permeated the western world.

During the days of Ezra the repentant Jews returned to Judea where they experienced a religious revival and eventually developed into the Mosaic Pharisees who lived at the advent of Christ.

Meanwhile the Jews who chose to remain in the dispersion became centered in Alexandria Egypt, Babylon and Rome; adopting and increasingly applying Hellenic reasoning to the scriptures.

This split Judaism into two parts with one group in Judaism using pagan Greek reasoning's about the scriptures and the others sitting in Moses seat at Jerusalem.

The pushing back and forth between the Babylonian and the Egyptian kingdoms eventually resulted in Babylon taking control of Palestine for a brief period by Antiochus Epiphanes.

**Antiochus IV Epiphanes** ( /æn'taɪ.əkəs ɛ'pɪfəniːz/; Ancient Greek: Ἀντίοχος Ἐπιφανής, 'God Manifest';c. 215 BC – 164 BC) ruled the Seleucid Empire from 175 BC until his death in 164 BC. He was a son of King Antiochus III the Great. His original name was Mithridates; he assumed the name Antiochus after he ascended the throne.

Antiochus, with the help of King Eumenes II of Pergamum, in 175 BC, seized the throne of Babylon Syria for himself, proclaiming himself co-regent for another son of Seleucus, an infant named Antiochus (whom he then murdered a few years later).

When the guardians of King Ptolemy VI of Egypt demanded the return of Coele-Syria in 170 BC, Antiochus launched a preemptive strike against

Egypt, conquering all but Alexandria and capturing King Ptolemy and taking Judea from Egypt.

**To control Judea Antiochus deposed the high Priest, Jason; who was of the loyal Mosaic faction and replaced him with a Hellenic High Priest, Menelaus.**

To avoid alarming Rome, Antiochus allowed Ptolemy VI to continue ruling as a puppet king. Upon Antiochus' withdrawal, the city of Alexandria chose a new king, one of Ptolemy's brothers, also named Ptolemy (VIII Euergetes). Instead of fighting a civil war, the Ptolemy brothers agreed to rule Egypt jointly.

In 168 BC Antiochus led a second attack on Egypt and also sent a fleet to capture Cyprus. Before reaching Alexandria, his path was blocked by a single, old Roman ambassador named Gaius Popillius Laenas, who delivered a message from the Roman Senate directing Antiochus to withdraw his armies from Egypt and Cyprus, or consider themselves in a state of war with the Roman Republic. Antiochus said he would discuss it with his council, whereupon the Roman envoy drew a line in the sand around him and said, "Before you cross this circle I want you to give me a reply for the Roman Senate" – implying that Rome would declare war if the King stepped out of the circle without committing to leave Egypt immediately. Weighing his options, Antiochus decided to withdraw. Only then did Popillius agree to shake hands with him.

**While Antiochus was busy in Egypt, a rumor spread that he had been killed.**

**The deposed High Priest of the Mosaic faction in Jerusalem, Jason; gathered a force of 1,000 soldiers and made a surprise attack on the city of Jerusalem.**

The Hellenic High Priest appointed by Antiochus, Menelaus; was forced to flee Jerusalem during a riot. On the return of Antiochus from Egypt in 167 BC enraged by his defeat in Egypt, and the affront to him by the insurrection against his appointed high priest, he attacked Jerusalem and restored the Hellenist Menelaus, and executed many Mosaic Jews.

" When these happenings were reported to the king, he thought that Judea was in revolt. Raging like a wild animal, he set out from Egypt and took Jerusalem by storm. He ordered his soldiers to cut down without mercy those whom they met and to slay those who took refuge in their houses. There was a massacre of young and old, a killing of women and children, a

slaughter of virgins and infants. In the space of three days, eighty thousand were lost, forty thousand meeting a violent death, and the same number being sold into slavery."
— 2 Maccabees 5:11–14

The Hellenized Jews did not reject holy days etc, but rather reinterpreted them according to Hellenic logic and exalted their own reasoning's above the literal scriptures.

In his rage Antiochus outlawed Mosaic practices around which the Mosaic Pharisees and Sadducees were rallying. However the Hellenizers also kept these things but did so according to their own logic; and the action of Antiochus, far from supporting one side against the other; brought the two sides into common resistance against Antiochus.

When Antiochus decided to outlaw the Holy Days, Sabbaths, circumcision, and ordered the worship of Zeus as the supreme god (2 Maccabees 6:1–12). This was anathema to both the faithful Mosaic Pharisees and to the Hellenic Pharisees.

They both rejected the decree and joined together to oppose Antiochus.

Antiochus then sent an army to enforce his decree and because of the resistance, the city was severely damaged, many were slaughtered, and a military Greek citadel called the Acra was established.

Not long after this the king sent an Athenian senator to force the Jews to abandon the customs of their ancestors and live no longer by the laws of God; also to profane the temple in Jerusalem and dedicate it to Olympian Zeus, and that on Mount Gerizim to Zeus the Hospitable, as the inhabitants of the place requested…They also brought into the temple things that were forbidden, so that the altar was covered with abominable offerings prohibited by the laws. A man could not keep the sabbath or celebrate the traditional feasts, nor even admit that he was a Jew. At the suggestion of the citizens of Ptolemais, a decree was issued ordering the neighboring Greek cities to act in the same way against the Jews: oblige them to partake of the sacrifices, and put to death those who would not consent to adopt the customs of the Greeks. It was obvious, therefore, that disaster impended. Thus, two women who were arrested for having circumcised their children were publicly paraded about the city with their babies hanging at their breasts and then thrown down from the top of the city wall. Others, who had assembled in nearby caves to observe the sabbath in secret, were betrayed to Philip and all burned to death."
— 2 Maccabees 6:1–11

The actions of Antiochus resulted in a joint alliance against him by both Jewish groups.

Taking advantage of Antiochus' western problems, King Mithridates I of Parthia attacked from the east and seized the city of Herat in 167 BC, disrupting the direct trade route to India and effectively splitting the Greek world in two.

Recognizing the potential danger in the east, but unwilling to give up control of Judea, Antiochus sent a commander named Lysias to deal with the Maccabees, while the King himself led the main Seleucid army against the Parthians. After initial success in his eastern campaign, including the reoccupation of Armenia, Antiochus died suddenly in 164 BC.

The Hasmonean Dynasty

> The Maccabee revolt against the Greek ruler led to the formation of an independent Jewish kingdom, known as the Hasmonaean Dynasty, which lasted from 165 BCE to 63 BCE.
>
> The Hasmonean Dynasty eventually disintegrated in a civil war between the Hellenizers and the Mosaic loyalists.
>
> Eventually the Mosaic element of the Hasmonaean Dynasty, appealed to Rome for intervention, leading to a total Roman conquest and annexation of Palestine,
>
> By the time of Christ, Judea was the center of the Mosaic Pharisees who taught the scriptures and had the temple and its rituals as re-established by Ezra; even though they had become self righteous and lacked understanding themselves.
>
> It was these Mosaic Pharisees who Christ said sat in Moses seat, until after his resurrection, when Christ was raised to sit in that seat of authority himself.
>
> Meanwhile the Hellenizers were widely spread through most of the Jewish world outside Judea - with some still in Judea - in the dispersion.
>
> When the Jews rebelled against Rome, Jerusalem, the Temple and Judea were destroyed by the Roman Prince Titus; leaving the Hellenized Pharisees to slowly gain control of Judaism in a rivalry with the scribes that lasted for another thousand years. The Hellenic Pharisees developed into Modern Rabbinic Judaism.

Modern Rabbinic Judaism is NOT the religion of Moses: It is an apostasy from Moses through Hellenic logic and the reasoning's of men about the scripture: In exactly the same way that modern "Christianity" is a perversion of the teachings of Christ.

This history set the conditions for the advent of Christ and his followers as the only remaining true religion, which adheres to the same religion that God gave to Moses and to "that prophet" which Moses spoke of; Messiah, Jesus Christ.

The "prince of the covenant" refers to the high priest.

**11:22** And with the arms of a flood shall they be overflown from before him, and shall be broken; yea, also the prince of the covenant.

**11:23** And after the league made with him he shall work deceitfully: for he shall come up, and shall become strong with a small people.

Antiochus first took over the kingdom of the North, Alexander's province of Babylon, by flatteries, and made his supporters very rich.

**11:24** He shall enter peaceably even upon the fattest places of the province; and he shall do that which his fathers have not done, nor his fathers' fathers;he shall scatter among them the prey, and spoil, and riches: yea, and he shall forecast his devices against the strong holds, even for a time.

Then Antiochus took over Egypt but allowed the boy king he controlled to remain under a regent. Then when Antiochus returned home a new king arose in Egypt which rebelled against Antiochus. In 168 BC Antiochus led a second attack on Egypt and was defeated.

While Antiochus was busy in Egypt, a rumor spread that he had been killed.

The deposed High Priest of the Mosaic faction in Jerusalem, Jason; gathered a force of 1,000 soldiers and made a surprise attack on the city of Jerusalem.

The Hellenized High Priest appointed by Antiochus, Menelaus; was forced to flee Jerusalem during the riot.

On the return of Antiochus from his defeat in Egypt in 167 BC, enraged by his defeat, he attacked Jerusalem and restored the Hellenist Menelaus, and executed many Mosaic Jews.

Antiochus sent troops to the Holy Land, who desecrated the Temple and sanctuary, abolished the daily sacrifice (see also Daniel 8:11, 24) and placed the abomination — an image of Jupiter Olympus [from which the modern supposed pictures of Christ are made] — on the altar in the Temple precincts, making it desolate (Rawlinson, p. 255).

**11:25** And he [Antiochus the king of the north] shall stir up his power and his courage against the king of the south with a great army; and the king of the south shall be stirred up to battle with a very great and mighty army; but he shall not stand: for they shall forecast devices against him.

Egypt fell to Antiochus, because of the intrigues of the Egyptian court and its child king.

**11:26** Yea, they that feed of the portion of his meat shall destroy him, and his army shall overflow: and many shall fall down slain.

**11:27** And both of these kings' hearts shall be to do mischief, and they shall speak lies at one table; but it shall not prosper: for yet the end shall be at the time appointed.

Egypt fell to Antiochus, and Antiochus enriched himself from the Egyptians and appointed an Hellenic high priest at Jerusalem as his agent to secure Palestine to follow him; before returning home

**11:28** Then shall he return into his land with great riches; and his heart shall be against the holy covenant; and he shall do exploits [Antiochus overthrew the lawful high priest with his own appointee from the Hellenists, which are the forefathers of modern Rabbinic Judaism], and return to his own land.

### Antiochus attacked Egypt the second time

**11:29** At the time appointed he shall return, and come toward the south; but it shall not be as the former, or as the latter [attacks on Egypt].

Egypt hired a foreign fleet to help her and had the backing of Rome against the second invasion by Antiochus; and Antiochus was forced to withdraw from Egypt and is enraged by the frustration of his purpose against Egypt and by the rebellion in Jerusalem against the Hellenic high priest he had appointed.

**11:30** For the ships of Chittim shall come against him: therefore he shall be grieved, and return, and have indignation against the holy covenant: so shall he do; he shall even return, and have intelligence with them that forsake the holy covenant [Antiochus tried to gain the support of the Hellenic Pharisees who had turned away from taking God's Word literally].

While Antiochus was busy in Egypt, a rumor spread that he had been killed.

The deposed High Priest of the Mosaic faction in Jerusalem, Jason; gathered a force of 1,000 soldiers and made a surprise attack on the city of Jerusalem.

The High Priest appointed by Antiochus, Menelaus; was forced to flee Jerusalem during a riot. On the return of Antiochus from Egypt in 167 BC enraged by his defeat, he attacked Jerusalem and restored the Hellenist Menelaus, and executed many Mosaic Jews.

Antiochus in his fury then outlawed all forms of "Judaism" and polluted the Most Holy Place; thus offending BOTH the Mosaic and Hellenized Pharisees!

**11:31** And arms shall stand on his part, and they shall pollute the sanctuary of strength, and shall take away the daily sacrifice, and they shall place the abomination that maketh desolate.

The BOTH the Mosaic and Hellenized Pharisees rose up against the pollution of the temple and the outlawing of true religion by Antiochus.

The Hellenized Pharisees continued to be corrupted, while the Mosaic Pharisees restored true religion in Judea, only to become corrupted by pride by the time that Messiah came.

Then from the time that Christ was physically on the earth until today, many of God's faithful have continued to do exploits by the power of God!

**11:32** And such as do wickedly against the covenant shall he corrupt by flatteries: but the people that do know their God shall be strong, and do exploits.

The prophecy now continues in a general way through the history of the faithful to God up to the end time. These things being applicable to the disciples of Christ as well as to the heroes of the Mosaic Covenant.

**11:33** And they that understand among the people shall instruct many: yet they shall fall by the sword, and by flame, by captivity, and by spoil, many days [years].

Always the called out are a very little flock of faithful, surrounded by a mixed multitude of tares, outright thorns and flatterers. The majority of most professing called out are not converted, although many will be very sincere they just do not really understand.

Satan sows tares of intelligent and charismatic men who rise quickly to the top and from there they mislead the brethren to follow their own imaginations and Hellenized [Aristotelian] reasoning's, contrary to the Word of God. The called out are warned to beware of this deception throughout the scriptures and especially by Jesus Christ.

**11:34** Now when they shall fall, they shall be holpen with a little help: but many shall cleave to them with flatteries.

Satan has always tempted, pressured and persecuted God's faithful to wear them out and quench their zeal to live by every Word of God.

**11:35** And some of them of understanding shall fall, to try them, and to purge, and to make them white, even to the time of the end: because it is yet for a time appointed.

### The Latter Days

### The prophecy now leaps to the events of the end time right before the coming of Messiah the Christ

Like Antiochus the final latter king of the north will seek to extirpate true religion from off the earth, and he shall prosper for a short time occupying Jerusalem and Judea for 42 months

**11:36** And the king shall do according to his will; and **he shall exalt himself, and magnify himself above every god, and shall speak marvellous things against the God of gods, and shall prosper till the indignation be accomplished: for that that is determined shall be done.**

**11:37 Neither shall he regard the God of his fathers, nor the desire of women, nor regard any god: for he shall magnify himself above all.**

This final king of the North [the now rising New Federal Europe] will put his trust in armies and will exalt himself and the false prophet above all that is called god, attempting to make themselves the ultimate moral authority of all humanity, regardless of the various religious traditions.

**11:38** But in his estate shall he honour the God of forces: and a god whom his fathers knew not shall he honour with gold, and silver, and with precious stones, and pleasant things.

The political leader of the coming New Europe will overcome many by stealth and trickery for a short time; and will divide the wealth of the nations among his followers, becoming very rich.

**11:39** Thus shall he do in the most strong holds with a strange god, whom he shall acknowledge and increase with glory: and he shall cause them to rule over many, and shall divide the land for gain.

This European Roman "Babylon" will become very rich for a short time [See Rev 18] but he shall then go to war with Asia and then with the coming Messiah; only to be destroyed.

Daniel 11 covers the history of the 2300 Day Prophecy (Dan 9) in detail, from the division of Alexander's empire into four parts (c 277 B.C,) up to and including Antiochus Epiphanes (c 167 B.C.).

Then the prophecy shifts to the end time in verse 40.

**Daniel 11:40** And **at the time of the end** shall the king of the south push at him [Egypt historically controlled Palestine and modern Israel [the Jewish state] is a part of the king of the south. Either Egypt or Israel will initially provoke the soon coming new Europe. For example the radical Jewish Settler Movement would do so by rejecting the coming peace deal and sabotaging it.]: and the king of the north [the Babylon of the New Europe which will rise up as the final ten nation revival of the Holy Roman Empire; ridden by the Roman Catholic church] shall come against him like a whirlwind [as a powerful irresistible force], with chariots [many modern military vehicles], and with horsemen [many soldiers particularly mobile forces], and with many ships; and he shall enter into the countries, and shall overflow and pass over.

The New Europe along with modern Jordan and the countries of Psalm 83, will invade the Jewish state. It is highly probable that the New Europe will have peace keepers as part of the coming peace deal (1 Thess 5:3) and being already in the area these forces could quickly take control of Jerusalem and Judea to stop the blood letting; when Jordan, Turkey, Gaza, the Palestinians and Arab's rush in upon a nation which has been abandoned by God for its many sins.

America and Britain will fall with Judah and Egypt (Hosea 5:5) but not necessarily occupied like Judea (Mat 24:15). The scriptures say that this latter day king of the north [Babylon the Great] will come to dominance by clever trickery and devious policies

Jerusalem and Judea will be occupied possibly at their own request to end the bloodshed of a losing war with the Palestinians and surrounding nations except Egypt

The other Israelite nations will be overcome peaceably by economic means, with nothing being said about them being occupied.

This New Europe will be allied with the Latin American nations and will also take over many American client states in the Middle East, Africa and elsewhere.

It should be noted that Israel, America, Britain and Egypt are extremely vulnerable with several Achilles heels to exploit. In the case of America an abandonment of the petrodollar by the Middle East energy producing countries for the Euro or its successor, would be all that is needed to bring economic collapse to the dollar dependent countries.

**11:41** He shall enter also into the glorious land [Palestine, the modern Jewish state], and many countries shall be overthrown: but these shall escape out of his hand, **even Edom, and Moab, and the chief of the children of Ammon.** [they will be allied with Assur (Germany) a part of the king of the North, Psalm 83]

With the collapse of the US dollar and economy Egypt, Libya and Africa will fall into the hands of Europe. Egypt with its canal being a key to controlling North Africa and commerce between Europe and Asia.

**11:42** He shall stretch forth his hand also upon the countries: and the land of Egypt shall not escape. **11:43** But he shall have power over the treasures of gold and of silver, and over all the precious things of Egypt: and the Libyans and the Ethiopians shall be at his steps [bow submissively at his feet to serve the New Europe].

After about two years of great prosperity the New Europe, the final revival of the scarlet beast of Revelation 17; will be distraught by the coming together of Asia [probably developing from the Shanghai Cooperation Organization] and will attack the Asian nations in the third year.

**11:44** But tidings out of the east and out of the north shall trouble him: therefore he shall go forth with great fury to destroy, and utterly to make away many.

Asia will counterattack, severely damaging Europe; and the king of the North, along with its religious leader will move to Jerusalem where their remaining forces are located.

**11:45** And he shall plant the tabernacles of his palace between the seas in the glorious holy mountain; yet he shall come to his end, and none shall help him.

Then the resurrection of the faithful dead will take place followed immediately by the marriage of the Lamb in heaven (Rev 15,19), and during that short period the seven last plagues will be poured out and the armies of Asia will come down to a staging area at Har Megiddo before attacking Jerusalem.

The Asian armies which were destroying the ten nation kingdom of the North in Europe, will turn south sweeping through the Middle East towards Jerusalem in hot pursuit of the political ruler and the false prophet, and the sixth angel's viol will open the way for them by drying up the river Euphrates allowing vast armies of men to pass over.

> **Revelation 16:12** And the sixth angel poured out his vial upon the great river Euphrates; and the water thereof was dried up, that the way of the kings of the east might be prepared.

When the Euphrates dries up demons will go forth [probably speaking through men] to encourage these armies of Asia and Europe to join forces to confront the coming Christ.

The language indicates that the spirits controlling the leaders of the New Federal Europe then staying in Jerusalem will convince the Asian nations to join with them to defend against this invasion from space.

> **16:13** And I saw three unclean spirits like frogs come out of the mouth of the dragon, and out of the mouth of the beast, and out of the mouth of the false prophet. **16:14** For they are the spirits of devils, working miracles, which go forth unto the kings of the earth and of the whole world, to gather them to the battle of that great day of God Almighty.

Jude declares that when Christ comes to destroy Babylon and establish the kingdom of God on the earth; that he is coming WITH his saints [his resurrected chosen who were first taken to heaven for the marriage of the Lamb and then will return to the earth to destroy rebellion and wickedness and to rule the earth is righteousness.

Blessed is the one who is watching and keeping himself from joining the rebellious!

> **16:15** Behold, I come as a thief. Blessed is he that watcheth, and keepeth his garments, lest he walk naked, and they see his shame.

> **16:16** And he gathered them together into a place called in the Hebrew tongue Armageddon.

Now the seventh angel pours out his viol [bowl] which is the seventh and last plague; and Christ comes WITH his saints and a mighty earthquake,

> **Zechariah 14:2** For I will gather all nations against Jerusalem to battle; and the city shall be taken, and the houses rifled, and the women ravished; and half of the city shall go forth into captivity, and the residue of the people shall not be cut off from the city.
>
> **14:3** Then shall the LORD go forth, and fight against those nations, as when he fought in the day of battle.
>
> **14:4** And his feet shall stand in that day upon the mount of Olives, which is before Jerusalem on the east, and the mount of Olives shall cleave in the midst thereof toward the east and toward the west, and there shall be a very great valley; and half of the mountain shall remove toward the north, and half of it toward the south.
>
> **14:5** And ye shall flee to the valley of the mountains; for the valley of the mountains shall reach unto Azal: yea, ye shall flee, like as ye fled from before the earthquake in the days of Uzziah king of Judah: and the LORD my God shall come, and all the saints with thee.
>
> **14:6** And it shall come to pass in that day, that the light shall not be clear, nor dark:
>
> **14:7** But it shall be one day which shall be known to the LORD, not day, nor night: but it shall come to pass, that at evening time it shall be light.

> **Revelation 16:17** And the seventh angel poured out his vial into the air; and there came a great voice out of the temple of heaven, from the throne, saying, It is done.
>
> **16:18** And there were voices, and thunders, and lightnings; and there was a great earthquake, such as was not since men were upon the earth, so mighty an earthquake, and so great.
>
> **16:19** And the great city was divided into three parts, and the cities of the nations fell: and great Babylon came in remembrance before God, to give unto her the cup of the wine of the fierceness of his wrath.
>
> **16:20** And every island fled away, and the mountains were not found.

**16:21** And there fell upon men a great hail out of heaven, every stone about the weight of a talent: and men blasphemed God because of the plague of the hail; for the plague thereof was exceeding great.

Consider that all these seven last plague events including the movement of mighty armies could not take place in the one day of the resurrection of the bride as the seventh trump begins to sound. Also consider that these plagues were poured out while the saints stood before the Temple of God in heaven.

The key to understanding these things and the difference between the 1,290 days and the 1,335 days of Daniel 12:

The resurrection is at the end of the 1,290 days and the final plagues take in the few remaining days while the resurrected chosen are at the marriage of the Lamb in heaven (Rev 15,19); after which Christ comes WITH his saints to destroy wickedness from off the earth and establish the Kingdom of God!

## Daniel 12

Just before this man of sin is set up working miracles in the Vatican there will be war in heaven; as Satan realizing his time is now ending rises up to attack God and is cast down.

Then being defeated, Satan will set up his man of sin, the final miracle working abomination, and the final revival of the scarlet beast (Rev 17) will come to pass.

Then within 75 days after this miracle working pope is set up to do miracles in the Vatican, he will go to the holy mount triggering the 42 month tribulation; at the end of which Messiah the Christ will come with his resurrected chosen.

**Daniel 12:1** And at that time shall Michael stand up, the great prince which standeth for the children of thy people: and there shall be a time of trouble, such as never was since there was a nation even to that same time: and at that time thy people shall be delivered, every one that shall be found written in the book.

**12:2** And many of them that sleep in the dust of the earth shall awake, some to everlasting life, and [the unrepentant evil doers] some to shame and everlasting contempt.

> **Revelation 12:7 And there was war in heaven: Michael and his angels fought against the dragon; and the dragon fought and his**

> **angels, 12:8** And prevailed not; neither was their place found any more in heaven. **12:9** And the great dragon was cast out, that old serpent, called the Devil, and Satan, which deceiveth the whole world: he was cast out into the earth, and his angels were cast out with him.

Daniel 12:1 tells us that Michael will stand up to fight against Satan - when Satan rises up to attack God , and Michael will cast Satan and his demons down to the earth, which will be right before the beginning of the tribulation.

**Daniel 12:1** And at that time shall Michael stand up, the great prince which standeth for the children of thy people: and **there shall be a time of trouble, such as never was since there was a nation even to that same time: and at that time thy people shall be delivered, every one that shall be found written in the book.**

Knowing that his imprisonment is near at hand, Satan rises up to attack God one more time and is defeated and thrown down again.

> **Revelation 12:10** And I heard a loud voice saying in heaven, Now is come salvation, and strength, and the kingdom of our God, and the power of his Christ: for **the accuser of our brethren is cast down**, which accused them before our God day and night.
>
> **12:11** And they overcame him by the blood of the Lamb, and by the word of their testimony; and they loved not their lives unto the death.
>
> **12:12** Therefore rejoice, ye heavens, and ye that dwell in them. **Woe to the inhabiters of the earth and of the sea! for the devil is come down unto you, having great wrath, because he knoweth that he hath but a short time** [there will be only 3 1/2 years remaining].

After being defeated by Michael and cast down, Satan the dragon, represented by the scarlet beast of the new Europe ridden by the Roman Catholic church; empowers the physical leader to make war and to persecute the called out of God. Then the faithful will flee to the place prepared of God just as they fled to Pella from Jerusalem and Judea in the first century.

> **12:13** And when the dragon saw that he was cast down unto the earth, he persecuted the woman which brought forth the man child. **12:14** And to the woman were given two wings of a great eagle, that she might fly into the wilderness, into her place, where she is

> nourished for a time, and times, and half a time [42 months or 1,260 days], from the face of the serpent [dragon, Satan].
>
> **12:15** And the serpent [Satan inspired an army to chase the faithful to God] cast out of his mouth water as a flood after the woman, that he might cause her to be carried away of the flood. **12:16** And the earth helped the woman, and the earth opened her mouth [a great earthquake will swallow up this Jordanian army and save the faithful to God], and swallowed up the flood which the dragon cast out of his mouth.

Satan deprived of the object of his hatred, will then go back to attack those who did not respond to the warnings and who lacked zeal to live by every Word of God.

God will allow Satan to attack them to bring them to sincere repentance and to test that repentance in great adversity.

> **12:17** And the dragon was angry with the woman, and went to make war with the remnant of her seed, which keep the commandments of God, and have the testimony of Jesus Christ.

The zealous for God who are passionate to live by every Word of God are the spiritually wise and they will shine brightly in the family of God forever!

**Daniel 12:3** And they that be wise shall shine as the brightness of the firmament; and they that turn many to righteousness as the stars for ever and ever.

This Book of Daniel which is the KEY to all end time prophecy was Sealed until the end time, when God will unseal the book (Rev 5) and open up a great increase in spiritual knowledge and understanding. An increase in spiritual understanding which is rejected by most of the Ekklesia today.

**12:4,** but thou, O Daniel, shut up the words, and **seal the book, even unto the time of the end**: [when] many shall run about to and fro, and [The book being unsealed. spiritual understanding will be greatly increased.] **knowledge shall be increased**.

The book was sealed until the end, just before the words are to be fulfilled; and since Daniel is a key to understanding all end time prophecy; the understanding of latter day prophecy was also sealed until the end time.

No one who is not zealous to learn and to live by every Word of God can understand these things, and nobody writing a few hundred years ago could have understood these things. No one writing even 40 or 50 years ago could have understood these things because these things were sealed until their fulfillment becomes imminent. We have the word here of the angel of God written in Holy Scripture.

**12:5** then I Daniel looked, and, behold, there stood two, the one on this side of the bank of the river, and the other on the other side of the bank of the river.

**12:6** And the one said to the man clothed in linen, which was upon the waters of the river, how long shall it be to the end of these wonders?

**12:7** And I heard the man clothed in linen, which was upon the waters of the river, when he held up his right hand and his left hand unto heaven, and swore by him that lives for ever that **it shall be for a time, times, and a half** [42 months]. . .

We see here, the same period of times that was mentioned in Revelation 12. These are the "Times of the Gentiles" spoken of by Jesus Christ.

The word "time" can be shown to be a year, the plural times would be 2 years and half a time is half a year.

**Time, times, and half a time therefore represent three 3 ½ years, or 42 months.**

It will take 1,260 days to scatter the power of the holy people.

. . . And when he shall **have accomplished to scatter the power of the holy people, all these things shall be finished.**

Here we are specifically told that **the tribulation period will be 42 months**.

We are also told that the scattering of the power of the people will be a progressive ongoing process lasting 42 months, rather than one massive nuclear attack.

The scriptures say that Jerusalem will be occupied for 42 months and how long Judea and Egypt are to be occupied is not specifically stated but would be very close to that figure. The 42 months will begin with Jerusalem being taken, but it may take a few days or even weeks of hard fighting before the rest of the Jewish State is completely subdued.

America and the other Israelite countries will also be overcome by peaceful devious economic strategies but nothing is said about them being occupied, and we are told that it will take 42 months to scatter their power.

This seems to indicate economic collapse, agricultural collapse, natural disasters, disease epidemics and famine, internal strife and possible cyber attacks rather than an immediate massive nuclear attack.

**12:8** And I heard, but I understood not: then said I, O my Lord, what shall be the end of these things?

**12:9** And he answered and said, go thy way, Daniel: for **the words are closed up and sealed till the time of the end.**

The tribulation begins when Jerusalem and Judea are occupied and the other Israelite tribes like the British peoples and America begin to collapse.

The United States and the British nations will endure a catastrophic decline until they are at the point of total destruction; then Jesus Christ [Hebrew: Yeshua Mashiach] will come to deliver all the tribes of Israel and all humanity, and totally destroy the scarlet beast of the Federal European "Babylonian" church state system.

Remember that the Jews are the tribe of Judah with many Levites and some others mixed in; while the latter day descendants of the ten tribes of Israel are primarily the Anglo Saxons, Normans, Dutch, Belgian and Scandinavian peoples.

Then Daniel was told the second time that all these things are sealed until the time of the end.

Nobody before now, nobody writing many years ago; could have understood these things. Not because they were not godly or converted, but because God himself had sealed the book and concealed its meaning until the very end time.

**Who are the wise?**

The wise are those who recognize and understand that the source of all true wisdom is the Eternal God. The wise are those who know that the beginning of wisdom is the fear of the Lord. It is respect for God and for his Word which makes one wise. The wise know that through living by every Word of God and believing and doing what God says they will learn the true wisdom of God.

From the very creation of man and through the coming 42 month trial many have been and will be purified from sin, but unrepentant evil doers will not understand the things of God.

**Daniel 12:10,** many shall be purified, and made white, and tried; but the wicked shall do wickedly: and **none of the wicked shall understand** [until after it actually happens].

Who are the wicked? It is written, sin is the transgression of the law, and sin is wickedness. Therefore those who transgress the law of God, and the Word of God, those who despise and have no zeal to learn and to live by every Word of God, are the wicked and they will not understand.

**The book of Daniel, which is the key to understanding latter day prophecy; was sealed until the latter days.**

We have to become wise: We have to become righteous by zealously believing God and living by every Word of God in order to have any chance at understanding these things.

If we are living in the last days, and if we are wise because we zealously live by every Word of God; then we shall understand. We have the promise of Holy Scripture!

Those people who have no zeal to live by every Word of God, who pollute his Sabbaths and Holy Days and then try to justify their sins; are the wicked and they will not understand.

Only those who put God first, only those who seek God's wisdom and believe and live by God's Word, only they, the wise; shall understand.

Anybody who despises any zeal for God's Word, who pollutes God's [Friday sunset to Saturday sunset] Sabbath, who treads all over God's annual Holy Days, who rejects God's law and despises God's Word to follow the false traditions of men; are not wise, they are among the wicked.

Those who have no zeal for keeping the Word of God cannot understand God's Word and their explanations of prophecy simply cannot be accurate. Their positions cannot be correct, cannot be true; for the wicked cannot understand.

**12:9** And he said, Go thy way, Daniel: for **the words are closed up and sealed till the time of the end.**

Even at the end time: ONLY those who are zealous to learn and to keep the whole Word of God will understand; while those who follow idols of men instead of living by Every Word of God: Shall NOT understand!

Some will leave before this trial begins, understanding and heeding the warnings, because of their zeal for God and his Word; and many others will remember the warnings and repent as they are tried in the furnace of affliction; and some of the wicked shall continue in their wickedness right up until the coming of Christ and shall not understand.

Brethren, even in the tribulation there will be many in denial who will believe that this is not really the end time tribulation, but just another war!

**12:10** Many shall be purified, and made white, and tried; but the wicked shall do wickedly: and **none of the wicked shall understand; but the wise shall understand.**

Now we come to another period of days which appears to contradict the first oath and proclamation that the tribulation will last 42 months [1,260 Days] made by the angel on the river.

**The Daily Sacrifice**

The Daily Sacrifice was offered by the physical high priest each morning and each evening as an example that the spiritual High Priest Jesus Christ intercedes day and night before the heavenly throne of God the Father for the Ekklesia. It is this intercession by the spiritual High Priest Jesus Christ which restrains the setting up of the final man of sin and the final hour of trial (2 Thess 2:7)

The PHYSICAL daily was STOPPED by Prince Titus in 70 A.D. with his destruction of Jerusalem and the temple there. The physical temple was to remain desolate until Messiah comes to build the Ezekiel Temple and restart the physical Daily Sacrifice at that time (Ezek 40-48).

See **Daniel 9: The 70 Weeks Prophecy**

> **2 Thessalonians 2:7** For the mystery of iniquity doth already work: only he who now letteth [restrains] will let [will restrain], until he [the restraining one] be taken out of the way [stop his restraining].
>
> **2:8** And then shall that Wicked be revealed, whom the Lord shall consume with the spirit of his mouth, and shall destroy with the brightness of his coming:

Yes, Jesus Christ has been restraining Satan and this deceitful system until the appointed time, and the restraint, which is the daily intervention of Jesus Christ in heaven on behalf of today's Laodicean Assemblies will be STOPPED and the miracle working abomination will be set up.

## The final days before the coming of Christ

**Daniel 12:11** And from **the time that the daily sacrifice shall be taken away, and the abomination that maketh desolate set up,** there shall be a thousand two hundred and ninety days [1,290].

Here we are told that the final abomination will be set up at the same time that the daily is removed [the restraints holding back the rise of the final revival of Babylon] and that 1290 or 1335 days would then remain.

Since we know that Prince Titus destroyed the temple and the daily was stopped in c 70 A.D. The next question is; what about the 1290 and the 1335 days. Counting forward 1290 years from 70 A.D. we reach 1360 A.D., or counting 1335 days from 70 A.D. we reach 1405 A.D. Neither of which dates has any end time significance.

Since Daniel 9 tells us that the temple would be destroyed. which was fulfilled by Prince Titus in c 70 A.D., and writes that the temple would remain desolate and the sacrifice stopped until Messiah came to build the Ezekiel Temple: What is the daily in this passage?

Clearly in this passage of Daniel 12:11 the term daily is referring to the restraints (2 Thess 2:7) placed on Satan until the appointed time by the daily spiritual intersession of our spiritual High Priest Jesus Christ!

Where do the scriptures speak of the daily spiritual intercession of the spiritual High Priest Jesus Christ ending? The intercession of the spiritual High Priest for the corporate Ekklesia will end when Jesus Christ rejects today's Laodicean Ekklesia.

> **Revelation 3:16** So then because thou art lukewarm, and neither cold nor hot, I will spue thee out of my mouth [reject you from my body, reject you from being my people, reject you into the terrible furnace of correction of the final 42 month tribulation] . See the message of Jesus Christ to Laodicea.

Yes, Jesus Christ will reject today's corporate Ekklesia; into great tribulation: and that rejection of stopping of his intercession for the corporate assemblies, also ends the restraint on Satan and the final revival of the Babylonian system, which has protected us so far!

What of the few who are faithful? The physical daily was offered on behalf of the whole nation; and the spiritual daily intercession is on behalf of the whole body of believers.

However the daily sacrifice is only a part of the sacrificial system, and there remain the personal sacrifices.

Today Jesus Christ is about to cast out the whole collection of corporate entities claiming to be his people, because they reject any zeal for living by every Word of God in favor of their own false traditions; and in so doing Jesus Christ will STOP his night and day intercession holding back the final 42 months of severe trial.

However our spiritual High Priest will still accept and intercede for the personal individuals who are indeed faithful to live by every Word of God!

**The 1,290 and 1,335 days**

**Daniel 12:11** And from the time that the [spiritual intercession of Jesus Christ for the Laodicean Ekklesia in heaven is stopped (Rev 3:14-22, 2 Thess; see the Sacrificial System article or the Leviticus studies)] daily sacrifice shall be taken away, and the abomination that maketh desolate set up, there shall be a thousand two hundred and ninety days. **12:12** Blessed is he that waiteth, and cometh to the thousand three hundred and five and thirty days.

Once the miracle working man of sin is set up after Christ's spiritual daily intervention on behalf of the corporate Ekklesia [which is restraining the final rise of the Babylonian system] is stopped with the rejection of today's corporate Ekklesia [who are overwhelmingly Laodicea], there will be 1,290 days and every person who continue and reach the 1,335th day will be greatly blessed. This blessing is not pronounced on any particular people but on all people.

At the end of the 1,290 days the faithful will be blessed because the resurrection to spirit will take place at the the end of the 1290 days.

Then the resurrected chosen will be married to the Lamb before the throne of God in heaven, and during the marriage feast in heaven (Rev 15, 19) the seven last plagues will be poured out on the earth.

Then within 45 days after the resurrection the changed to spirit chosen will come to the earth with Christ, to put down the wicked and to receive their portion and to "stand in their lot."

The resurrected chosen will return to the earth and receive their responsibilities at the END of the 1,335 days and all people will be blessed by the removal of Satan; then God's Spirit will be poured out on all flesh establishing the kingdom of God over all the earth on that Feast of Pentecost.

The faithful will be blessed immediately after the end of the 1,290 days when they are changed to spirit, and then the whole earth will be blessed when the resurrected chosen return to the earth to put away all wickedness and establish the Kingdom of God over all peoples: after which God's Spirit is poured out on all flesh (Joel 2:28) on the Feast of Pentecost.

It is not clear whether this means that all people will be blessed by the outpouring of the Spirit on Pentecost at the precise end of the days, or whether the people will be blessed by the coming of Christ with his resurrected saints and the removal of Satan at the end of the days, followed by a few days of repentance while waiting for Pentecost.

Consider that Israel had arrived at Sinai and then had to wait for a few days before Pentecost came and God appeared on the Mount.

**Daniel 12:12** Blessed is he **that waiteth, and cometh to the thousand three hundred and five and thirty days.** **12:13** But go thou thy way till the end be: for thou shalt rest, and **stand in thy lot at the end of the days**.

The resurrected bride will be married to the Lamb before the throne of God the Father in heaven (Rev 15) while the seven last plagues are poured out, and will then return to the earth, where on the Feast of Pentecost God will pour out his Spirit on all flesh establishing the kingdom of God over all the earth (Joel 2:28)!

See the articles on the Marriage of the Lamb and Pentecost.

## Daniel 9: Dating the Ministry of Jesus Christ!

The Daniel 9:1 to 9:23 covers the first 69 weeks of the 70th week of the Seventy Weeks Prophecy accurately predicting the first coming of Jesus Christ; hundreds of years before it happened!

Then the Daniel 9:24 Seventieth Week of the Prophecy provides vital information concerning the Latter Days and the Return of Christ, which will be covered in Part 2.

**Dating the Ministry of Jesus Christ!**

Building the Temple

The deportations from Babylon began with the children of certain nobles including Daniel at about the age of 17, being taken to Babylon in 604 B.C. Then in 597 B.C. there was a major forced deportation, this was followed by another deportation in 586 B.C. when Nebuchadnezzar put down the rebellion of Zedekiah.

The city Jerusalem and temple were demolished and the deportation of the middle and upper class to Babylon [leaving the farmers to till the land] took place in 586 B.C.

The completion of the seventy years pronounced on Jerusalem through Jeremiah ended in 516 B.C., seventy years after the city and temple were destroyed in 586 B.C. the temple would again be completed.

Now consider the actual prophecy: In **Jeremiah 29:10**, God had promised, **"After seventy years** be accomplished at Babylon I will visit you, and perform my good word toward you, in causing you to return to this place" and Isaiah records that God had appointed Cyrus for this task. **Isaiah 44:28 "That saith of Cyrus, He is my shepherd, and shall perform all my pleasure: even saying to Jerusalem, Thou shalt be built; and *to the temple, Thy foundation shall be laid.*"**

Daniel recognizing that the 70 years pronounced on Jerusalem and specifically to the temple was nearing completion and seeing that construction on the temple had been suspended, fasted and prayed for the city in 522 B.C.

Daniel fasted and prayed [522 B.C.] that the city could be built and the prophecy of Jeremiah would be fulfilled.

**Daniel 9:1** **In the first year of Darius** the son of Ahasuerus, of the seed of the Medes, which was made king over the realm of the Chaldeans;

**9:2** In the first year of his reign (522 B.C.) I Daniel understood by books the number of the years, whereof the word of the LORD came to Jeremiah the prophet, that he would accomplish seventy years in the desolations of Jerusalem.

**The Fasting Prayer of Repentance by Daniel**

There is a reason why this prayer of repentance is recorded for us: This is an example of the kind of sincere repentance prayer that God accepts from his people. Please spend some time in carefully thinking about what a proper repentant attitude is, in the eyes of God.

**9:3** And I set my face unto the Lord God, to seek by prayer and supplications, with fasting, and sackcloth, and ashes:

**9:4** And I prayed unto the LORD my God, and made my confession, and said, O Lord, the great and dreadful God, keeping the covenant and mercy to them that love him, and to them that keep his commandments;

**9:5** We have sinned, and have committed iniquity, and have done wickedly, and have rebelled, even by departing from thy precepts and from thy judgments:

**9:6** Neither have we hearkened unto thy servants the prophets, which spake in thy name to our kings, our princes, and our fathers, and to all the people of the land.

**9:7** O LORD, righteousness belongeth unto thee, but unto us confusion of faces, as at this day; to the men of Judah, and to the inhabitants of Jerusalem, and unto all Israel, that are near, and that are far off, through all the countries whither thou hast driven them, because of their trespass that they have trespassed against thee.

**9:8** O Lord, to us belongeth confusion of face, to our kings, to our princes, and to our fathers, because we have sinned against thee.

**9:9** To the Lord our God belong mercies and forgivenesses, though we have rebelled against him; **9:10** Neither have we obeyed the voice of the LORD our God, to walk in his laws, which he set before us by his servants the prophets.

**9:11** Yea, all Israel have transgressed thy law, even by departing, that they might not obey thy voice; therefore the curse is poured upon us, and the oath that is written in the law of Moses the servant of God, because we have sinned against him.

**9:12** And he hath confirmed his words, which he spake against us, and against our judges that judged us, by bringing upon us a great evil: for under the whole heaven hath not been done as hath been done upon Jerusalem.

**9:13** As it is written in the law of Moses, all this evil is come upon us: yet made we not our prayer before the LORD our God, that we might turn from our iniquities, and understand thy truth.

**9:14** Therefore hath the LORD watched upon the evil, and brought it upon us: for the LORD our God is righteous in all his works which he doeth: for we obeyed not his voice.

**9:15** And now, O Lord our God, that hast brought thy people forth out of the land of Egypt with a mighty hand, and hast gotten thee renown, as at this day; we have sinned, we have done wickedly.

**9:16** O LORD, according to all thy righteousness, I beseech thee, let thine anger and thy fury be turned away from thy city Jerusalem, thy holy mountain: because for our sins, and for the iniquities of our fathers, Jerusalem and thy people are become a reproach to all that are about us.

**9:17** Now therefore, O our God, hear the prayer of thy servant, and his supplications, and cause thy face to shine upon thy sanctuary that is desolate, for the Lord's sake.

**9:18** O my God, incline thine ear, and hear; open thine eyes, and behold our desolations, and the city which is called by thy name: for we do not present our supplications before thee for our righteousnesses, but for thy great mercies.

**9:19** O Lord, hear; O Lord, forgive; O Lord, hearken and do; defer not, for thine own sake, O my God: for thy city and thy people are called by thy name. Gabriel is sent to Daniel with the prophetic words of encouragement.

**9:20** And whiles I was speaking, and praying, and confessing my sin and the sin of my people Israel, and presenting my supplication before the LORD my God for the holy mountain of my God; **9:21** Yea, whiles I was speaking in prayer, even the man Gabriel, whom I had seen in the vision at the beginning, being caused to fly swiftly, touched me about the time of the evening oblation.

**9:22** And he informed me, and talked with me, and said, O Daniel, I am now come forth to give thee skill and understanding.

All understanding of spiritual things comes from God. Gabriel was sent the moment that Daniel began his prayer of repentance and supplication for himself, for the temple, for Judah/Israel and for Jerusalem.

**9:23** At the beginning of thy supplications the commandment came forth, and I am come to shew thee; for thou art greatly beloved: therefore understand the matter, and consider the vision.

### The Prophecy to build the city and the appearance of Messiah

Please note that this prophecy was given long after the decree to build the temple by Cyrus (536 B.C.) and speaks of a yet, at that time still future, decree to build the city. The actual decree to build the city Jerusalem was given to Ezra by Ahaseurus the husband of Esther in 457 B.C.

**9:24** Seventy weeks are determined upon thy people and upon thy holy city, to finish the transgression, and to make an end of sins, and to make reconciliation for iniquity, and to bring in everlasting righteousness, and to seal up the vision and prophecy, and to anoint the most Holy. **9:25** Know therefore and understand, that from the going forth of the commandment to restore and **to build Jerusalem** [the city, NOT the temple] unto the Messiah the Prince shall be seven weeks (49 days, which is 49 years at a day for a year Ezekiel 4), and three score and two weeks (a total of 434 years): the street shall be built again, and the wall, even in troublous times.

There is ample proof that this command to BUILD THE CITY was issued in the seventh year of the reign of Artaxerxes Longimanus, in 457 B.C.

It was during the 49 year period from 457 B.C. when the original decree was given to build the city, that the city was built under extremely trying circumstances, being completed as the angel had foretold to Daniel in 49 years in 408 B.C. After which another 62 weeks (434 years) would pass before the revealing of the Christ.

The dating of this decree marks the starting point of the entire prophecy of the physical ministry of Christ and is of vital importance in understanding the prophecy about the date of the death of Christ.

**The Four Different Decrees**

1. **The decree of Cyrus recorded in Ezra 1:1-4**

In Jeremiah 29:10, God had promised, "After seventy years be accomplished at Babylon I will visit you, and perform my good word toward you, in causing you to return to this place."

**Ezra 1:1** "Now in the first year of Cyrus king of Persia, that the word of the Lord by the mouth of Jeremiah might be fulfilled, the Lord stirred up the spirit of Cyrus, king of Persia, that he made a proclamation throughout all his kingdom...."

The royal decree went forth in the year 536 B.C., at which time nearly 50,000 Jews returned to their homeland.

Two centuries earlier, God had appointed Cyrus for this task: **Isaiah 44:28** "That saith of Cyrus, He is my shepherd, and shall perform all my pleasure: even saying to Jerusalem, Thou shalt be built; and *to the temple, Thy foundation shall be laid.*"

Ezra recorded the decree of Cyrus as an historical record.

Recognizing in Isaiah's prophecy a personal directive, Cyrus began his decree with these words, **Ezra 1:2** "The Lord God of heaven hath given me all the kingdoms of the earth; and *he hath charged me to build him an house* at Jerusalem, which is in Judah."

Cyrus continued, "Who is there among you of all his people? his God be with him, and let him go up to Jerusalem, which is in Judah, and *build the house of the Lord* God of Israel, (he is the God,) which is in Jerusalem." **Ezra 1:3.**

This first decree authorized the Jews to return to Jerusalem and rebuild the *temple*. Ezra chapter 3 tells us that those who returned to Judea gathered in Jerusalem to observe the feast of tabernacles in the seventh month, and the following spring, "in the second month," they "set forward the work of the house of the Lord" (verses 1, 4, 8).

After the foundation of the temple had been laid, "the adversaries of Judah and Benjamin," "the people of the land," being prohibited from participating in the project, "weakened the hands of the people of Judah, and troubled them in building, and hired counsellors against them, to frustrate their purpose, all the days of Cyrus king of Persia, even until the reign of Darius king of Persia." **Ezra 4:1-5.**

"Then ceased the work of the house of God which is at Jerusalem. So it ceased unto the second year of the reign of Darius king of Persia." **Ezra 4:24.**

There was no more construction after the Altar had been built and the foundation laid.

Then, the adversaries came and asked the workers, "Who hath commanded you to build this house?" **Ezra 5:3.** They replied, "In the first year of Cyrus the king of Babylon the same king Cyrus made a decree to build this house of God." **Ezra 5:13.**

So governor Zerubbabel and his officials wrote a letter to King Darius I, saying, "If it seem good to the king, let there be search made in the king's treasure house, which is there at Babylon, whether it be so, that a decree was made of Cyrus the king to build this house of God at Jerusalem, and let the king send his pleasure to us concerning this matter." **Ezra 5:17.**

   2.  **The decree of Darius I** recorded in Ezra 6:1-12

Under the inspiration of Haggai and Zechariah, the governor Zerubbabel sent a letter Darius and a search was made, and Cyrus' original decree was found.

Darius then issued his own decree reinforcing the decree of Cyrus, saying, "Let the governor of the Jews and the elders of the Jews build this house of God in his place." Darius instructed his governor to supply the Jews with money or whatever else they needed, that "the building of this house of God . . . be not hindered." (Ezra 6:7, 8).

Based on Ezra 4:24, this decree was **issued in 520 B.C., the second year of the solo reign of Darius.** With the hinderances now removed, the temple was completed in the sixth solo year of Darius (516 B.C.) on the third day of the twelfth month, and in the following month they kept the Passover (Ezra 6:15, 19).

3. **The decree of Artaxerxes I [Ahaseurus Longimanus, Esther's husband] recorded in Ezra 7:12-26**

King Artaxerxes Longimanus, during the seventh year of his reign (457 B.C.), authorized Ezra the priest and scribe, and all who wished to join him, to go to Jerusalem. It was Ezra's desire to instruct the Jews in the Word of God.

Artaxerxes granted him large amounts of silver and gold to furnish the temple, and gave instruction that his treasurers on that side of the river should provide whatever was needed to beautify the Lord's house, revive the religion and build the city.

In the decree, Artaxerxes Longimanus commanded Ezra to "set magistrates and judges, which may judge all the people that are beyond the river, all such as know the laws of thy God; and teach ye them that know them not. And whosoever will not do the law of thy God, and the law of the king, let judgment be executed speedily upon him, whether it be unto death, or to banishment, or to confiscation of goods, or to imprisonment." (Ezra 7:25, 26).

4. **The second decree of Artaxerxes Longimanus [Esther's husband] mentioned in Nehemiah chapters 1 and 2**

The story of Nehemiah begins in the 20th year of Artaxerxes Longimanus' reign. Nehemiah, a Jew, was the king's cupbearer. One day some of his brethren from Judah arrived in Shushan where king's palace was. Nehemiah inquired of them about the condition of things in Jerusalem.

"The remnant that are left of the captivity there in the province are in great affliction and reproach," they replied. "The wall of Jerusalem also is broken down, and the gates thereof are burned with fire."

Nehemiah sat down and wept. For several days he mourned and fasted and prayed. His prayer is remarkably similar to that of Daniel in Daniel 9. He prayed that somehow God would "grant him mercy in the sight of" the king.

Four months later, Nehemiah was serving wine to the king, and Artaxerxes noticed a sadness on Nehemiah's countenance. "Why is thy countenance sad?" the king asked.

Nehemiah explained that Jerusalem was still in ruins, the wall and the gates were still not repaired. When the king asked what he would like to do, Nehemiah answered, "If it please the king, and if thy servant have found favour in thy sight, that thou wouldest send me unto Judah, unto the city of my fathers' sepulchres, that I may build it." [Build the city walls of Jerusalem]

Artaxerxes Longimanus consented, and sent with him letters for the governors of the region, authorizing the rebuilding project. This commission confirming the original decree and authorizing the work to be renewed was issued in the spring of 444 B.C., in Artaxerxes' 20th year of reign.

**Evaluating the four decrees**

**Daniel 9:25** "Know therefore and understand, that **from the going forth of the commandment to restore and to build Jerusalem** [the city, not the temple] unto the Messiah the Prince shall be seven weeks, and threescore and two weeks: the street shall be built again, and the wall, even in troublous times."

This is an important verse to understand. It is the only prophecy in the Bible which tells us precisely when the Messiah would arrive. It is extremely vital therefore to know exactly when that time period began.

The event to mark the beginning of the seventy weeks is stated to be **"the commandment to restore and to build Jerusalem."** But to which "commandment" does it refer? We have just seen that there were four different decrees, all of which seem quite similar. If we use the wrong starting point, the whole prophecy will be off.

As always, it is essential to pay close attention to the words of the text. We are looking for a command to **"*restore* and to build *Jerusalem*."** The decree of Cyrus, recorded in Ezra 1, gave instruction only for the rebuilding of the *temple* in Jerusalem. It said nothing about restoring the whole city.

The decree of Darius, recorded in Ezra 6, was simply his endorsement of the decree of Cyrus. It mentioned only the building of the **"house of God."**

**But in the decree of Artaxerxes Longimanus, recorded in Ezra 7, provision is made for the complete restoration of the Jewish state, including the right to appoint magistrates and judges, hold trials, and pass and execute sentence upon violators of their own national laws.**

This was clearly understood to be an authorization for the full reestablishment **of Jerusalem** and the Jewish nation; for shortly after this the enemies of the Jews wrote to the king complaining that "the Jews which came up from thee to us are come unto Jerusalem, *building the rebellious and the bad city*, and have set up the walls thereof, and joined the foundations" **Ezra 4:12.** That the walls had been completely set up was obviously an exaggeration, as verse 13 reveals. Yet this incident shows that for the first time there was actual work being done to **rebuild the** *city*. This had not been the case under the previous decrees.

The fourth decree (Nehemiah 2), the wording of which has not been preserved, was simply a reinstatement of Artaxerxes' original authorization, this time naming Nehemiah to take charge of the project.

Considering all the options, the decree which most correctly answers to the specifications of Daniel 9:25 was the decree of Artaxerxes to Ezra, recorded in Ezra chapter 7.

**We should therefore date the beginning of the 70 week prophecy of Daniel 9 from that command of Artaxerxes made in 457 B.C.**

It was during the 49 year period from 457 B.C. when the original decree was given to build the city that the city was built under extremely trying circumstances, being completed as the angel had foretold to Daniel in 49 years in 408 B.C. After which another 62 weeks (434 years) would pass before the revealing of the Christ.

The decree to restore and build Jerusalem was issued in the seventh year of Artaxerxes' reign (Ezra 7:7, 8).

Ezra left Babylon on the first day of the first month [about April] **in 457 B.C.** arriving on the first day of the fifth month [approximately August] after which the command of Artaxerxes was then officially read out, to all the people (Ezra 7).

**Therefore, the prophecy of Daniel 9 began,** *with the command to build the city, in summer 457 B.C.*

### The Work of Messiah the Christ

Seventy weeks are determined upon thy people and upon thy holy city, to FINISH TRANSGRESSION, and to make an END OF SINS, and to make RECONCILIATION FOR INIQUITY, and to BRING IN EVERLASTING

RIGHTEOUSNESS, and to SEAL UP THE VISION AND PROPHESY, and to ANOINT THE MOST HOLY.

Notice that it is at THE END of the full Seventy Weeks that reconciliation for iniquity, the anointing of the Most Holy and an end to sin and bringing in everlasting righteousness will occur.

When Jesus Christ was on the earth the first time, these things happened only in part. **Reconciliation was offered to only a very few.** Transgressions have not yet been finished, nor has sin been ended.

Therefore it is when he comes the second time that he will be Anointed King over all the earth and put an end to all wickedness.

**Timeline**

**The Building of the Temple**

- The people went up to Jerusalem with Zerubbabel to build the temple according to the decree of Cyrus in 536 B.C.
- Cyrus appointed Sheshbazzar [the Persian name for Zerubbabel] governor of the Jews in Jerusalem and Judea, Ezra 5:16.
- Zerubbabel and Joshua went with the people out of Babylon to Jerusalem under the governor and they build the Altar in time to sacrifice during the Feasts of the seventh month.
- Construction of the temple foundation began in the second year, Ezra 3.
- Little progress was made due to the opposition of the local people and lack of support
- Then Haggai and Zechariah began to prophesy and encourage the people and construction resumed
- Then construction was halted by Artaxerxes [Darius] in 522 B.C. due to complaints from the local people [which came during a period of uprisings in the empire], Ezra 5.
- Then Daniel fasted and prayed for Jerusalem and the Daniel 9 prophecy was given.
- Then the Persian governor Tatnai wrote to Darius explaining that Cyrus had ordered the construction of the temple.
- After seeing God's deliverance of Daniel from the lions (Dan 6) Darius then ordered the construction to resume in 520 B.C. and the

temple was completed in 516 B.C. fulfilling the Jeremiah prophecy precisely, Ezra 6.

## Timeline

### Restoring true religion and building the city

- Artaxerxes [Ahaseurus Longimanus] put away queen Vashti in his second year (461 B.C.) for her example of rebellion and disobedience.

- He became the husband of Esther in his third year (c 460 B.C.)

- In his seventh year (457 B.C.) king Artaxerxes [Ahasuerus Longimanus], disposed to hold the Jews in favor due to the influence of queen Esther and Mordachi, sent Ezra to rebuild the city Jerusalem.

- Ezra as the high priest was sent to restore the religion and build the city in 457 B.C., Ezra 7

- In Ezra 9, Ezra learns of the marriages to unconverted spouses and idolatry among the people and separates them calling them to repentance Ezra 10.

- Ezra concentrates on restoring true religion and building the city but does not build the walls.

- In the twelfth year (452 B.C.) of king Artaxerxes [Ahasuerus Longimanus], the Jews were saved from Haman who was incensed by the favours granted to the Jews and conspired to destroy them.

- In 444 B.C. Nehemiah was appointed governor and is sent to help Ezra the high priest, and as the governor he begins construction of the city walls to protect the city, Nehemiah 3-8, leaving Ezra to fulfill his religious function of teaching the people and restoring true religion as the high priest.

- Nehemiah as Terhasha [governor] and the high priest Ezra read the book of the law before all the people at the Fall Festivals, Nehemiah 9

- On the second day after the Feast of the Eighth Day they held a day of fasting and repentance Nehemiah 10, and many people recommitted themselves to the Covenant, Nehemiah 11

- Ezra died in 440 B.C.

- After 12 years as governor, during which he ruled with justice and righteousness, Nehemiah returned to visit king Ahaseurus at Susa in 432 B.C.
- After some time he returned to Jerusalem and was horrified to find that the people had fallen back into their evil ways. Unconverted people were permitted to conduct business with Jews inside Jerusalem on the Sabbath and the Jews did business with them. Greatly angered, he purified the temple and the priests and Levites and again separates them from their unconverted spouses and decries their sins of idolatry and Sabbath breaking, Nehemiah 13.
- The city was completed in 408 B.C.

It was during the 49 year period from 457 B.C. when the original decree was given to build the city, that the city was built under extremely trying circumstances, being completed as the angel had foretold to Daniel in 49 years in 408 B.C. After which another 62 weeks (434 years) would pass before the revealing of the Jesus Christ when his ministry began at the age of 30 in autumn 27 A.D.

**The city of Jerusalem was built over seven weeks (49 years)** (Dan 9:25).

It was during the 49 year period from 457 B.C. when the original decree was given to build the city, that the city was built under extremely trying circumstances, being completed as the angel had foretold to Daniel in 49 years in 408 B.C. After which another 62 weeks (434 years) would pass before the revealing of Messiah the Christ.

**And sixty-two weeks** (434 years) **after the city was built, Messiah was to appear** (Dan 9:25).

And AFTER [the] three score and two weeks shall Messiah be cut off, but not for Himself (Dan 9:26).

We know that the entire ministry of Jesus Christ; from the time that He began [in the autumn of 27 A.D.] until His crucifixion at Passover was 3 1/2 years.

We see that: **beginning with the decree to build the city, until the Messiah appears Verse 25 there shall be 7+62=69 weeks, or 483 days and at a day for a year, this is 483 years.**

Let us then do the math and we will see when Messiah would appear. -457 B.C. + 483 years = 26 A.D.. Now add one for the lack of a zero between AD and BC and:

**We come to the appearance of Messiah in autumn 27 A.D.! Which is absolutely consistent with Luke 3!**

**Christ was then to be "Cut Off" some time AFTER the 483 years but it does not say how long after.** That information can be learned by determining the years of the ministry of Christ.

From here we can determine the date of the crucifixion of Jesus Christ the Messiah. Knowing that he was baptized in the early spring before Passover [beginning his ministry in the autumn]; and that from his ministry beginning in the autumn of 27 A.D. there were four Passovers, with His death coming on the last [fourth] Passover; we see that he died on Passover in 31 A.D.

In 31 A.D. Passover, according to the Biblical Mosaic Calendar in use in Judea at that time; which relied upon the first light of the new moon to start the month; was Wednesday April 25th!

The modern Rabbinic Calendar places Passover on a Monday in 31 A.D. however that Rabbinic Calendar was not finalized until 1178 A.D. and was not in use until centuries later in 1178 A.D.

**This is confirmed in the scriptures** [Luke 3] **which say that Christ's ministry began in the 15th year that Tiberius FIRST ascended the throne 12 A.D. + 15 = 27 A.D.!**

See New Moon dates: Passover Date


**The Birth Year of Jesus Christ**

The birth of Christ is generally dated through certain comments of Josephus about the death of Herod the Great. Josephus writes that after an eclipse Herod slaughtered certain Jews, then he went to the Dead Sea for a cure of his ailments and then observed Passover in Jerusalem before dying.

A theory is that the lunar eclipse of September 15 of 5 B.C. was the lunar eclipse preceding the death of Herod. That eclipse occurred 7 lunar months before the Passover of 4 B.C.

Thus the eclipse either occurred in the month of Elul or in the month of Tishri, but with the addition of the month of Adar II before the Nisan of 4 B.C. But Josephus clearly describes Herod's eclipse as occurring after the removal from office of the high priest—the same high priest whom Josephus describes as still being in office on the fast day of Tishri 10. Neither could Herod's eclipse have occurred in Tishri, for at that time there would have been huge crowds gathered for the Feast of Tabernacles. These crowds would not have permitted such an offense [as the slaughter of many leading Jews], nor would Herod have dared to outrage them and risk a riot or rebellion. Therefore, 4 B.C. cannot be the year of Herod's death".

1. The only date for **Herod's death**, fulfilling all the criteria presented by Josephus would have been 1 B.C.

2. There is nothing in the Bible to indicate that the Family spent two years in Egypt. It is only said that children of two years and younger were killed. Herod was a thorough man and would have certainly doubled the age [to make sure] as indicated by the men of the East. Even then the killing could have taken some time and after that more time would have to pass before Herod died. The amount of time spent in Egypt is unknown, but may have been more or less than two precise years.

3. The ministry of Messiah began when he was about 30 years old. We are told that this ministry began in the 15th year of Tiberius, Luke 3. Tiberius became co-ruler with Augustus in 12 AD and sole ruler after the death of Augustus in 14 A.D.

Fifteen years after the co ruler-ship from 12 A.D., would be 27 A.D. for the beginning of the ministry of Christ when he was coming to the age of 30 years, with his birth being in 4 B.C. [adding a year to compensate for no year zero]. This would put the birth of Christ in autumn 4 B.C.; which would fit with the death of Herod after Passover in 1 B.C. From fall 4 BC to spring 1 B.C. being about 2 1/2 years. Time enough for the birth, the period of uncleanness and the traveling to and stay in Egypt. This date would put the Sacrifice of Christ at Passover on Wednesday in 31 A.D.

4. If the count is from the **death of Augustus and the sole ruler-ship of Tiberius in 14 AD,** then Christ would have become about 30 in 29 A.D.: 14 A.D. + 15 = 29 A.D.; and that would have required the birth of Christ in the year 1 B.C., which would be out of sync with the death of Herod in 1 BC. It would also be contrary to the 70 Weeks Prophecy which puts the appearance of Christ in 27 A.D. This error taught by many would wrongly put the Sacrifice of Christ on a Friday Passover in 33 A.D.

**Conclusion:** The birth of Christ was in 4 B.C.; His ministry began in the 15th year that Tiberius FIRST ascended the throne 12 A.D. + 15 = 27 A.D.; and Christ died on Passover 31 A.D..

### The Beginning of the Ministry of Jesus Christ and the Passover of His Death

**Daniel 9:25** Know therefore and understand, that from the going forth of the commandment to restore and to build Jerusalem unto the Messiah the Prince shall be seven weeks (49 days, which is 49 years at a day for a year, Ezekiel 4), and three score and two weeks (434 years): the street shall be built again, and the wall, even in troublous times.

There is ample proof that this command was made in the seventh year of the reign of Artaxerxes 1 Longimanus, in 457 BC.

The city Jerusalem was built in seven weeks [49 years[ (Dan 9:25). And AFTER another 62 [434 years] weeks Messiah was to begin his ministry and then later to be cut off.

After three score and two weeks shall Messiah be cut off, but not for Himself (Dan 9:26).

How long AFTER the 62 weeks when he shall be cut off? It does not say, but we know that the entire ministry of Jesus Christ; from the time that He began until His crucifixion was 3 1/2 years.

We can see that beginning with the decree [457 B.C.] to build the city, until the Messiah appears Verse 25; there shall be 7+62=69 weeks, or 483 days and at a day for a year, this is 483 years.

Let us then do the math and see when Messiah would appear. –457 B.C. + 483 years = 26 A.D. Now add one for the lack of a zero between A.D. and B.C. and we come to the appearance of Messiah in 27 A.D.

From here we can determine the date of the birth of Christ by subtracting 30 [Christ being 30 years old in 27 A.D.] from 27 A.D. adjusting for no year zero and we get 4 B.C.

### We can also determine the date of the crucifixion of Jesus Christ the Messiah.

Knowing that he was baptized in the early spring of 27 A.D., and that His ministry began in the autumn of 27 A.D. and covered four Passovers, with His death on the last [fourth] Passover; we can conclude that he died on Passover Wednesday in 31 A.D.

Therefore the Passover of 31 A.D. fell on a Wednesday by the Mosaic Calendar in use at that time; while today's Rabbinic Calendar was not finalized until 1178 A.D!

The crucifixion of Jesus Christ was on Wednesday, NOT ON FRIDAY!

## Daniel 9: The 70th Week

Daniel 9:24-27 The 70th Week Prophecy

There are those who believe that the full 70th week of Daniel 9 is still to come with a period of 3 1/2 years after a peace deal in the Middle East before the tribulation begins.

There are a variety of explanations concerning the Seventieth or Last Week, of the Seventy Weeks Prophecy. Most of which have been around for a long time and were first put forth as a part of the Protestant Reformation. We know that these explanations cannot be true because the understanding of these things has been sealed until the last days.

> **Daniel 12:9** And he said, Go thy way, Daniel: for **the words are closed up and sealed till the time of the end.**

A common explanation of the seventieth week put out by certain folks, is that the False Prophet will make a peace deal with Judah, possibly allowing them to build a temple or set up a tabernacle and start sacrifices.

Then after 3 1/2 years that peace covenant will be broken, the sacrifices stopped and the tribulation will begin and last for a second 3 1/2 years. This explanation gives rise to the theory that a temple, or at least some kind of tabernacle must be built and physical sacrifices must start.

We KNOW that this explanation CANNOT BE TRUE for the scripture says that when "Peace and Safety" is declared; SUDDEN, IMMEDIATE,

AT THAT TIME; destruction will come: 1 Thes 5:3. There will be NO 3 1/2 years of peace!

Jesus Christ said that when the abomination spoken of by Daniel goes to the Holy Place; sudden, immediate great tribulation will begin (Mat 24:15).

Daniel tells us that his prophetic words are SEALED UNTIL THE END (Dan 12:9). This means that explanations written many years ago: CANNOT BE CORRECT.

**The seventieth week of the prophecy is found in Daniel 9:24-27.**

Each week is seven days; so seven weeks is forty nine days and sixty two weeks is four hundred and thirty four days.

Each day representing one year, therefore the city would be built in forty nine years, then Messiah would come after another four hundred and thirty four years. Indicating that Messiah would come four hundred and eighty three years after the commandment to rebuild the city was issued.

Then at an unspecified point after the four hundred and eighty three years, Messiah would be cut off, but not for Himself: and then after Christ's death, resurrection and ascension, came the fist half of the 70th week when the Ekklesia fled to Pella and the first century destruction of Jerusalem and the temple by Titus stopped the daily sacrifice after a 42 month siege and BEFORE the second 42 months of tribulation.

**Daniel 9:24** Seventy weeks are determined upon thy people and upon thy holy city, to finish the transgression, and to make an end of sins, and to make reconciliation for iniquity, and to bring in everlasting righteousness, and to seal up the vision and prophecy, and to anoint the most Holy.

In the first century reconciliation was offered to only a very few and transgressions have not yet been finished on this earth, nor yet in Judah, nor has sin been ended. It is when He shall return that Messiah shall be Anointed King over all the earth and will put an end to all wickedness.

**Titus and the first Roman destruction of Jerusalem ending the Daily**

**9:25** And the people of the prince that shall come shall destroy the city and the sanctuary: and the end thereof shall be with a flood, and unto the end of the war desolations are determined.

And He [Messiah] shall CONFIRM A COVENANT [the New Covenant] for one week [seven years]:

The prophecy now addresses the siege of Jerusalem by Prince Titus

. . . and in the midst of the week [at the end of the first 3 1/2 years, after a 42 month siege during which the Ekklesia had fled to Pella]; He [The Roman Prince Titus besieged Jerusalem and after 42 months the city fell and the temple was burned stopping the daily sacrifice.] shall cause the sacrifice and oblation to cease and for the overspreading of abominations He shall make it desolate [This was fulfilled at the end of the first half of the week when God allowed Prince Titus to destroy the temple.], even until the consummation [The temple would remain destroyed and the daily sacrifice stopped until the end of the age and the completion of the seventy weeks, when Christ comes to build the Ezekiel Temple!], and that determined shall be poured upon the desolator [the final abomination will be destroyed at the coming of Messiah, Daniel 9:27].

At that time, the New Covenant of espousal between Jesus Christ and the called out was confirmed for the first half of the 70th week when the Ekklesia fled to Pella about c 66 A.D., to be preserved from the destruction of the Roman war against Jerusalem! This fulfilled the first 3 1/2 years or the first half of the 70th week, as I shall presently show!

Once the Romans had destroyed the temple and ended the Daily Sacrifice; at the END of three and a half years of war [in the midst of the week of seven years]; it is prophesied that **the temple will not be rebuilt, and that the Daily Sacrifice will not be renewed and not resume; until the end of the second half of the week and the coming of Messiah:** Until the consummation, or end, of the 70 weeks!

**The time line of The Seventy Weeks Prophecy**

1) The decree goes out to build the city; Messiah appears and begins his ministry in autumn 27 A.D. 483 years after the command to rebuild the city,

He is cut off 3 1/2 years later and resurrected; only then does the New Covenant officially begin, and verse 27,

2) Jesus Christ confirms the New Covenant with many by taking them and preserving them in Pella during the 42 month siege of Jerusalem for the first half of the 70th week or 3 1/2 years, fulled in years for days!

3) Then after a 3 1/2 year siege, at the end of the first half of the seventieth week and before the second half of the seventieth week, God caused the sacrifice and oblation to cease by allowing Prince Titus to

conquer Jerusalem and destroy the city and the temple; stopping the daily sacrifice!

Brethren, the physical daily sacrifice has already been stopped! and it is to remain stopped until the consummation of the end of the 70th week and the coming of Christ!

NOTICE: The seventieth week does NOT BEGIN until after the resurrection of Jesus Christ. It is not until c 66 A.D. that the first half of the seventieth week is confirmed for three and one half years by the protection of the faithful in Pella during the siege of Jerusalem by the Romans; and it is not until our day that the second half of the 70th week will come, as per Daniel 9.

**What covenant is being talked about?**

Why, the New Covenant; which was not made sure until after the sacrifice of Christ was accepted by God the Father on Wave Offering Sunday. The MARRIAGE Covenant of Espousal, of Betrothal; between Jesus Christ and His called out first fruits, His bride; was then made official at Pentecost 31 A.D.

Jesus Christ the espoused Husband, promised to cherish and nurture the bride; and the espoused bride [the sincerely repentant person as part of the collective bride] promises to love, to follow and to faithfully obey Him.

The New Covenant like the Mosaic Covenant is a Marriage Covenant!

Jesus Christ would then confirm His New Covenant with His espoused bride when the city (Jerusalem) was under siege and destroyed after 42 months in circa 70 A.D. (Dan 9:26-27).

In the first century, the faithful fled to Pella in Jordan and remained there for the first 1/2 week (a day for a year; 3 1/2 years) preserved by Jesus Christ from the Roman armies, in a first century fore-type of the final 42 month great tribulation.

This refuge in Pella for 1,260 days, fulfilled the first half of the 70th week

The people of the prince that shall come shall destroy the city and the sanctuary; and the end thereof shall be with a flood, and unto the end of the war desolations are determined (Dan 9:26).

Messiah had no sin and did not die for His own sin, but died for the sins of mankind. AFTER His death and resurrection, Judah rebelled against Rome and was destroyed, Jerusalem falling in c 70 AD. This was a precursor of or a fore-type of; the final great tribulation.

And He [Christ] shall CONFIRM A COVENANT for one week: and in the midst of the week He [Christ] shall cause the sacrifice and oblation to cease and for the overspreading of abominations [Christ shall give the city over to a desolator, the Roman prince Titus; and this will be repeated in the last days with the second half of the week (3 1/2 years)].

The Roman Prince Titus made the temple and the Daily Sacrifice desolate, and it will remain desolate, even until the consummation [the end of the 70th week and the coming of Messiah, and that determined [When the King of kings comes he will destroy the desolating political leader and his false prophet with their armies.] shall be poured upon the desolator (Dan 9:27).

Notice the time-line. The seventieth week, of seven years; does not begin until after the death and resurrection of Jesus Christ!

Jesus Christ was to appear at the end of the seven plus sixty-two weeks (69 weeks) Dan 9:26, which was in 27 A.D.

There is no way that the ministry of Christ could have fulfilled the first half of the 70th week since this could ONLY be fulfilled AFTER he was "Cut Off," AFTER he was killed and resurrected!

The first half or the 70th week was fulfilled when the faithful fled Jerusalem for Pella in c 66 A.D.

According to the time line and the flow of events, the 70th week could not begin until Messiah had been "Cut Off" and resurrected, rising to be accepted by God the Father on Wave Offering Sunday for us.

ONLY when Christ was accepted as our sacrifice and High Priest, could there be a Covenant to confirm; for the Mosaic Covenant was ended by his death as Husband of Israel, and the New Covenant did not officially begin until Christ was accepted by the Father.

Then He, Jesus Christ, PERSONALLY; not some apostle or disciple, shall confirm a covenant for seven years, or one prophetic week after His resurrection.

The New Covenant could NOT OFFICIALLY BEGIN until Jesus Christ fulfilled His mission and died to pay the penalty for the sins of men. Therefore only after Messiah had died and been resurrected could the New Covenant be confirmed.

ONLY AFTER THE DEATH AND SACRIFICE OF JESUS CHRIST COULD THE NEW COVENANT BE CONFIRMED; the first half of the last seventieth week could not begin until after the death and resurrection of Christ!

Therefore Messiah could not have been confirming a part of the 70th week covenant during His physical earthly ministry; as some wrongly teach.

In the midst of the week, after three and one half years of siege and before the final three and one half years; God caused the daily sacrifice to be stopped by allowing Prince Titus to destroy the temple in c 70 A.D.

As Jerusalem will once again be given over to her enemies (Rev 11:2, Rev 12:6), Jesus Christ will protect the faithful bride once again, for 1/2 week (3 1/2 years) thus confirming the New Covenant of ESPOUSAL with His Bride for the second half of the 70th week.

What covenant is being confirmed? The ONLY covenant mentioned in scripture to exist after the resurrection of Christ; THE NEW COVENANT, between Christ and those called out of season as a kind of first fruits of the NEW COVENANT of Jeremiah 31:31!

What does confirmed mean? To fulfill, to make sure. What is this covenant? A marriage agreement to PROTECT, NOURISH and CARE FOR His espoused bride, those who KEEP HIS COMMANDMENTS!

**PROOF:** The true explanation of the whole 70th Week is found in Revelation 12.

> **Revelation 12:1** And there appeared a great wonder in heaven; a woman clothed with the sun, and the moon under her feet, and upon her head a crown of twelve stars: **12:2** And she being with child cried, travailing in birth, and pained to be delivered.

This speaks of the mother of Christ, as an allegorical type of the called out faithful Ekklesia.

> **12:3** And there appeared another wonder in heaven; and behold a great red dragon, having seven heads and ten horns, and seven crowns upon his heads.

This is Satan, and later Satan's system on the earth is described as the scarlet beast; Scarlet being red. This is explained in Revelation 17 which will be included in a future book.

> **12:4** And his tail drew the third part of the stars of heaven, and did cast them to the earth: and the dragon stood before the woman which was ready to be delivered, for to devour her child as soon as it was born.

Satan at his original fall, led a third of the angels with him, and as the Christ was ready to be born, he stood up to destroy him.

> **12:5** And she brought forth a man child, who was to rule all nations with a rod of iron: and her child was caught up unto God, and to his throne.

The child being spoken of, is identified as Christ the Messiah; for ONLY Christ has died and been resurrected to spirit and ascended to the Father's throne.

Now we come to the first half of the 70th week; the first 3 1/2 year flight of the faithful, which was to Pella; NOT Petra!

> **12:6** And the woman fled into the wilderness, where she hath a place prepared of God, that they should feed her there a thousand two hundred and threescore days.

This was the first one half of the 70 Weeks, for 1,260 days, which is 42 months, or one half of seven years. The 70th Week, being 7 years, or 2520 days.

The first 3 1/2 years were fulfilled when the saints fled from Jerusalem to Pella, when the Romans besieged Jerusalem.

Now NOTICE that; at an unspecified time [in this prophecy; but actually specified in the 2,300 day prophecy] AFTER that; there was war in heaven. This is clearly at the end time, for it begins after the first half, and before the second half of the week.

> **12:7** And there was war in heaven: Michael and his angels fought against the dragon; and the dragon fought and his angels, [This is AFTER the first half of the week has passed, and just before the second half of the 70th week begins.]
>
> **12:8** And prevailed not; neither was their place found any more in heaven. **12:9** And the great dragon was cast out, that old serpent, called the Devil, and Satan, which deceiveth the whole world: he was cast out into the earth, and his angels were cast out with him.

Daniel 12:1 tells us that Michael will stand up to fight against Satan and will cast him to the earth, which will be right before the beginning of the tribulation.

**Daniel 12:1** And at that time shall Michael stand up, the great prince which standeth for the children of thy people: **and there shall be a time of trouble, such as never was since there was a nation even to that same**

**time:** and at that time thy people shall be delivered [Rescued by the coming of Messiah!], every one that shall be found written in the book.

Just before the onset of the latter 42 month tribulation, Satan rises up to fight against God, knowing that his imprisonment is at hand, and is defeated and thrown down

> **Revelation 12:7** And there was war in heaven: Michael and his angels fought against the dragon; and the dragon fought and his angels,
>
> **Revelation 12:10** And I heard a loud voice saying in heaven, Now is come salvation, and strength, and the kingdom of our God, and the power of his Christ: for the accuser of our brethren is cast down, which accused them before our God day and night.
>
> **12:11** And they overcame him by the blood of the Lamb, and by the word of their testimony; and they loved not their lives unto the death [they died for godliness].
>
> **12:12** Therefore rejoice, ye heavens, and ye that dwell in them. Woe to the inhabiters of the earth and of the sea! for the devil is come down unto you, having great wrath, because he knoweth that he hath but a short time [That is 3 1/2 years remaining to him].

All converted faithful believers are to rejoice and to hold their heads up high (Luke 21:28), as they see the imminence of the resurrection to eternal life and the Marriage to the Lamb of God!

The sinful need fear great sorrows because they must go through great tribulation for their sins.

> **12:13** And when the dragon saw that he was cast unto the earth, he persecuted the woman which brought forth the man child.

Obviously Mary could not have lived into the end time; therefore the woman is the body of the faithful believers and doers of the will of God.

Satan through his human instruments works to destroy all who will not bow to him. This is fully empowered by the setting up of the Abomination in Rome, the setting up of the New Europe and the Beast Emperor and the subsequent wars. This will be discussed in future volumes.

This miracle working abomination [false prophet, son of perdition.] will then go to the Holy Place to trigger the war within 75 days AFTER he is set up in Rome. Just before the second half of the seventieth week [just before the final 42 months] the woman [the Ekklesia] flees to Pella for the second time!

> **12:14** And to the woman were given two wings of a great eagle, that she might fly into the wilderness, into her place, where she is nourished for a time, and times, and half a time, from the face of the serpent.

The time, times and half a time are 3 1/2 years or 1,260 days, or 42 months; the second half of the 70th Week!

The "Great Eagle" is God, to whom the saints are faithful; and the two wings that are given to the saints that remove them to the place prepared: Are the Two Prophets of Zechariah 4 and Revelation 11, sent by God!

> **12:15** And the serpent cast out of his mouth water as a flood after the woman, that he might cause her to be carried away of the flood.

> **12:16** And the earth helped the woman, and the earth opened her mouth, and swallowed up the flood which the dragon cast out of his mouth.

When the faithful arrive in Moab in the near future, Satan will inspire an army to chase and attack the Ekklesia, and Jordan will be allied with the New Europe and Beast Emperor, Psalm 83.

The flood is a flood of men, a pursuing army; and God will cause an earthquake to destroy them.

Then Satan will turn back to attack the majority of the Ekklesia who have initially not believed the warnings, but who after this tribulation begins, will then remember and believe and bitterly sincerely repent.

> **12:17** And the dragon was wroth with the woman, and went to make war with the remnant of her seed, which keep the commandments of God, and have the testimony of Jesus Christ.

At the moment that the faithful escape, Satan will turn to attack the wayward Spiritual Ekklesia and those who make a show of keeping the commandments; while being lukewarm for the things of God and idolizing those organizations and false prophets who have convinced them to ignore and reject the warnings from God through his servants and in particular the warnings from God's Two Prophets.

Jesus Christ will protect and nourish those people who are faithful to him! He did this for the first half of the 70th week during the siege of Jerusalem after his resurrection; and he will do this for second half of the 70th week at this end time!

**The two halves complete one full week; the 70th Week of the prophecy!**

Remember that one half of a week is three and one half days, which is three and one half years [at a day for a year] or forty two months or 1260 days. The explanation is found in the twelfth chapter of Revelation!

A woman clothed with the sun (the brightness of the LIGHT), and the moon under her feet (the power of the night, darkness) and wearing a crown of twelve stars (a Queen) brought forth a man child who was to rule all nations (Jesus Christ).

She fled into the wilderness where she was fed (nourished) by God for 1260 days [1/2 week =42 months = 3 1/2 days = 3 1/2 years = 1,260 days].

Later there was war in heaven and Satan was cast out (triggering a great time of trouble in the later days Dan 12:1) and he went to persecute that same woman, who again fled, INTO HER PLACE, where she is again nourished for a time, times and half a time; the times of the Gentiles Daniel 12:7, or 1260 days.

The woman is symbolic of the faithful who KEEP THE COMMANDMENTS of God, HAVING THE LAW OF GOD WRITTEN IN THEIR HEARTS (Heb 8:10). And the nourishing for these two halves of the week; is the confirming of the husband's part of the New Covenant by Jesus Christ!

This was just before the city was destroyed in the Jewish-Roman wars. See: Josephus, Wars of the Jews, the fall of Jerusalem. The city was surrounded in c 66 A.D. and then Vespasian was recalled to Rome after the suicide of Nero. the siege was slightly relaxed and a voice was heard in the temple declaring: "let us remove hence." The faithful then fled to Pella in what is now Jordan.

Then Vespasian on becoming emperor sent his son, Prince Titus to continue the war. Titus himself later became emperor in 79 A.D.

The Daily Sacrifice was offered on behalf of the entire nation and represents the bearing of the national sins of the entire nation! The physical daily was stopped by God at the END of the first 41 months through the instrument of Prince Titus!

Now the High Priest of the New Covenant, Melchizedek [Jesus Christ], intercedes day and night for a spiritual people with God the Father. That daily intercession will be stopped because of the apostasy of today's Spiritual Ekklesia, and the restraints will be removed to allow the correction of the wayward brethren.

Seek the LORD with all your hearts; Turn to a zeal for God to learn and to keep his Word; and he will deliver us, for those who love God enough to learn and to keep his Word are his precious jewels.

The Eternal is a RIGHTEOUS GOD, who KEEPS HIS COVENANTS; He will fulfill His role as a loving husband to a faithful wife.

Yes Jesus Christ loves his bride as only he can love therefore, FEAR NOT and HOLD YOUR HEADS UP, YOU WHO LOVE YOUR GOD AND DO HIS WILL Luke 21:28 FOR YOUR REDEMPTION DRAWS NEAR.

Be strong and of a good courage to follow the Mighty One who inhabits eternity!

These two periods of 3 1/2 years each, total the seven years of the last 70th week of the prophecy.

Yes; He, Jesus Christ will confirm His New Marriage Covenant with His loyal faithful espoused Bride for a full week!

1. The first half of the 70th week was fulfilled in the first century when the Ekklesia fled to Pella as the Romans besieged Jerusalem for 42 months, stopping the daily at the end of that 42 months.

2. The temple and the daily sacrifice will remain desolate until Messiah comes to build the Ezekiel Temple.

3. The second half of the 70th week will begin with the taking of Jerusalem in the latter days (Rev 13:5, Rev 11:2, Luk 21:24 and Rev 12:6), and Jesus Christ will take his faithful espoused bride to the place which God has prepared and nourish her there for 42 months: The second time!

When ALL the Biblical signs are present; when the final false prophet goes to the Holy Mount as Peace and Safety is being declared: sudden destruction [severe correction] will come upon a stubborn and rebellious people (Mat 24:14, 1 Thess 5:3).

Many lukewarm people in the faith who have lost their zeal for living by every Word of God and fallen into a lukewarm complacency, will lack the oil of God's Spirit to respond to the warnings; and will become the victims of a strong delusion.

Preferring to lean on their own false traditions and looking to idols of corporate organizations and men, instead of standing on the Word of God; they will fall into the correction of great tribulation.

## Daniel 6

After taking over Babylon in 539 B.C., the Persian empire replaced the Chaldean's and continued the same Babylonian religious political system.

Later when Darius the Mede ascended the throne in 522 B.B. after the death of Cyrus and his son Cambyses 2, Darius organized his kingdom into 120 provinces and made Daniel his prime minister.

**Daniel 6:1** It pleased Darius to set over the kingdom an hundred and twenty princes, which should be over the whole kingdom;

The kingdom was divided into 120 province with a governor over each one, and three presidents over the governors to serve the king. Daniel was made chief ruler or prime minister under the king.

**6:2** And over these three presidents; of whom Daniel was first: that the princes might give accounts unto them, and the king should have no damage.

**6:3** Then this Daniel was preferred above the presidents and princes, because an excellent spirit was in him; and the king thought to set him over the whole realm.

Political intrigue enters and the others conspire against Daniel.

## The Fascinating Background to Daniel 6
## The Building of the Temple

- The people went up to Jerusalem with Zerubbabel to build the temple according to the decree of Cyrus in 536 B.C.

- Cyrus appointed Sheshbazzar [the Persian name for Zerubbabel] governor of the Jews in Jerusalem and Judea, Ezra 5:16.

- Zerubbabel and Joshua went with the people out of Babylon to Jerusalem under the governor and they build the Altar in time to sacrifice during the Feasts of the seventh month.

- Construction of the temple foundation began in the second year, Ezra 3.

- Little progress was made due to the opposition of the local people and lack of support

- Then Haggai and Zechariah began to prophesy and encourage the people and construction resumed

- Then construction was halted by Artaxerxes [Darius] in 522 B.C. due to complaints from the local people [which came during a period of uprisings in the empire], Ezra 5.

- Then Daniel fasted and prayed for Jerusalem and the Daniel 9 prophecy was given.

- Then the Persian governor Tatnai wrote to Darius explaining that Cyrus had ordered the construction of the temple.

- It was in this poisoned political atmosphere that the nobles in Babylon thought that they could conspire and get rid of Daniel the Jew by contriving to have him cast into the lion's den.

- After seeing God's deliverance of Daniel from the lions (Dan 6) Darius then ordered the construction to resume in 520 B.C. and the temple was completed in 516 B.C. fulfilling the Jeremiah prophecy precisely, Ezra 6.

In 536 B.C. Cyrus had decreed that the various people could send delegations to their native lands and restore the temples of their gods. Zerubbabel was appointed governor of a delegation which returned to Jerusalem to rebuild the temple. They quickly left off from the work due to extreme poverty and local opposition.

Then about 521 B.C. God sent Haggai and Zechariah to exhort the people to resume construction and Zerubbabel. Inspired they resumed construction which greatly angered the Samaritans and Ammonites who wrote a letter of complaint to the newly crowned king Darius in his first year 522 B.C. Thinking the construction unlawful and a rebellious act he ordered it stopped. It was in this poisoned political atmosphere that the nobles in Babylon thought that they could conspire and get rid of Daniel the Jew.

Then Tatnai the Persian governor of Palestine wrote king Darius on behalf of Zerubabbel informing Darius that Cyrus had ordered the construction. His letter came just after Daniel was delivered from the den of lions and Darius ordered an urgent search of the archives for the decree of Cyrus.

Deeply impressed by the deliverance of Daniel by God, Darius immediately ordered the construction of the temple to resume as soon as the decree of Cyrus was found.

Based on Ezra 4:24, this decree was **issued in 520 B.C., the second year of the solo reign of Darius.**

With the hinderances now removed, the temple was completed in the sixth solo year of Darius (516 B.C.) on the third day of the twelfth month, and in the following month they kept the Passover (Ezra 6:15, 19).

Darius went further and made it a capital offense to interfere with the construction and ordered all necessary materials to be supplied. Construction resumed and the temple was completed in 516 B.C., exactly 70 years after it was burned by Nebuchadnezzar in 586 B.C.

**6:4** Then the presidents and princes sought to find occasion against Daniel concerning the kingdom; but they could find none occasion nor fault; forasmuch as he was faithful, neither was there any error or fault found in him.

They concluded that Daniel was blameless and decided to contrive a cause from his faith in the Eternal.

**6:5** Then said these men, We shall not find any occasion against this Daniel, except we find it against him concerning the law of his God.

These top leaders then conspired against Daniel and appealed to king Darius using flattery to establish a foolish decree.

**6:6** Then these presidents and princes assembled together to the king, and said thus unto him, King Darius, live for ever.

The king's vanity was appealed to, and he approved the decree.

**6:7** All the presidents of the kingdom, the governors, and the princes, the counsellors, and the captains, have consulted together to establish a royal statute, and to make a firm decree, that whosoever shall ask a petition of any God or man for thirty days, save of thee, O king, he shall be cast into the den of lions.

**6:8** Now, O king, establish the decree, and sign the writing, that it be not changed, according to the law of the Medes and Persians, which altereth not.

Then Darius approved the decree which could not afterwards be altered.

**6:9** Wherefore king Darius signed the writing and the decree.

What did Daniel do? He put God first!

He put God first and does so openly! Daniel does not hide in a closet, NO he opens his window shutters and sets an example for those folks, for us and for all humanity; for all eternity of godly courage based on a profound faith!

Who has a Bible and has not heard of the faith and courage of Daniel?

Let all the called of God: Dare to be like Daniel, and: Dare to take a stand for what is godly and right!

Daniel made known his faith and fealty to the Eternal above the word of any man, even the emperor of the known world!

The Eternal is the Mighty God and King of our salvation ;not any man! To follow men and not the Word of God is IDOLATRY, and NO idolater will be in the resurrection to spirit!

> **Revelation 22:14** Blessed are they that do his commandments, that they may have right to the tree of life, and may enter in through the gates into the city. **22:15** For without are dogs, and sorcerers, and whoremongers, and murderers, and idolaters, and whosoever loveth and maketh a lie.

**Daniel 6:10** Now when Daniel knew that the writing was signed, he went into his house; and his windows being open in his chamber toward Jerusalem, he kneeled upon his knees three times a day, and prayed, and gave thanks before his God, as he did aforetime.

It is interesting that these rulers KNEW that Daniel would do this! They knew Daniel and his love and passion for the Eternal, so they knew that they could trap him in this way; they KNEW that Daniel was faithful to God and chose to make no secret of it. Indeed he opened his windows and openly flaunted his zeal for the Eternal Almighty God as an example for all!

When an elder asks you to take part in polluting God's Sabbath by taking part in some catered meal or inappropriate activity on God's Sabbath or Holy Days: Do you refuse to sin like Daniel did? Do you dare to be like Daniel and serve the Eternal God with all your heart regardless of what men may say or do?

**6:11** Then these men assembled, and found Daniel praying and making supplication before his God.

Just as they foresaw these people found Daniel praying to God and reported the matter to the king as breaking the command of the king.

When you are zealous for the whole Word of God, God's weekly Sabbath and his Holy Days; do you fear being reported for your zeal, or are you ready to give an answer from the Word of God and courageously declare that you will obey the Word of God like Daniel did?

**6:12** Then they came near, and spake before the king concerning the king's decree; Hast thou not signed a decree, that every man that shall ask a petition of any God or man within thirty days, save of thee, O king, shall be cast into the den of lions? The king answered and said, The thing is true, according to the law of the Medes and Persians, which altereth not.

**6:13** Then answered they and said before the king, That Daniel, which is of the children of the captivity of Judah, regardeth not thee, O king, nor the decree that thou hast signed, but maketh his petition three times a day.

Then king Darius repented of his law because he loved Daniel, but it could not be undone in his kingdom.

**6:14** Then the king, when he heard these words, was sore displeased with himself, and set his heart on Daniel to deliver him: and he laboured till the going down of the sun to deliver him.

**6:15** Then these men assembled unto the king, and said unto the king, Know, O king, that the law of the Medes and Persians is, That no decree nor statute which the king establisheth may be changed.

This king Darius also had hope that God would deliver his faithful servant.

**6:16** Then the king commanded, and they brought Daniel, and cast him into the den of lions. **Now the king spake and said unto Daniel, Thy God whom thou servest continually, he will deliver thee.**

This unconverted emperor had more faith than the called out of today's Spiritual Ekklesia!

Yes, Darius spoke the truth; and if we are zealous for our Mighty One; even if we are rejected by our friends or die in HIS service; HE WILL RAISE US UP ON THAT DAY!

The lion's den was sealed so that no friend could come and rescue Daniel.

Brethren, if we are ostracized and made friendless, **God is testing us and teaching us to trust in God alone for our salvation!**

If we are rejected for our zeal to learn and keep the whole Word of God; then "Bury yourself in the Book!" Run to HIM! For God alone is worthy of our trust and obedience!

**6:17** And a stone was brought, and laid upon the mouth of the den; and the king sealed it with his own signet, and with the signet of his lords; that the purpose might not be changed concerning Daniel.

Darius spent the night fasting, sleepless for his friend Daniel.

**6:18** Then the king went to his palace, and passed the night fasting: neither were instruments of musick brought before him: and his sleep went from him.

The king rushed to Daniel as soon as he could see in the morning.

**6:19** Then the king arose very early in the morning, and went in haste unto the den of lions.

**6:20** And when he came to the den, he cried with a lamentable voice unto Daniel: and the king spake and said to Daniel, O Daniel, servant of the living God, is thy God, whom thou servest continually, able to deliver thee from the lions?

Daniel answered the king, and was released. God defends his faithful because they are innocent before him.

Brethren this deliverance of Daniel from the lions and death; was an example that Almighty God will deliver his beloved passionately faithful [faithful as Daniel was faithful] from the "Roaring Lion" Satan himself, and from the grave of certain death.

**1 Peter 5:8** Be sober, be vigilant; because your adversary the devil, as a roaring lion, walketh about, seeking whom he may devour:

**Daniel 6:21** Then said Daniel unto the king, **O king, live for ever.**

**6:22 My God hath sent his angel, and hath shut the lions' mouths, that they have not hurt me: forasmuch as before him innocency was found in me; and also before thee, O king, have I done no hurt.**

Daniel was faithful in all things before God and the king

**6:23** Then was the king exceedingly glad for him, and commanded that they should take Daniel up out of the den. So Daniel was taken up out of the den, and **no manner of hurt was found upon him, because he believed in** [and obeyed the Eternal] **his God.**

Then the leaders who had sinned against God's faithful were themselves punished.

It is one thing for professing Christians to say they do not agree with our zeal; and it is quite another thing to take on the role of Satan and actively persecute those zealous for God.

**Matthew 18:4** Whosoever therefore shall humble himself as this little child, the same is greatest in the kingdom of heaven.

The humble and sincerely repentant who eagerly follow the Eternal will be in the resurrection to eternal life; and those who receive [accept] such a spiritual childlike brother full of love and zeal for the word of God, does good to Christ.

**18:5** And whoso shall receive one such little child in my name receiveth me.

Anyone who rejects or persecutes the zealous to learn and to keep the whole word of God; offends Jesus Christ!

**18:6** But whoso shall offend one of these little ones [any brethren faithfully submissive to live by Every Word of God] which believe in me, it were better for him that a millstone were hanged about his neck, and that he were drowned in the depth of the sea.

**Matthew 18:10** Take heed that ye despise not one of these little ones; for I say unto you, That in heaven their angels do always behold the face of my Father which is in heaven.

**Daniel 6:24** And the king commanded, and they brought those men which had accused Daniel, and they cast them into the den of lions, them, their children, and their wives; and the lions had the mastery of them, and brake all their bones in pieces or ever they came at the bottom of the den.

Then Darius made a decree to all of his kingdom.

This decree is a prophecy that when Messiah the King of kings comes and establishes the kingdom of God over all the earth; all people will sincerely repent and worship the Eternal, turning to live by every Word of God!

**6:25** Then king Darius wrote unto all people, nations, and languages, that dwell in all the earth; Peace be multiplied unto you.

**6:26** I make a decree, **That in every dominion of my kingdom men tremble and fear before the God of Daniel: for he is the living God, and stedfast for ever, and his kingdom that which shall not be destroyed, and his dominion shall be even unto the end.**

**6:27** **He delivereth and rescueth, and he worketh signs and wonders in heaven and in earth, who hath delivered Daniel from the power of the lions.**

May all of God's called out, be as faithful, as bold and courageous, as zealous as Daniel!

Let us all stand wholeheartedly on every Word of God, without any compromise; forever!

**6:28** So this Daniel prospered in the reign of Darius, and in the reign of Cyrus the Persian.

Daniel's faith and courage led to the decree of Darius to resume rebuilding the temple at Jerusalem and so fulfill the 70 Years Prophecy of Jeremiah.

> Isaiah records that God had appointed Cyrus for this task. **Isaiah 44:28** That saith of Cyrus, He is my shepherd, and shall perform all my pleasure: even saying to Jerusalem, Thou shalt be built; and to the temple, Thy foundation shall be laid.
>
> And in **Jeremiah 29:10,** God had promised, **After seventy years be accomplished at Babylon I will visit you, and perform my good word toward you, in causing you to return to this place.**

### The decree of Cyrus is found and re-issued by Darius

Based on Ezra 4:24, this decree was issued in 520 B.C., the second year of the solo reign of Darius.

**Ezra 6:1** Then Darius the king made a decree, and search was made in the house of the rolls, where the treasures were laid up in Babylon. **6:2** And there was found at Achmetha, in the palace that is in the province of the Medes, a roll, and therein was a record thus written:

The 70 Weeks Prophecy of Daniel used the decree **to build the City Jerusalem** as its starting point, This Decree of Cyrus was about building the temple only.

**6:3 6:4** With three rows of great stones, and a row of new timber: and let the expenses be given out of the king's house:

**6:5** And also let the golden and silver vessels of the house of God, which Nebuchadnezzar took forth out of the temple which is at Jerusalem, and brought unto Babylon, be restored, and brought again unto the temple which is at Jerusalem, every one to his place, and place them in the house of God.

Darius instructed the construction to resume and ordered the surrounding peoples NOT to interfere with the king's command. The king then ordered these people to support the work by paying tribute for its furtherance.

God the great King will intervene to help his people who are building themselves into a fit Spiritual Temple for God and his Spirit, by internalizing the whole Word of God!

**6:6** Now therefore, Tatnai, governor beyond the river, Shetharboznai, and your companions the Apharsachites, which are beyond the river, be ye far from thence:

**6:7** Let the work of this house of God alone; let the governor of the Jews and the elders of the Jews build this house of God in his place.**6:8** Moreover I make a decree what ye shall do to the elders of these Jews for the building of this house of God: that of the king's goods, even of the tribute beyond the river, **forthwith expenses be given unto these men, that they be not hindered.**

Darius then commanded these people to supply animals for sacrifice on the altar.

**6:9** And that which they have need of, both young bullocks, and rams, and lambs, for the burnt offerings of the God of heaven, wheat, salt, wine, and oil, according to the appointment of the priests which are at Jerusalem, let it be given them day by day without fail: **6:10** That they may offer sacrifices of sweet savours unto the God of heaven, and pray for the life of the king, and of his sons.

The king adds the pain of death for any disobedience.

**6:11** Also I have made a decree, that whosoever shall alter this word, let timber be pulled down from his house, and being set up, let him be hanged thereon; and let his house be made a dunghill for this.

Then, undoubtedly because of Daniel, Darius goes even further and curses anyone who interferes with the temple construction with destruction. Spiritually, if we are faithful to internalize and keep the whole Word of God; things many seem difficult; but the Eternal goes before us!

**6:12** And the God that hath caused his name to dwell there destroy all kings and people, that shall put to their hand to alter and to destroy this house of God which is at Jerusalem. I Darius have made a decree; let it be done with speed.

# Revelation

# Revelation 1

The book of Revelation is a direct revealing of latter day events by Jesus Christ to John, and through John to the faithful disciples of Christ.

The Book is about events FUTURE from the time these things were revealed to John.

The messages to ALL of the seven churches are instructive for the present situation and for very called out individual.

**Revelation 1:1** The Revelation of Jesus Christ, which God gave unto him, to shew **unto his servants things which must shortly come to pass;** and he sent and signified it by his angel unto his servant John: **1:2** Who bare record of the word of God, and of the testimony of Jesus Christ, and of all things that he saw.

The prophecies were sealed until the end time, when the time of their fulfillment is at hand (Dan 12), Revelation 5 will confirm this.

At the very End Time the Sealed Books will be unsealed and spiritual knowledge and understanding will be increased (Dan 12) for the faithful to God. We have the promise of God in Daniel 12, and confirmed in Revelation 5. The books of the prophecies will be opened to the understanding of the faithful when their redemption is at hand!

We are not only to hear and understand, we are to KEEP the words of the book of Revelation! A blessing is pronounced on those who faithfully KEEP the words of Revelation including messages to all seven churches by correcting their faults as identified by Jesus Christ.

**1:3 Blessed is he that readeth, and they that hear the words of this prophecy, and keep those things which are written therein: for the time is at hand.**

ALL of the seven churches existed together at the same time in the first century when John wrote this, and ALL seven attitudes, strengths and issues have always existed at the same time together through history from the first century to today; and all seven attitudes, strengths and issues exist together at the same time today!

All of these seven churches existed together at the same time and all of these messages are for us today.

The seven churches are about seven different attitudes, strengths and problems in the Ekklesia and are written to the WHOLE of the Ekklesia, to each one of us; and all of these messages were written for the guidance of the New Covenant Ekklesia through the centuries from the first century to today, so that each and every one of us may examine ourselves as to our own spiritual condition.

Of course different attitudes may dominate organizations at different times, however this idea of seven consecutive eras is simplistic and seems designed to justify ignoring most of the messages by claiming that they are for others: When we are to apply ALL scripture to ourselves for our own benefit.

Brethren, as verse 3 makes clear, ALL of this Book was written for EVERY PERSON in the Ekklesia at all times!

Nowhere does John record that this was on some mail route and that these churches represent consecutive eras! That thought is not in the scriptures and such an assumption amounts to obscuring the meaning by adding something which is not there: When the meaning is that EVERY message applies to EVERY person

> **2 Timothy 3:16** All scripture is given by inspiration of God, and is profitable for doctrine, for reproof, for correction, for instruction in righteousness:

ALL seven churches existed at the same time together in the first century; and all of these problems have existed in the Ekklesia throughout history since the first century, and they all exist in the Ekklesia today!

The true Ekklesia has always been a mix of people with every one of these attitudes! In today's corporate Ekklesia; ALL of these messages are applicable because each group is a mix of all of these different attitudes in its individual brethren, as well as briers and tares.

In fact this situation is climaxing today at the end time, fulfilling the prophecies of a great falling away from true godliness!

This study will demonstrate that the problems of all of these seven churches exist in the Ekklesia at the same time today, as they have existed throughout the period from the first century to today; which is what the Revelation messages from Jesus Christ are all about.

Every one of these messages from Jesus Christ is a personal message to each and every one of us, alerting us to what we should look out for, and warning us what to examine ourselves for.

All seven church attitudes exist today and ALL of these messages are for every one of us today! Each of us needs to examine himself honestly to see if we have any of these problems. We all need to remember that NO corporate church is a true church of God at all, and that the true Ekklesia is made up of every called out person!

**2 Timothy 3:16 All scripture [including the Seven Messages] is given by inspiration of God, and is profitable for doctrine, for reproof, for correction, for instruction in righteousness: 3:17 That the man of God may be perfect, thoroughly furnished unto all good works.**

**1 Corinthians 10:1** Moreover, brethren, I would not that ye should be ignorant, how that all our fathers were under the cloud, and all passed through the sea; **10:2** And were all baptized unto Moses in the cloud and in the sea; **10:3** And did all eat the same spiritual meat [the Word of God]; **10:4** And did all drink the same spiritual drink [in the physical sense; just as we must do in both the physical and the spiritual sense]: for they **drank of that spiritual Rock that followed them: and that Rock was Christ.**

**10:5** But with many of them God was not well pleased: for they were overthrown in the wilderness. **10:6** Now **these things were our examples, to the intent we should not lust after evil things, as**

**they also lusted. 10:7 Neither be ye idolaters** [referring to today's spiritual idolatry], as were some of them; as it is written, The people sat down to eat and drink, and rose up to play.

**10:8** Neither let us commit fornication [Pornea, means any disloyalty to our spouse; today referring to following any other than the whole Word of God as inspired by Jesus Christ our espoused Husband], as some of them committed, and fell in one day three and twenty thousand.

**10:9 Neither let us tempt Christ** [by not being faithful to His Word and so challenging his authority as our head], as some of them also tempted, and were destroyed of serpents.

**10:10** Neither murmur ye [We are not to complain against and blame Christ and the Father for our trials and we are not to try to mitigate trials by compromising with God's Word; instead we are to run to God and cry out to our Mighty Deliverer for salvation.], as some of them also murmured, and were destroyed of the destroyer.

**10:11** Now **all these things happened unto them for examples: and they are written for our admonition, upon whom the ends of the world are come. 10:12 Wherefore let him that thinketh he standeth take heed lest he fall.**


### The Seven Churches

Each one of the seven spirits is the spiritual overseer [angel spirit] of one of the seven churches, helping Christ who is over all.

**Revelation 1:4** John to the seven churches which are in Asia: Grace be unto you, and peace, from him which is, and which was, and which is to come; and from the seven Spirits which are before his throne; **1:5** And from Jesus Christ, who is the faithful witness, and the first begotten of the dead, and the prince of the kings of the earth. Unto him that loved us, and washed [the sincerely repentant] us from our sins in his own blood,

The reward of those chosen to be changed to spirit at the early harvest is to be made eternal kings and priests of the order of Jesus Christ unto God the Father.

As kings [rulers] and priests [teachers of godliness] it will be our mission to bring many to the righteousness of understanding and zealously living by every Word of God!

Most tend to think that today's terrible example of elders dominating the brethren is the right way to go, and look forward to dominating others in the Kingdom.

NO, NO, NO, Absolutely NOT. The Nicolaitane attitude of most elders today in coming between the brethren and God and dominating the brethren is an abomination to Jesus Christ.

> **Matthew 20:25** But Jesus called them unto him, and said, Ye know that the princes of the Gentiles exercise dominion over them, and they that are great exercise authority upon them. **20:26** But it shall not be so among you: but whosoever will be great among you, let him be your minister; **20:27** And whosoever will be chief among you, let him be your servant:

**Revelation 1:6** And **hath made us kings and priests unto God and his Father** [Did you catch that? Jesus is here referred to a God and with God the Father!]; to him be glory and dominion for ever and ever. Amen.

Jesus Christ shall come from heaven and will be seen in the skies of the earth, and all who live at that time will see him. Later in their own time of physical resurrection, those who killed him will also see him and will weep and deeply repent.

When Christ comes all humanity alive after the last battle, when the political and spiritual rulers of spiritual Babylon are destroyed and Satan with his demonic followers are imprisoned; will sincerely repent and turn to God the Father, and the Holy Spirit will be poured out on all flesh (Joel 2:28).

**1:7** Behold, he cometh with clouds; and every eye shall see him, and they also which pierced him: and **all kindreds of the earth shall wail because of him**. Even so, Amen.

Jesus Christ existed from the beginning and will exist until the end. Of God's family there shall be no end; and all of the wicked will have their end in the lake of fire by the power of Jesus Christ! He will NOT tolerate any willful sin, but will cast the unrepentant who will not stop sinning into the fire of eternal destruction.

**1:8 I am Alpha and Omega, the beginning and the ending, saith the Lord, which is, and which was, and which is to come, the Almighty.**

John had been exiled to the island of Patmos because of his preaching of Christ.

**1:9** I John, who also am your brother, and companion in tribulation, and in the kingdom and patience of Jesus Christ, **was in the isle that is called Patmos, for the word of God, and for the testimony of Jesus Christ.**

John was in spirit; that is, he saw a vision.

The term Lord's Day refers to the latter day "Day of the Lord" when Christ comes, so the vision regarding the seven churches was a vision that the end time seven churches which are all together at the Day of the Lord when Christ comes, and the issues being revealed are the issues in the Ekklesia TODAY!

This vision was about seven contemporaneous churches in the first century which all existed at the same time, this is NOT about any first century mail route which is NOT scriptural and is a false assumption of men added to the scriptures! The vision is dual using the conditions in the first century seven churches to reveal that these same conditions would exist today!

The vision is about seven church problems which exist during the latter days, our time today: the Day of the Lord's coming!

**1:10 I was in the Spirit on the Lord's day**, and heard behind me a great voice, as of a trumpet,

The whole Book of Revelation is addressed to the seven brother churches as types representing the seven primary issues of the end time Ekklesia.

**1:11** Saying, I am Alpha and Omega, the first and the last: and, What thou seest, write in a book, and send it unto the seven churches which are in Asia; unto Ephesus, and unto Smyrna, and unto Pergamos, and unto Thyatira, and unto Sardis, and unto Philadelphia, and unto Laodicea.

The whole Book of Revelation was to be sent to every one of the seven churches of Asia in John's time; and doubtless while a particular problem might be dominate, the specific messages to each of the seven churches did apply at that time to all of them!

In John's time the seven churches all existed at the same time; and in this latter day; all seven messages are applicable for OUR instruction!

**The Lamp Stand**

In King James England the use of candles was the common method of lighting in the land, so they improperly translated oil burning lamps [lamp stands] as candlesticks; and olive oil lamps as candles. When you see the terms candles or candlesticks: read oil burning lamps or oil lamps [Menorah].

The olive oil represents the Holy Spirit which is in the Ekklesia and in converted individuals; which if used produces the light of a godly example for all others to see.

Today, the flow of the oil of the Holy Spirit has been quenched because the Ekklesia is spiritually asleep; and must be awakened and must fill their lamps with the oil of the Holy Spirit in sincere repentance so they can be resurrected to life eternal.

It is explained in Zechariah 4 that the latter day Ekklesia is about to die and it is God's two prophets who God will use to revive them; turning them to a passion for godliness and reviving them so that the oil of God's Spirit might make them shine brightly in passionate godliness.

In Zechariah 4 the golden lamp or menorah is presented, which is a single lamp stand with seven branches, each branch representing one of the latter day churches of Revelation. God's two servants revive all seven branches of the lamp stand; therefore of necessity all seven Revelation churches must exist at the same time that these two are working.

**1:12** And I turned to see the voice that spake with me. And being turned, I saw seven golden candlesticks; **1:13** And in the midst of the seven candlesticks [Oil Burning Lamps] one like unto the Son of man,

**Jesus Christ and the Seven Spirits**

. . . clothed with a garment down to the foot, and girt about the paps with a golden girdle. **1:14** His head and his hairs were white like wool, as white as snow; and his eyes were as a flame of fire; **1:15** And his feet like unto fine brass, as if they burned in a furnace; and his voice as the sound of many waters.

**1:16** And he had in his right hand seven stars [The seven spirits of the seven latter day churches in his hand serve Christ over the seven churches, each church represented by a branch of the Menorah lamp stand.]: and out of his mouth went a sharp twoedged sword [The sharp sword if the TRUTH of God; which most of the brethren reject today to maintain their false traditions.]: and his countenance was as the sun shineth in his strength.

John worships Christ and faints in awe of him.

**1:17** And when I saw him, I fell at his feet as dead. And he laid his right hand upon me, saying unto me, Fear not; I am the first and the last:

Jesus Christ has the keys of judgment to save the godly faithful and to condemn the wicked who stray away from a zeal to follow the whole Word of God and instead follow idols of men.

**1:18** I am he that liveth, and was dead; and, behold, I am alive for evermore, Amen; and have the keys of hell and of death.

John is commanded to write what he sees.

**1:19** Write the things which thou hast seen, and the things which are, and the things which shall be hereafter;

**1:20** The mystery of the seven stars which thou sawest in my right hand, and the seven golden candlesticks. **The seven stars are the angels of the seven churches: and the seven candlesticks** [the seven oil burning lamps; Menorah] **which thou sawest are the seven churches.**

## Revelation 2

### The Seven Churches

ALL the words of this Book are for the instruction of ALL of God's people.

Each one of us needs to take a very serious look at every one of the messages and examine ourselves closely as to whether we can learn from them about our own condition; and so profit from these messages in our own personal spiritual growth.

> **2 Timothy 3:16** All scripture is given by inspiration of God, and is profitable for doctrine, for reproof, for correction, for instruction in righteousness: **3:17** That the man of God may be perfect, thoroughly furnished unto all good works.

Brethren, How long will we cherry pick scripture to claim the good things are about us and any correction is about others; refusing to examine ourselves by the WHOLE Word of God? How long will we justify our sins by claiming that certain instructions apply only to others and not to ourselves?

ALL of these messages are for EVERYONE who reads the Book. That means that EVERY message is a personal message to each one of us today!

Saying that these messages are for sequential periods and not for us today is rejecting the loving instructions of Jesus Christ as he works to save us!

**Ephesus**

Jesus Christ speaks directly to those who have lost their first love and zeal to live by every Word of God.

Do you remember the passion of your first love of God and the scriptures? Do you remember how we eagerly rushed to the scriptures to see whether some new thing we were learning was true? Do you remember how we tested many things to discern right from wrong? and the joy of discovery we had at finding some truth?

Do you remember how we lay awake at night trying to understand God's Word and meditated on the Word of God every moment we could?

Did we not Hunger and Thirst; BURNING with passion to learn - to understand - to know the whole Word and Will of God? Did we not want to learn the things of God; to be like God our Father and passionately, joyously, wholeheartedly follow God's every Word?

Our burning love for our God and his Word was like the passion of a starving man for food, or a thirsty man for water; Or as a man and his bride yearning to be one with each other on their wedding day!

**Revelation 2:1** Unto the angel of the church of Ephesus write; These things saith he that holdeth the seven stars in his right hand, who walketh in the midst of the seven golden candlesticks;

Can you remember how we loved good and hated evil and tested all men and all things, seeking to live by every Word of God? Can you remember the joy we felt in our study of God's Word at every new truth we discovered and how we rushed to embrace it and to keep it? Do you remember how we eagerly rushed to repudiate sin and turn to truth as soon as we learned the Will of God in some matter?

Remember how we tested by the scriptures all those who made claims of godliness and rejected all error for the truth of God?

Remember how much we endured for our love of God? How we were make a laughingstock by our friends, family and neighbours? Yet we patiently endured the pain and the disgrace heaped upon us, because of our passionate love for God and his Word.

**2:2** I know thy works, and thy labour, and thy patience, and how thou canst not bear them which are evil: and thou hast tried them which say they are apostles, and are not, and hast found them liars: **2:3** And hast borne, and hast patience, and for my name's [to exalt the authority of God] sake hast labored [to grow in knowledge and understanding of true godliness], and hast not fainted.

**2:4** Nevertheless I have somewhat against thee, because thou hast left thy first love.

Brethren, generally in today's Spiritual Ekklesia we have grown weary with well doing and have fallen away from our first passionate love and zeal for godliness! We have fallen spiritually asleep content to follow idols of men and corporate institutions in place of following our espoused Husband and living by the Will and by every Word of God.

We have lost our fire of passionate love for God the Father and for our Husband Jesus Christ; we have turned to other lovers by embracing idols of men and calling the promised latter day advances in knowledge and understanding: contemptible.

Jesus Christ admonishes us to REMEMBER our first love and passion for Him, God the Father, and His Word. Our Husband stands and calls out to his bride: Remember me and return to me, rekindle your burning fire of passion for me [Christ], God the Father and His Word!

So many of us have lost our first passionate zeal for the whole Word of God and turned to a zeal for corporate idols, idols of men and false traditions.

Oh, how we loved God and his Word! But deceitful men came in and taught us that they were between us and God, and that we should blindly obey them without question as the supposed chosen leaders of God; and so we became passionate for men, being deceived that this was the same as a passion for God! Today we love our corporate assemblies and its leaders, elders and our friends in the congregation: MORE THAN WE LOVE OUR GOD!

Today many gladly do what men say, even in contradiction to God's Word! We no longer have a zeal to run to the whole Word of God to prove all things, instead we look at only the out of context scriptures given to us by deceivers trying to justify the sins of men!

Brethren, the vast majority of brethren TODAY have left their first love! We have left off from any zeal to learn and to keep the whole Word of God, and we have left off from any zeal for the TRUTH of God, to follow idols and false traditions of men.

Jesus Christ admonishes us to REPENT from turning away from our zeal for Him, His Father and His Word. He commands us to run back to our first passionate zealous enthusiasm for the righteousness of the whole Word of God to follow the espoused Husband of our baptismal commitment!

Jesus Christ warns each one of us that if we do not quickly and sincerely repent: He will remove our Light [the Holy Spirit in us] and reject us [into the great correction of tribulation] for turning away from our zeal for God's Word to follow idols of men and ungodly traditions.

Today our sins are many; such as calling the Sabbath and High Days holy, and then openly polluting them; or rejecting the newly revealed knowledge of God's Biblical calendar, for the unscriptural Rabbinic calendar; even knowingly lying to justify making an idol of the unconverted Rabbinate.

**2:5** Remember therefore from whence thou art fallen, and repent, and do the first works; or else I will come unto thee quickly, and will remove thy candlestick out of his place, except thou repent.

Yes, some of us hate the deeds of the Nicolaitanes; which is the domination system of the Nicolaitane Babylonian Mysteries form of church governance adopted by most of the Ekklesia today. The ministry are to be helps for the brethren to focus us on God; they are not to dominate and demand that the brethren follow their false traditions instead of being zealous for God.

**2:6** But this thou hast, that **thou hatest the deeds of the Nicolaitanes, which I also hate.**

Brethren, IF we sincerely repent and turn back to our first love the whole Word of God; to prove all things by the whole Word of God and to make God's Word our ultimate moral authority: and if we overcome our tendency to exalt anything else to love it as much or more than we love the whole Word of God; We shall be saved into the promised land of a change to spirit and eternal life by our sincere repentance from this terrible sin.

**2:7** He that hath an ear, let him hear what the Spirit saith unto the churches; To him that overcometh will I give to eat of the tree of life, which is in the midst of the paradise of God.

If only the brethren, leaders and elders of today's Spiritual Assemblies would open up the scriptures and instead of saying the first five messages to the churches, or Ezra and Nehemiah, or such and such, do not apply to us, but apply to others: we would apply EVERY WORD of God to ourselves!

If they would only say that ALL scripture is for our instruction; and that we NEED to wholeheartedly REPENT of polluting the Sabbath and Holy Days, and we NEED to STOP cooking and paying other to cook for and serve us on God's holy time; that we NEED to stop marrying outside the faith; that we need to STOP idolizing men and the false traditions of men and turn with passionate zeal to the Word of God!

**If such a thing were to be done; the whole heavens would erupt with a uncontainable rejoicing!**

As Paul told Timothy, all scripture is for OUR instruction. These scriptures apply to us: and if we will only acknowledge that and correct ourselves, we shall be saved.

**Smyrna**

A message to those who are physically poor yet faithfully following every Word of God and spiritually rich. Jesus reminds us that he died for us and is now alive by the power of God the Father; implying that we too as flesh will die, but if we are faithful to God the Father and live by every Word of God as Christ does. we will also be resurrected to eternal life.

**2:8** And unto the angel of the church in Smyrna write; These things saith the first and the last, which was dead, and is alive [Jesus Christ];

Those who are faithful in their godly actions [works of faith] to zealously KEEP the whole Word of God, may suffer physical poverty and persecution in this world, but they will become spiritually rich and will have riches in the world to come.

Those who claim to be Christians [spiritual Jews] and then follow men away from and contrary to the Word of God, are of Satan. This includes the Church of God groups who idolize men and reject zealous obedience to live by every Word of God.

Does this seem harsh? The Spirit of God leads us into an enthusiastic passion to become like God, by learning and keeping the whole Word and Will of God; which is TRUTH.

It is the spirit of Antichrist, the spirit of Satan, which leads people to follow idols of men and to leave our first love of godliness to reject any zeal to follow the whole Word and Will of God.

Those who know better and even stoop to LYING to themselves and others, to justify idolizing men and the false traditions of men are not of God. Neither are those who call God's Sabbaths holy and then routinely and deliberately pollute them, or those who reject the truth to maintain their false traditions.

**2:9** I know thy works [works of faith], and tribulation [trials], and [physical] poverty, (but thou art [spiritually] rich) and I know the blasphemy of them which say they are [converted spiritual New Covenant called out] Jews, and are not, but are the synagogue of Satan.

The faithful to God and his Word, will suffer in this life; even from the hands of their families and friends in their beloved Church corporations. God allows us to be tried so that we may grow in godliness and bring forth much fruit (John 15).

Christ encourages us that our trials will bring forth much fruit and are for our ultimate good; revealing that through patient endurance of trials we shall inherit a crown of eternal life.

**2:10** Fear none of those things which thou shalt suffer: behold, the devil shall cast some of you into prison, that ye may be tried; and **ye shall have tribulation ten days** [years]: be thou faithful unto death, and I will give thee a crown of life.

The faithful in Smyrna suffered a great persecution for ten years during which Polycarp was killed in 157 A.D. Polycarp had known and was ordained bishop of Smyrna by the apostle John. In his youth Polycarp also personally knew many other witnesses of the resurrection.

Whether or not one wants to argue that Smyrna was dominant for a specific period of time: Who among those trying to live by every Word of God has not had their faith tested by many trials? This applies to us, as an encouragement, that though we may have many trials in this life, if we rely on our great God and continue to zealously live by every Word of God, we shall become spiritually rich and have a good reward.

> **Hebrews 10:32** But call to remembrance the former days, in which, after ye were illuminated, ye endured a great fight of afflictions; **10:33** Partly, whilst ye were made a gazingstock both by

reproaches and afflictions; and partly, whilst ye became companions of them that were so used.

This is a promise from Jesus Christ that all of those who are adamantly enthusiastic and full of love for God and his Word, will suffer in this world for their zeal, but they will become spiritually rich forevermore!

**John 15:19** If ye were of the world, the world would love his own: but because ye are not of the world, but I have chosen you out of the world, therefore the world hateth you.

**15:20** Remember the word that I said unto you, The servant is not greater than his lord. If they have persecuted me, they will also persecute you; if they have kept my saying, they will keep yours also.

**15:21** But all these things will they do unto you for my name's sake, because they know not him that sent me.

The message ends with the promise to Smyrna and to all those who are zealous to live by every Word of God; that if we are willing to suffer for our passion or even to die for the faith, we shall receive the gift of eternal life.

This is a particular encouragement for most of today's Spiritual Ekklesia who will soon be in the correction of great tribulation. If we sincerely repent and overcome and turn to live by every Word of God, we will surely be persecuted, many to the death. But if we are faithful to God to steadfastly put God first above any trial and are even willing to die for love of God we shall receive eternal life and will be delivered from the second death.

The vast majority of today's called out brethren are zealous for God and his Word; but they have been deceived into thinking of their leaders and elders as being between them and God; and they falsely believe that loyalty to these men is the same as loyalty to God: That is the sin of idolatry: And that is the lesson that God is teaching his people today!

**Follow men ONLY as they follow God!**

**1 Thessalonians 5:19** Quench not the Spirit.

**5:20** Despise not prophesyings [warnings and correction].

**5:21** Prove all things; hold fast that which is good.

**3:22** Abstain from all appearance of evil.

**Revelation 2:11** He that hath an ear, let him hear what the Spirit saith unto [All the called out, the Ekklesia] the churches; **He that overcometh shall not be hurt of the second death.**

The Word of God is sharper than any two edged sword, to divide the holy from the profane. If we loved the truth we would never knowingly lie to justify our own positions, therefore it is obvious that many today have no love for the truth.

Nothing negative is said of Smyrna, only encouragement to be steadfast in trials.


**Pergamos**

**Revelation 2:12** And to the angel of the **church in Pergamos** write; These things saith he which hath the **sharp sword with two edges**;

The Pergamos attitude holds fast to the name [the authority of God the Father and Jesus Christ] even though they dwelt at the very seat of Satan in Pergamos [the Greeks moved the seat of the Babylonian Mysteries from Babylon to Pergamos] and were among the martyrs. These people exalted the authority [name] of Christ and God the Father above all else even to death.

This is a prophecy that there are still some in the Ekklesia today who exalt the "name" the AUTHORITY of the Word of God, Jesus Christ and God the Father.

They accept the authority of the Word of God as their ONLY moral authority even under persecution for doing so; this applied in the first century and it applies today as many such faithful people are cast out of the Assemblies of the called out for not bowing to the Nicolaitane governance used in much of the latter day Ekklesia.

**2:13** I know thy works, and where thou dwellest, even where Satan's seat is: and thou holdest fast my name [God's authority], and hast not denied my faith [by turning away from the works of faith], even in those days wherein Antipas was my faithful martyr, who was slain among you, where Satan dwelleth.

**2:14** But I have a few things against thee, because thou hast there them that hold the doctrine of Balaam, who taught Balac to cast a stumblingblock before the children of Israel, to eat things sacrificed unto idols [to accept false doctrines of idols of men], and to commit fornication [pornea; spiritually, disloyalty to our espoused husband Jesus Christ].

Balaam taught Balac how to entice Israel into sin to bring a curse upon themselves, by tempting them into fornication and idolatry.

It is the same today, as Satan has enticed us to follow idols of men and to commit spiritual adultery against our espoused Husband. We follow the false teachings of the heathen like the Nicolaitane Babylonian church governance system which puts the ministry as a layer of authority between us and God, to be blindly followed and obeyed in place of God's Word. And by teaching for doctrine the commandments of men we bring the curse of rejection from Christ and his correction down upon ourselves.

**2:15 So hast thou also them that hold the doctrine of the Nicolaitanes, which thing I hate.**

Just as the ancients exalted men, placing them between men and God [the doctrine of the Nicolaitanes] today's Ekklesia is also full of the abominable doctrine of the Nicolaitanes and most maintain the doctrine of a layer of ministry between the brethren and God to this very day. Jesus Christ says he HATES this false doctrine, because it separates him from his people and attempts to give an authority that belongs to God the Father alone, to mere mortal men.

Jesus Christ says very clearly that this condition will exist when he comes and that Christ WILL FIGHT against those who hold to this abominable teaching when he comes.

**2:16 Repent; or else I will come unto thee quickly, and will fight against them with the sword of my mouth [the TRUTH].**

We are commanded to REPENT of the spiritual adultery of following men in place of the Husband of our baptismal espousal. We are commanded by Jesus Christ to REPENT of the Nicolaitane church governance system of exalting idols of men above the Word of Almighty God!

I am NOT against godly leaders and governance!

Godly leadership points all men to obey and zealously learn, Keep and Live By EVERY WORD OF GOD! Nicolaitane leadership says obey us because we are God's appointed leaders; and so exalts men as little idols, placing men between the brethren and God!

Those who overcome the spiritual chains of exalting men and thinking of loyalty to idols of men as loyalty to God; will be delivered from slavery to men and will be fed the true heavenly manna of the Bread of Life, the whole Word of God!

Just as the physical temple was built of stones so the overall collective spiritual temple is built of the stones of the faithful chosen of humanity.

> **Ephesians 2:20** And are built upon the foundation of the apostles and prophets, Jesus Christ himself being the chief corner stone; **2:21** In whom all the building fitly framed together groweth unto an holy temple in the Lord: **2:22** In whom ye also are builded together for an habitation of God through the Spirit.

Those who overcome the abominable church governance system of following men and not living by every Word of God, will each be given a white [white being a symbol of purity from sin] stone; and a place among the stones [the spiritual stones of faithful overcomers] which will constitute the collective spiritual temple, the dwelling of God through the Holy Spirit.

They will receive a new name; that is a title [God calls things what they are] reflecting their new life and responsibilities in the government of God!

**Revelation 2:17** He that hath an ear, let him hear what the Spirit saith unto the churches; To him that overcometh will I give to eat of the hidden manna [Which means to internalize the Bread of Life, the whole Word of God and to understand of the things of God.], and will give him a white stone, and in the stone a new name written, which no man knoweth saving he that receiveth it.

## Thyatira

Pride in good works toward men while lacking any zeal to love God and live by EVERY Word of God; is exalting a love of men above our duty to follow and keep the whole Word and Will of God: This is idolatry!

Christ is described as like a flame of fire. Flames are a fire that purifies all things. Jesus Christ will purify all things by forgiving sincerely repented sins and destroying all willful sinners in the lake of fire.

**Revelation 2:18** And unto the angel of the **church in Thyatira** write; These things saith the Son of God, who hath his eyes like unto a flame of fire, and his feet are [shine] like fine brass;

There are people who have many good works and much good in them, who still sin and tolerate sin. A little leaven [leaven as a type of sin] leavens the whole lump.  Let us not deceive ourselves that because we have some good or do some good works; that a few good things mixed with sins, makes us acceptable to God.

It is not a few good things which make us acceptable to God;  but that we should live by EVERY WORD of God!  Many sinners are charitable and do many good things, but they fall short because they will not live by every Word of God!

The problem that many fine generous people have is the putting of the first great commandment second and putting the secondary commandment first.  They get so immersed in doing good for mankind that they forget any zeal to put God FIRST so that their good works become an idol replacing God as their primary concern.

> **Matthew 22:37** Jesus said unto him, Thou shalt love the Lord thy God with all thy heart, and with all thy soul, and with all thy mind. **22:38** This is the first and great commandment. **22:39** And the second is like unto it, Thou shalt love thy neighbour as thyself. **22:40** On these two commandments hang all the law and the prophets.

Friends we ought to be charitable and serve others, but we ought to put God FIRST and serve God FIRST!  We ought to live by EVERY WORD of God, FIRST; and after that to do good to all people.

**Revelation 2:19** I know thy works, and charity, and service, and faith, and thy patience, and thy works; and the last to be more than the first. **2:20** Notwithstanding I have a few things against thee, because thou sufferest that woman Jezebel, which calleth herself a prophetess, to teach and to seduce my servants to commit fornication [spiritually to follow others and not be absolutely faithful to God], and to eat things sacrificed unto idols [to seek after and internalize false teachings].

Thyatiran's are generally humanly good folks in the Ekklesia who love their neighbor and are very kind and charitable, but lack a zeal to live by every Word of God.

Jezebel is an allegory of Baalism, or the Babylonian Nicolaitane system of making idols of men instead of fully zealously obeying and living by every Word of God.

In the name of a false kind of love, Thyatiran's tolerate sin and permit seducers and deceivers to teach the false traditions of men and entice the brethren away from any zeal to learn and keep the whole Word and Will of

God. They tolerate people's sins out of a misguided concept of love while overlooking the effect that such sin has on the brethren and the Ekklesia as a whole.

Those with the Thyatira attitude, tolerate sin, false teachings and teaching people to commit spiritual adultery against our espoused spiritual Husband, under the false impression that they are godly because they are generous toward men.

Yes, generosity toward men is a godly thing, as long as it is kept secondary to putting every Word of God first. If we give vast sums to charitable enterprises and we do not regard the sanctity of the Sabbath, all our charitable works will be accounted as nothing when we are judged.

> **Matthew 7:21** Not every one that saith unto me, Lord, Lord, shall enter into the kingdom of heaven; but he that doeth the will of my Father which is in heaven.
>
> **7:22** Many will say to me in that day, Lord, Lord, have we not prophesied in thy name? and in thy name have cast out devils? and in thy name done many wonderful works?
>
> **7:23** And then will I profess unto them, I never knew you: depart from me, ye that work iniquity.

Today's church of God has been warned and given time to repent of this same sin of exalting a layer of men as our idols and allowing them to come between the brethren and God.

Elders and leaders can be excellent helps as long as they focus on God; yet they can be a curse if they exalt their own ways above the Word of God. The brethren MUST prove all things and follow ONLY what is consistent with the whole Word of God!

**Revelation 2:21** And I gave her space to repent of her fornication [putting men above God]; and she repented not.

Those with this attitude of tolerating the sin of idolizing men above the whole Word of God, to obey men without question and to follow them contrary to the Word of God: are proud of their misguided love of exalting people above any zeal to live by every Word of God and they will not repent therefore they will be cast into great tribulation.

This proves that there will be those with this problem at the end time. In fact this is an overspreading sin in the vast majority of the Ekklesia today. Nearly all of today's congregations exalt some man above the Word of God or put good works above a zeal to put God first.

Jesus Christ calls on us to repent of this sin and threatens us with the tribulation if we refuse to do so.!

**2:22** Behold, I will cast her into a bed, and them that commit adultery with her into **great tribulation, except they repent of their deeds**.

The correction of the great tribulation will fall on six of the seven "churches" in this latter day; and being corrected they will learn to exalt the Eternal and the whole Word and Will of God above all else! Jesus Christ will judge us by ALL of our deeds, not just by those deeds that are good, but by ALL of our works good and bad!

Appearances can be deceiving. Some great charities can hide much evil!

**2:23** And I will kill her children with death; and all the churches shall know that I am he which searcheth the reins [the hidden sensitive places] and hearts: and **I will give unto every one of you according to your works.**

Brethren all of us will be judged by what we say and do, therefore this instruction is for us today!

They were not criticized for doing good works, but for lacking in zeal to live by every Word of God. They were/are proud of their good works towards men, not understanding that they lack the good works of obeying God in other things. Jesus Christ tells us that this exalting of love of men above any zeal for God is a "Doctrine of Satan!"

Jesus then comforts those who are full of the good works of Thyatira, telling them that if they do sincerely repent and put God first and reject making idols of men; that they will be covered by His sacrifice and will be made blameless; and instructs them to hold fast until he comes.

This love of men to idolize men above being zealous to live by every Word of God is called a doctrine of Satan by Jesus Christ! This instruction to Thyatira clearly says that those with the Thyatiran attitude will be cast into great tribulation in our day and that this attitude will be present at the coming of Christ.

**2:24** But unto you I say, and unto the rest in Thyatira, as many as **have not this doctrine, and which have not known the depths of Satan**, as they speak; I will put upon you none other burden. **2:25** But that which ye have already **hold fast till I come.**

Christ has received rulership over the whole earth and it is the people of faith and service to GOD and to others without the sins of Thyatira [exalting serving people above serving God] who will rule the nations with him.

To the Thyatira attitude people who are proud of their good works toward humanity and are not zealous to learn and to keep the whole Word and Will of God, Jesus Christ says that this is a "doctrine of Satan" and that God the Father and Jesus Christ will reject them into the correction of great tribulation in the hope that they will sincerely repent.

Those who overcome the sin of pride in exalting love of mankind or anything else above loving God; need to sincerely repent and turn to zealously live by every Word of God as Jesus lived and lives.

**2:26** And he that overcometh [repents of serving people while neglecting the service of God], and keepeth my works [has the works of faith in keeping the whole Word and Will of God] unto the end, to him will I give power over the nations: **2:27** And he [the faithful overcomer] shall rule them [his heritage] with a rod of iron [refusing to tolerate any law breaking]; as the vessels of a potter shall they [The resurrected godly will crush rebellion and refusal to put God FIRST in the position which they will receive.] be broken to shivers: even as I received of my Father.

Once they learn to put God first they will serve God with the same zeal with which they had served men, and the sincerely repentant of Thyatira will shine brightly in the government of God forever.

> **Daniel 12:3** And they that be wise shall shine as the brightness of the firmament; and they that turn many to righteousness as the stars for ever and ever.

**Revelation 2:28** And I will give him the morning star.

The sincerely repentant will be one in unity with Jesus Christ at his coming.

Brethren, these messages are for our instruction at the end of this present age. It is not wise to neglect these things as only ancient history. All of these attitudes and problems are climaxing in the Ekklesia TODAY!

All of these messages are absolutely applicable to today's Spiritual Ekklesia.

May those with God's Spirit, understand what the Spirit is saying to them.

**2:29** He that hath an ear, let him hear what the Spirit saith unto the churches.

# Revelation 3

## Sardis

**Revelation 3:1** And unto the angel of the church in Sardis write; These things saith he that hath the seven Spirits of God, and [which are] the seven stars; I know thy works, that thou hast a name that thou livest, and art dead.

These are folks who call themselves God's people and are spiritually dead in terms of any zeal for godliness. They are physically alive and claiming to be God's people but they are spiritually dead; following their own ways, false traditions of men and idols of men, instead of being alive and full of the fire of zeal to live by every Word of God. The Sardis warning applies to the vast majority of today's Spiritual Ekklesia.

**3:2** Be watchful, and strengthen the things which remain, that are ready to die: for I have not found thy works perfect before God.

We have some things right but instead of truly GROWING in knowledge, understanding and the works of faith; we are stagnant and even letting those right things that we knew in the past slip away.

Today the Ekklesia is doing exactly that: As was prophesied, they are turning from any zeal to learn and keep the whole Word and Will of God in a great falling away from the Word of Life.

**Matthew 24:5** For many shall come in my name, saying, I am Christ; and shall deceive many.

**2 Timothy 4:3** For the time will come when they will not endure sound doctrine; but after their own lusts shall they heap to themselves teachers, having itching ears;

**Matthew 22:14** For many are called, but few are chosen.

**2 Thessalonians 2:3** Let no man deceive you by any means: for that day shall not come, except there come a falling away first, and that man of sin be revealed, the son of perdition;

Jesus then warned that if these folks are not watching for him, his coming will catch them by surprise. This means that this attitude will exist at his coming. It also means that even in the midst of the great tribulation some will be in denial, too spiritually dead to realize what is taking place.

**Revelation 3:3** Remember therefore how thou hast received and heard, and hold fast, and repent. If therefore thou shalt not watch, I will come on thee as a thief, and thou shalt not know what hour I will come upon thee.

Yet, there are a few who will sincerely repent and turn to a zeal for godliness; then the sacrifice of Christ will be applied to them, purifying them and making their garments pure [imputing godly righteousness], clean and white.

**3:4** Thou hast a few names even in Sardis which have not defiled their garments; and they shall walk with me in white: for they are worthy.

With God all things are possible and even some of those who are spiritually dead [which is the vast majority of today's Ekklesia] will be saved and turned to God, receiving the gift of the oil of the Holy Spirit; so that their light which has gone out, might be reignited that they may shine brightly with godliness.

**3:5** He that overcometh, the same shall be clothed in white raiment; and I will not blot out his name out of the book of life, but I will confess his name before my Father, and before his angels.

**3:6** He that hath an ear, let him hear what the Spirit saith unto the churches.

### Philadelphia

Jesus begins his message to Philadelphia by remarking that He is the Door and the Way and the Key into the kingdom of God and eternal life.

It is Jesus Christ who judges us and who can let us in or shut us out of the resurrection to eternal life. No man can take away our promise of eternal life by casting us out of some corporation; nor does belonging to some corporate church a pass to enter eternal life!

Only fidelity to our espoused Husband and God the Father alone will bring eternal life!

When men say that questioning them is questioning God and that leaving them is leaving God: They LIE! It is not blindly following idols of men that brings eternal life; only being a part of the true Spiritual Ekklesia who live by every Word of God brings acceptance by God and eternal life!

**3:7** And to the angel [one of the seven spirits] of the **church in Philadelphia** write; These things saith he that is holy, he that is true, he that hath the key of David, **he that openeth, and no man shutteth; and shutteth, and no man openeth;**

Those with a Philadelphian attitude of absolute faith in God and a full wholehearted zeal for learning and living by every Word of God, have an open door to God the Father and into eternal life!

Jesus Christ is the door of salvation to those who are faithful and He will open the way to eternal life if we are diligent to internalize the very nature of God the Father like he did!

Those who are diligent to keep the Word of God and who do not deny the name [authority] of God and his Word over his people; will be changed to spirit on that day!

I capitalize the word "Word" for a reason; Jesus Christ is the Logos, the Word; summing up the whole of Holy Scriptures with God the Father! To break any art of the Word of God, is to break the teachings of Jesus Christ, the WORD who inspired all of scripture!

ONLY those who keep the whole Word of God and exalt the name [authority] of God above all others will have access to God the Father through the door of Jesus Christ to eternal life!

A Philadelphian is weak having only a little strength, he knows that and therefore relies on the strength of the Eternal Almighty God! He knows that in the flesh he is weak and seeks spiritual strength from God to overcome; he runs to and takes refuge in the Mighty God!

**3:8** I know thy works: behold, I have set before thee an open door, and no man can shut it: for **thou hast a little strength,** and **hast kept my word, and hast not denied my name.**

Those who are full of zeal to live by every Word of God will be made eternal priests and kings [teachers and leaders] and those of the nations who hated the zealous for God will sincerely repent and they will worship God at the feet of [under the tutelage of] the Philadelphian attitude folks who are full of faithful zeal for godliness.

**3:9** Behold, I will make them of the synagogue of Satan, which say they are Jews, and are not, but do lie; behold, I will make them to come and worship before thy feet, and to know that I have loved thee.

If the zealous for God patiently endure and wait; they will be the wise (Dan 12), the "children of light" (1 Thess 5): They will not be taken by surprise when the tribulation and later Jesus Christ comes; they will understand the biblical signs and they will obey the words of God's prophets and so will be kept from the hour of trial.

Those who are full of zeal for godliness and study carefully, Watching for the coming of their LORD, will be preserved from the terrible correction of a righteous God on the earth.

Yes, there is a place of refuge, as David said; that refuge is in the arms of our Mighty Deliverer! Follow and zealously keep the whole Word and Will of God; and when God says to do this or to do that, or he says to go here or to go there: Follow him and DO IT!

**3:10 Because thou hast kept the word of my patience** [patiently lived by every Word of God], **I also will keep thee from the hour of temptation** [a 42 month period], **which shall come upon all the world,** to try them that dwell upon the earth.

**3:11** Behold, I come quickly: hold that fast which thou hast, that no man take thy crown.

A pillar is a supporting column that stands on a firm foundation, the pillars of God stand on the firm foundation of every Word of God and are full of a zeal to learn and live by every Word of God!

> **Ephesians 2:18** For through him we both have access by one Spirit unto the Father. **2:19** Now therefore ye are no more strangers and foreigners, but fellowcitizens with the saints, and of the household of God;

**2:20** And are built upon the foundation of the apostles and prophets [the scriptures], Jesus Christ himself being the chief corner stone; **2:21** In whom all the building fitly framed together groweth unto an holy temple [growing into a dwelling place for the Holy Spirit] in the Lord: **2:22** In whom ye also are builded together for an habitation of God through the Spirit.

A pillar helps to hold up the rest of the structure; the pillars of God will stand on the foundation of the whole Word of God and will help to hold up the rest of the Spiritual Ekklesia of the faithful.

If the zealous to keep the whole Word of God and endure all trials remain faithful; they will become permanent pillars in the eternal government of God; and they will have the name [authority] of God and of the capital of His eternal government, the New Jerusalem forever. They shall occupy positions of responsibility in God's government and will act on behalf of God and God's government, not just in the millennium, but forever!

**Revelation 3:12** Him that overcometh will I make a pillar in the temple of my God, and he shall go no more out: and I will write upon him the name of my God, and the name of the city of my God, which is new Jerusalem, which cometh down out of heaven from my God: and I will write upon him my new name.

**3:13** He that hath an ear, let him hear what the Spirit saith unto the churches.

The Philadelphian pillar is a person who is weak and knows it; therefore he relies upon God and seeks the strength of God rather than trying to stand on his own strength.

He is zealous to root out all error and internalize the truth of God. He is faithful to follow God in all things and will not turn aside to follow any man or spirit away from his zeal to follow the whole Word of God.

Yes, he makes mistakes and occasionally slips; and when he does instead of giving up, he admits his errors, sincerely repents and cries out to his heavenly Father for deliverance!

There are those who say that "I am a Philadelphian because God does not criticize that church." That is a proud, arrogant and totally ignorant attitude: ALL have sinned and come short of the glory of God!

Jesus Christ does not criticize Philadelphia because he does not have to! The Philadelphian pillar is well aware of his short comings, and he knows that he has no strength in himself; therefore he runs to the Eternal and takes refuge in the Eternal, the Mighty High Tower of Strength; to seek and find deliverance.

The true Philadelphian attitude is one of humility before God, relying totally on God; KNOWING that we are so weak and so sinful and knowing that God is so great, strong and powerful; that they RUN TO HIM and seek HIS STRENGTH to deliver!

The difference between the Philadelphian and the others is: HUMILITY and true LOVE for the Eternal and all his ways. They know that they are weak and fall short, and therefore they are filled with complete loving submission to the whole Word of God!

The true Philadelphian attitude person is usually someone who has been most wicked and is therefore often despised by others; however they, like David, have deeply repented and they KNOW how much God has forgiven him and are therefore full of the deepest passionate love for their Deliverer. They are so full of love for God that they would do anything to please God.

> **Luke 7:37** And, behold, a woman in the city, which was a sinner, when she knew that Jesus sat at meat in the Pharisee's house, brought an alabaster box of ointment, **7:38** And stood at his feet behind him weeping, and began to wash his feet with tears, and did wipe them with the hairs of her head, and kissed his feet, and anointed them with the ointment.
>
> **7:39** Now when the Pharisee which had bidden him saw it, he spake within himself, saying, This man, if he were a prophet, would have known who and what manner of woman this is that toucheth him: for she is a sinner.
>
> **7:40** And Jesus answering said unto him, Simon, I have somewhat to say unto thee. And he saith, Master, say on.
>
> **7:41** There was a certain creditor which had two debtors: the one owed five hundred pence, and the other fifty. **7:42** And when they had nothing to pay, he frankly forgave them both. Tell me therefore, which of them will love him most?
>
> **7:43** Simon answered and said, I suppose that **he, to whom he forgave most**. And he said unto him, Thou hast rightly judged.
>
> **7:44** And he turned to the woman, and said unto Simon, Seest thou this woman? I entered into thine house, thou gavest me no water for my feet: but she hath washed my feet with tears, and wiped them

with the hairs of her head. **7:45** Thou gavest me no kiss: but this woman since the time I came in hath not ceased to kiss my feet. **7:46** My head with oil thou didst not anoint: but this woman hath anointed my feet with ointment.

**7:47** Wherefore I say unto thee, **Her sins, which are many, are forgiven; for she loved much: but to whom little is forgiven, the same loveth little.**

**7:48** And he said unto her, Thy sins are forgiven.

**7:49** And they that sat at meat with him began to say within themselves, Who is this that forgiveth sins also?

**7:50** And he said to the woman, **Thy faith hath saved thee; go in peace.**

There were pillars throughout the physical temple; representing that the human spiritual pillars are also scattered throughout the Ekklesia. There is no such thing as a true Philadelphian corporate church of God today. The true Philadelphian pillars are scattered throughout the Ekklesia and are very often serving God independently.

**Laodicea**

To Laodicea Jesus identifies himself as the faithful and true witness of what they are truly like. They think themselves spiritually rich and have no idea what Jesus Christ really thinks of them. Jesus here tells them their problems straight out, but they are proud and willfully blind to reality.

**Laodicea means the people will be judged and corrected.**

Lao: the people:

Dike: judged [condemned by the law and punished, corrected]

> Definition: diké: right (as self-evident), justice (the principle, a decision or its execution)
> Original Word: d???, ??, ?
> Part of Speech: Noun, Feminine
> Transliteration: diké
> Phonetic Spelling: (dee'-kay)
>
> Short Definition: justice, judicial hearing, punishment
> (a) (originally: custom, usage) right, justice, (b) process of law,

judicial hearing, (c) execution of sentence, punishment, penalty, (d) justice, vengeance.   Cognate: 1349 díke – properly, right, especially a judicial verdict which declares someone approved or disapproved; a judgment (just finding) that regards someone (something) as "guilty" or "innocent." See 1343 (dikaiosyne).

[1349 (díke) is used in classical Greek for a legal decision – a recompense (based on justice). In the LXX, dike is used nine times to translate rî, the Hebrew term for "law-suit."]

Thayer's
STRONGS NT 1349:

1. custom, usage, (cf. Schmidt, chapter 18, 4 cf. 3).

2. right, justice.

3. a suit at law.

4. a judicial hearing, judicial decision, especially a sentence of condemnation; so in Acts 25:15 (L T Tr WH ?atad????).

5. execution of the sentence, punishment, (Wis. 18:11; 2 Macc. 8:11): d???? ?p??e??, Jude 1:7; d???? (Sophocles El. 298; Aj. 113; Euripides, Or. 7), to suffer punishment, 2 Thessalonians 1:9.

6. the goddess Justice, avenging justice: Acts 28:4, as in Greek writings often from Hesiod theog. 902 on; (of the avenging justice of God, personified, Wis. 1:8, etc.; cf. Grimm at the passage and commentary on 4 Macc., p. 318, (he cites 4 Macc. 4:13, 21; 8:13, 21; 9:9; 11:3; 12:12; 18:22; Philo adv. Flacc. § 18; Eusebius, h. e. 2, 6, 8)).

suffer, weep, ache, lament, sorrow, bewail

Strong's
penalty, punishment
Probably from deiknuo; right (as self-evident), i.e. Justice (the principle, a decision, or its execution) -- judgment, punish, vengeance.

see GREEK deiknuo

Jesus emphasizes that his message to Laodicea is true and is coming out of Christ's faithful love for them, in the hope that they might repent and be saved.

Jesus also calls himself the "beginning of the creation of God;" clearly meaning that Christ is the Creator who began the creation of all things. See Revelation 1:8. 1:11, 21:6, 22:13 I am the Alpha [Beginning]

**Revelation 3:14** And unto the angel of the church of the Laodiceans write; These things saith the Amen, the faithful and true witness, the beginning of the creation of God;

Laodicea is spiritually lukewarm, professing godliness while keeping the commandments according to their own imaginations instead of keeping them the way that God commands.

They pay lip service to godliness without any zeal to learn and keep the Word of God. Their zeal is for their own ways and what they think, for their own past false traditions and their idols of men and not for what God says. They stand on their false past traditions and proudly think they know it all; refusing any spiritual growth they are stagnant or even falling backward in their spiritual condition.

They are hot for their own traditions, and for the teachings of their idols of men about the Word of God, and cold for zealously keeping the whole Word as God, as God has commanded them. This mixture of hot for their idols of men and corporate entities, and a cold, lack of zeal to keep the Word of God, makes them lukewarm and revolting to God the Father and Jesus Christ.

They are idolaters of men and tradition; proud, thinking that they know it all spiritually and therefore they reject any correction from God or man; they reject the Word of God for their own ways and they reject any growth in truth and refuse to turn from error.

This is a clear, obvious, indisputable and precise explanation of the overwhelming majority in the Ekklesia today!

Because these folks have rejected Jesus Christ to follow him above our idols of men they will be rejected by Christ into the correction of great tribulation, in the hope that through the correction of the flesh the spirit may be saved.

**3:15** I know thy works, that thou art neither cold nor hot: I would thou wert cold or hot. **3:16** So then because thou art lukewarm, and neither cold nor hot, **I will spue thee out of my mouth** [They will be rejected by Christ into severe correction].

Proud and self-willed, they think they are spiritually rich and know it all, having no need of spiritual growth, and they reject the increase in spiritual knowledge and understanding promised for the last days, Daniel 12.

They reject any part of scripture which they do not want to follow, saying it is for others; and they are so proud and arrogant they have no idea how spiritually wretched, miserable, poor and naked of godly righteousness they really are.

They are willfully blind to their own condition and to the things of God that disprove their own false ways; They lack the garments of righteousness and are naked of any righteousness before God, their many sins being exposed to Him; beginning with the sins of pride and self-justification and self-approval.

**3:17** Because thou sayest, I am rich [spiritually], and increased with goods [spiritual knowledge], and have need of nothing [no one not even Jesus Christ (the Word of God) can tell them anything]; and knowest not that thou art [spiritually] wretched, and miserable, and [spiritually] poor [knowing almost nothing of God as they ought to know it], and blind [they are willfully blind to their wretched spiritual state], and naked [naked of any true godly righteousness, not being zealous to keep the Word of God]:

Jesus Christ counsels those with the Laodicean attitude which is by far the overwhelming majority of the major corporate Assemblies today, to buy spiritual gold in the fire of tribulation so that they may become spiritually rich.

They are bidden to sincerely repent of their prideful sins so that the nakedness of their wickedness may be covered by the application of the sacrifice of Christ; and so that they may receive God's Holy Spirit and the white raiment of the righteousness of the zealous keeping of the whole Word of God.

They are commanded to anoint their eyes and open them to see themselves as God sees them, and to sincerely repent from their pride and false ways and to turn away from their idols of men and false traditions to follow the Spirit of God into all truth; rejecting all error and sin to embrace godly truth so that they might be saved.

**3:18** I counsel thee to buy of me gold [spiritual wisdom] tried in the fire [during the period of our correction in the fire of tribulation], that thou mayest be rich [become spiritually rich]; and white raiment [the righteousness of zealously keeping the whole Word of God], that thou mayest be clothed, and that the shame of thy nakedness [that our sins might be covered by the righteousness of God] do not appear; and anoint thine eyes with eyesalve, [acquire the Holy Spirit through sincere repentance] that thou mayest see [We are told to open our eyes to see ourselves as God sees us, to see ourselves as we really are, so that we can repent and be saved].

Jesus reminds these folks that he rebukes them only because he truly loves them and is not willing that they should perish. They are rejected only because they first rejected Christ, refusing to keep the whole Word of God, refusing to follow Christ and refusing to live by every Word of God in Christ-like zeal.

Jesus Christ tells those of the Laodicean attitude which is the overwhelming attitude throughout the Ekklesia today; to REPENT of their pride and self-righteousness. and to REPENT of trusting in their idols of men and false traditions.

Jesus Christ tells us to turn to him and turn to a zeal for the whole Word of God, to learn it and to keep it; to turn from our false idols and false traditions and to become zealous to remove error and embrace the truth of God!

**3:19 As many as I love, I rebuke and chasten: be zealous therefore, and repent.**

Jesus is warning and calling each one of his straying sheep; He wants us to open up to him, to reject idols of men and false traditions and to follow him, to be zealous to remove sin and to embrace God's righteous truth and to internalize the solid meat of the Word of God in fellowship with Jesus Christ and God the Father.

We have an open invitation from Jesus Christ who is gladly willing to accept us, if we would only open up our eyes and turn to Him!

**3:20** Behold, I stand at the door, and knock: if any man hear my voice, and open the door, I will come in to him, and will sup [eat; internalize the Word of God] with him, and he with me.

Only those who overcome this Laodicean attitude of pride and self-will will be resurrected to spirit. Those who sincerely repent of the sins of Laodicea will be in the resurrection to eternal life and they will have a place in the eternal government of God.

**3:21** To him that overcometh will I grant to sit with me in my throne, even as I also overcame, and am set down with my Father in his throne.

**3:22** He that hath an ear, let him hear what the Spirit saith unto the churches.

As the seventh and last church addressed, Laodicea has all of the problems of the other six churches.

That is because pride is the chief cause of most of the various problems. Today all the major Assemblies and most of the smaller ones are full of pride and idolatry, rejecting any biblical thing they do not agree with, claiming it applies only to others.

They think of themselves as the repository of all wisdom and truth, and refuse any zeal to live by every Word of God in order to follow their corporate idols, idols of men and their own false traditions.

They call the Sabbath and High Days, Holy; and then they walk all over them, while claiming that the commandments not to cook or buy food on Sabbath somehow apply to others and not to themselves. They insist on following the apostate Rabbinic Calendar even resorting to lying to attempt to justify themselves, and they refuse to keep the Biblical Calendar of God even though the proofs are overwhelming.

They have almost no understanding of the Festivals, rejecting the true meanings of the Festivals; even still claiming that the seven day Feast of Tabernacles somehow represents only one thousand years. They reject any zeal for keeping the Word of God, and insist on a zeal for their corporate idols, idols of men and past false traditions, insisting that people should obey them above the Word of God.

### The Mosaic Pharisees were a type of Laodicea

The Laodicean attitude is an exact replica of the primary attitude of the Mosaic Pharisees during the physical ministry of Christ.

Contrary to popular belief the Mosaic Pharisees were NOT zealous for the law, rather they made the law of God of no effect by their own false traditions just as today's modern Ekklesia does!

In Matthew 15:9 Jesus said of the Mosaic Pharisees; and this is a very precise description of today's Spiritual Ekklesia:

> **Matthew 15:7** Ye hypocrites, well did Esaias prophesy of you, saying, **15:8** This people draweth nigh unto me with their mouth, and honoureth me with their lips; but their heart is far

> from me. **15:9 But in vain they do worship me, teaching for doctrines the commandments of men.**

Matthew 23 describes the attitude during the physical ministry of Jesus Christ; and it also accurately describes the church of God groups right before Christ comes to rule: today!

## Matthew 23

Jesus speaks privately to his disciples and begins to criticize the Mosaic scribes and Pharisees; which are analogous to today's Nicolaitane Laodiceans.

Jesus begins by saying that the scribes and Pharisees sat in Moses seat. Of course that was overturned when they had Christ killed; and Jesus Christ replaced the Levitical priesthood as the new High Priest of the ancient order of Melchisedec, and God's faithful became the Royal Priesthood of the New Covenant.

> **1 Peter 2:7** Unto you therefore which believe [believe and obey] he is precious: but unto them **which be disobedient** [to the Word of God], the stone which the builders disallowed, the same is made the head of the corner,

This is not just talking about Judaism rejecting Jesus Christ! It is talking about ALL those who will not enthusiastically live by every Word of God as Jesus taught (Mat 4:4)!

What? I mean that many of those called to God refuse to follow Jesus Christ in living by every Word of God as Jesus commanded us, rejecting parts of God's Word for our own false ways and traditions; bowing to idols of men and committing spiritual adultery against our Lord.

Today most professing Christians stumble at Christ, wrongly thinking that his sacrifice made keeping much of the Word of God no longer binding. Such people are rejecting Jesus Christ!

We stumble at Christ with many teaching a false Christ who will tolerate sin and forgives any sin we might do in future in advance: Thus making Christ's sacrifice a license to continue in sin.

They say "keep the commandments" and then they say that we are weak and Jesus understands that, so if we sin here and there Jesus will automatically forgive because he has paid for sin in advance, thus making a mockery of the sacrifice of Christ.

Mainstream Christianity has been taken in by this lie and so have very many in the Ekklesia.

**We have misunderstood and so stumbled at Jesus Christ!**

> **2 Timothy 3:4** Traitors [against the Word of God] , heady [intoxicated with pride], highminded [exalting our own ways], lovers of pleasures more than lovers of God [paying others to serve us on God's Sabbath for our own pleasure]; **3:5** Having a form [an appearance, a put on, a show] of godliness, but denying the power [exalting themselves above the authority of the Word of God] thereof: **from such turn away.**

Of course we are weak and cannot overcome on our own; but with the indwelling strength of God's Spirit and our faithful following of God's Word we shall be overcomers. Not by our own strength, but by the power of that ultimate over comer, Jesus Christ!

> **3:8** And a stone of stumbling, and a rock of offence, even **to them which stumble at the word, being disobedient**: whereunto also they were appointed.

The Called Out, the passionately obedient and faithful to God the Father and Jesus Christ, zealously learning and keeping the whole Word of God like Christ commanded us to, are qualifying to enter the Royal Priesthood of Jesus Christ which transcends and replaces the seat of Moses!

> **1 Peter 2:9** But ye are a chosen generation, a royal priesthood, an holy nation, a peculiar people; that ye should shew forth the praises of him who hath called you out of darkness into his marvellous light;

**Matthew 23:1** Then spake Jesus to the multitude, and to his disciples, **23:2** Saying The scribes and the Pharisees sit in Moses' seat: **23:3** All therefore whatsoever they bid you observe, that observe and do; but do not ye after their works: for they say, and do not.

Just like many elders today the Mosaic scribes and Pharisees bound heavy burdens on the people which they would not bear themselves. They were hypocrites not keeping what they taught.

**23:4** For they bind heavy burdens and grievous to be borne, and lay them on men's shoulders; but they themselves will not move them with one of their fingers.

With the death of the Husband of Israel the marriage between Israel and Christ ended and so did the authority of the Mosaic Levitical Priesthood, the scribes and the Mosaic Pharisees; and the Hellenized Rabbins NEVER had any right to Moses seat!

When Christ ascended to heaven and was accepted as a sacrifice for us; he became our High Priest and the King of the world in waiting; the Mosaic priesthood was superseded by a reestablishment of the High Priesthood of Melchizedek[See the Hebrews studies].

When he comes Jesus Christ will build a new physical temple and those Levites descended from Zadok will again serve in that physical temple; doing those physical things necessary for that physical temple service (Ezek 40-48). Yet they will also be converted to Christ and grafted into the Royal Priesthood of Jesus Christ in the New Covenant at that time.

The only true Priesthood now and forever more; is that of our High Priest Jesus Christ [Melchizedek] and those called out with the potential to become priests of the priesthood of Jesus Christ forever in the coming Kingdom of God. All of God's faithful are in training to become priests forever in that spiritual priesthood of Jesus Christ [Melchizedek].

We are to rely on the example and teachings of our Lord Jesus Christ and the whole body of scriptures that was inspired by HIM, for our religion!

**23:5** But all their works they do for to be seen of men: they make broad their phylacteries, and enlarge the borders of their garments,

**23:6** And love the uppermost rooms at feasts, and the chief seats in the synagogues, **23:7** And greetings in the markets, and to be called of men, Rabbi, Rabbi.

**23:8** But be not ye called Rabbi: for one is your Master, even Christ; and all ye are brethren. **23:9** And call no man your father upon the earth: for one is your Father, which is in heaven. **23:10** Neither be ye called masters: for one is your Master, even Christ.

This is about the Mosaic Pharisees love of titles and the chief seats, and love of being preeminent above the brethren; not about calling your true father "father" nor is it about calling some man Mr. in common usage; it is talking about a love of ecclesiastical titles. This is about elders demanding to be called father or Mr. or Rabbi as an ecclesiastical title to create a hierarchy of men between the brethren and God.

Sound familiar? Just substitute the word Master or "father" or padre etc with Rabbi, Mister, Reverend etc! Oh, how we love to put on a show and impress people; Oh, how church elders love titles, the pre-eminence and the chief seats today.

From this instruction of Jesus it has always been customary in the Spiritual Ekklesia to call everyone brothers and sisters, including elders and leaders in the Ekklesia, until this leaven of pride infected us.

> **1 Timothy 2:5** For **there is one God, and one mediator between God and men, the man Christ Jesus; 2:6** Who gave himself a ransom for all, to be testified in due time.

The idea of a pyramidal structure of layers of authority between men and God is an abomination to God. It is the job of ALL elders to focus all people on God the Father and Christ: NEVER to come between the people and God; but to act as facilitators in helping people to focus DIRECTLY on God the Father through their ONLY High Priest and Mediator; Jesus Christ!

We are to prove the words of ALL men by the Word of Almighty God! We are NOT to interpret God's Word by the words of men; we are to prove the words of men by the Word of Almighty God!

**Matthew 23:11** But he that is greatest among you shall be your servant.

We are all to desire to serve our God and not to exalt ourselves. God will exalt or abase as HE sees fit.

**23:12** And **whosoever shall exalt himself shall be abased; and he that shall humble himself shall be exalted.**

All of those men who love to exalt themselves over the people with grand titles as they spurn any zeal for God's Word will be abased in due time; being cast into the furnace of correction.

Those who humble themselves to be zealous to learn and to keep the whole Word of God, shall be exalted by Almighty God in due time.

**23:13** But woe unto you, scribes and Pharisees, hypocrites! for ye shut up the kingdom of heaven against men: for ye neither go in yourselves, neither suffer ye them that are entering to go in.

How? By paying lip-service to God's Word while making it of no effect with the false traditions of men, and through rejection of scripture or compromise in the practical application of God's Word.

**23:14** Woe unto you, scribes and Pharisees, hypocrites! for ye devour widows' houses, and for a pretence make long prayer: therefore ye shall receive the greater damnation.

Demanding money of poor widows, taking the inheritances of orphans and making a show of prayer.(Mat 6 and Luk 18).

**23:15** Woe unto you, scribes and Pharisees, hypocrites! for ye compass sea and land to make one proselyte, and when he is made, ye make him twofold more the child of hell than yourselves.

How? By teaching people to obey men, organizations and false traditions, instead of focusing them on sincere repentance and a diligent passionate obedience of God's Word.

People have been deceived into thinking that the Mosaic Pharisees were zealous for the letter of law; when in fact they were zealous for their own traditions above the Word of God!

Today the Spiritual Ekklesia focus on their own false traditions of men as being so important that they exalt them over the scriptures and make the Word of God of no effect by their false traditions; exactly like the Mosaic Pharisees did!

**23:16** Woe unto you, ye blind guides, which say, Whosoever shall swear by the temple, it is nothing; but whosoever shall swear by the gold of the temple, he is a debtor! **23:17** Ye fools and blind: for whether is greater, the gold, or the temple that sanctifieth the gold? **23:18** And, Whosoever shall swear by the altar, it is nothing; but whosoever sweareth by the gift that is upon it, he is guilty. **23:19** Ye fools and blind: for whether is greater, the gift, or the altar that sanctifieth the gift? **23:20** Whoso therefore shall swear by the altar, sweareth by it, and by all things thereon.

Today's major professing Christians exalt their corporate idols and exalt obedience to men above obedience to God. They place mammon and numbers above sincere repentance, faith and a zeal to obey God.

To a lesser or greater degree in the different groups, we commit the exact same sin as Jesus rebuked the Mosaic Pharisees for:

> **Matthew 15:4** For God commanded, saying, Honour thy father and mother: and, He that curseth father or mother, let him die the death.
>
> **15:5** But ye say, Whosoever shall say to his father or his mother [or wife or children who God has blessed us with, and given us responsibility to care for], It is a gift [ offering for the church], by whatsoever thou mightest be profited by me;
>
> **15:6** And honour not his father or his mother, he shall be free. **Thus have ye made the commandment of God of none effect by your tradition.**

**15:7** Ye hypocrites, well did Esaias prophesy of you, saying,

**15:8** This people draweth nigh unto me with their mouth, and honoureth me with their lips; but their heart is far from me.

**15:9** But in vain they do worship me, teaching for doctrines the commandments of men.

Jesus said that God and God's Word are everything!

**Matthew 23:21** And whoso shall swear by the temple, sweareth by it, and by him that dwelleth therein. **23:22** And he that shall swear by heaven, sweareth by the throne of God, and by him that sitteth thereon.

In preaching the important thing is NOT the numbers of responses, but the quality of the message! The important thing is not the building [the organization] but serving and obeying the Eternal God on his throne who sits in absolute authority over all things! God will most certainly judge us by our works; whether of faithful uncompromising obedience, or of rebellious compromising with HIS Word!

**23:23** Woe unto you, scribes and Pharisees, hypocrites! for ye pay tithe of mint and anise and cummin, and have omitted **the weightier matters of the law, judgment, mercy, and faith: these ought ye to have done, and not to leave the other undone.**

Demanding every last cent that can be demanded or extorted while ignoring and not teaching sincere repentance from evil doing, and faith, mercy and sound judgment based on God's Word, is an unbalanced priority.

We are to be merciful to the poor in their needs; and we are to be merciful to the sincerely repentant instead of condemning them for being over righteous.

We are to preach a message of warning and repentance and teach a zeal for God and his Word; so that the mercy of God who gave his only begotten Son for us, might be applied to the sincerely repentant to reconcile sinners to God the Father.

**23:24** Ye blind guides, which strain at a gnat, and swallow a camel.

This is a figure of speech that simply means that we strain at the little unimportant things like money and numbers; and neglect the really important things like an enthusiastic zeal to live by every Word of God.

**23:25** Woe unto you, scribes and Pharisees, hypocrites! for ye make clean the outside of the cup and of the platter, but within they are full of extortion and excess. **23:26** Thou blind Pharisee, cleanse first that which is within the cup and platter, that the outside of them may be clean also. **23:27** Woe unto you, scribes and Pharisees, hypocrites! for ye are like unto whited sepulchres, which indeed appear beautiful outward, but are within full of dead men's bones, and of all uncleanness. **23:28** Even so ye also outwardly appear righteous unto men, but within ye are full of hypocrisy and iniquity.

Likewise today's Ekklesia try to put up a good appearance outside, and we are full of sin inside ourselves and our organizations!

We need to clean up our own spiritual lives and get right with God. We need to rekindle our passionate zeal for God to live by every Word of God; we need to get rid of all false traditions of men not consistent with scripture!

We need to stop rejecting those scriptures that we do not like because they destroy our false traditions, and we need to start setting a godly example instead of acting so shamefully!

We need to stop exalting men and organizations above God and God's Word; equating loyalty to men as being equal to loyalty to God. We need to sincerely repent and turn to our God with passionate enthusiastic zeal; and we need to begin to preach the Gospel of warning and sincere repentance that Jesus Christ has commanded us to preach.

**23:29** Woe unto you, scribes and Pharisees, hypocrites! because ye build the tombs of the prophets, and garnish the sepulchres of the righteous, **23:30** And say, If we had been in the days of our fathers, we would not have been partakers with them in the blood of the prophets.

Today we claim to honor the prophets and ancient men of God while persecuting those who are filled with a similar zeal: Showing ourselves that we are no better than those who persecuted the saints of old.

**23:31** Wherefore ye be witnesses unto yourselves, that ye are the children of them which killed the prophets. **23:32** Fill ye up then the measure of your fathers.

Today many persecute the zealous just as was done in the past.

Jesus says of the Mosaic Pharisees in those days; and he says the same things to today's Spiritual Ekklesia:

**23:33** Ye serpents, ye generation of vipers, how can ye escape the damnation of hell?

Jesus prophesies that the religious establishment of that day and of today will reject the prophets and spiritually wise and persecute them; rejecting godliness to follow their own idols of men and false traditions.

**23:34** Wherefore, behold, I send unto you prophets, and wise men, and scribes: and some of them ye **shall** kill and crucify; and some of them shall ye scourge in your synagogues, and persecute them from city to city: **23:35** That upon you may come all the righteous blood shed upon the earth, from the blood of righteous Abel unto the blood of Zacharias son of Barachias, whom ye slew between the temple and the altar.

Those who reject the scriptures and persecute the zealous for the Word of God in the Ekklesia today are no different than the Mosaic Pharisees who are likened to vipers which hide along the path waiting to strike the unwary.

When a person goes to today's corporate Ekklesia with questions; very many of the leaders and elders reason with them that they should not be zealous for the Word of God, but should follow their traditions just like the ancient Pharisees did!

Then if the zealous will not be dissuaded from their zeal for God; they persecute such zeal by calling the zealous Pharisaic; when it is they themselves who are Pharisaic: Filled with zeal for their own groups, their idols of men and their false traditions, while rejecting any scripture that contradicts their false ways!

Since Cain slew Abel it has ever been thus; the faithless and compromising have always persecuted the faithful and zealous. Those who exalt the Lord their God; will face resistance from outside and from inside these latter day church organizations, just as they did from the Mosaic Pharisees.

Such persecuted people should REJOICE for they are being tempered and tested to become pillars in the Temple of The Great God for all eternity.

If they stand on the foundation of the Word of Almighty God without turning aside, no matter what the stress; they will be made fit by God to stand on that sure foundation for all eternity!

**23:36** Verily I say unto you, All these things shall come upon this generation.

These persecutions came upon the saints by the religious establishment of that day, and have continued to this day.

Now in this generation; which is the last generation before the resurrection to spirit of the chosen and the coming of Christ to establish the Kingdom of God over all the earth; the majority of the called out to God have fallen away and will not endure sound doctrine; rejecting the scriptures and rejecting all those who love and keep the whole Word of God.

**2 Timothy 4:3** For the time will come when they [today's Spiritual Ekklesia i.e. Laodicea; Rev 3:15] will not endure sound doctrine; but after their own lusts shall they heap to themselves teachers, having itching ears; **4:4** And they shall turn away their ears from the truth, and shall be turned unto fables.

**Matthew 23:37** O Jerusalem, Jerusalem [the actual city and also as the capital representing all physical and spiritual Israel], thou that killest the prophets, and stonest them which are sent unto thee, how often would I have gathered thy children together, even as a hen gathereth her chickens under her wings, and ye would not!

**23:38** Behold, your house is left unto you desolate.

This is about the city Jerusalem and is figuratively about the faithless who persecute the faithful today and throughout history. Jesus Christ would have saved them, if only they would accept his deliverance and turn to him, away from sin and compromise with God the Father's Word.

Both Jerusalem and all faithless people will be made desolate in the tribulation; it is then that many will repent and turn to the ONLY ONE that can truly save!

**23:39** For I say unto you, Ye shall not see me henceforth, till ye shall say, Blessed is he that cometh in the name of [in the authority of] the Lord.

When Messiah the Christ comes, the people will be humbled and sincerely repentant and they will call him 'Blessed," acknowledging his Messiahship, accepting him and seeking his deliverance with shouts of Hosanna [Save Us]!

Then people will be sincerely repentant and will no longer reject the scriptures and reject any zeal to keep them; instead they will shout for joy at his appearance; crying out "Blessed is he ]The people will sincerely repent in great tribulation and when Christ comes they will call him Blessed] that cometh in the name [in the authority of] of the Lord"!

## Philadelphia and Laodicea

Jesus illustrated the difference between a Philadelphian and a Laodicean, the difference between a holy attitude and a profane and unacceptable attitude in this parable.

These prayers are not just words, they reveal the attitude of the person praying, for out of the abundance of the heart the mouth speaks.

> **Luke 18:9** And he spake this parable unto certain which trusted in themselves that they were righteous, and despised others:
>
> **18:10** Two men went up into the temple to pray; the one a Pharisee [Laodicean], and the other a publican [Philadelphian].
>
> **18:11** The Pharisee [Laodicean] stood and prayed thus with himself, God, I thank thee, that I am not as other men are, extortioners, unjust, adulterers, or even as this publican.
>
> **18:12** I fast twice in the week, I give tithes of all that I possess.
>
> **18:13** And the publican [Sincerely repentant sinner; Philadelphian], standing afar off, would not lift up so much as his eyes unto heaven, but smote upon his breast, saying, God be merciful to me a sinner.
>
> **18:14** I tell you, this man went down to his house justified rather than the other: for every one that exalteth himself shall be abased; and he that humbleth himself shall be exalted.

Today the true Philadelphian pillars are either standing alone or scattered throughout the overwhelmingly Laodicean Ekklesia.

Oh, why do we Laodiceans exalt ourselves to live by our own false traditions and reject any true humble passion for our Mighty One who could deliver us! Proud and thinking ourselves rich in spiritual things, thinking we know it all: We have become spiritually dead, apostate from our Master.


## Conclusion

The various church attitudes may have dominated at various historical tines, but the seven churches existed together at the same time in the first century and each one is an instructional example for us. All of these problems and strengths exist at the same time in these last days.

- Today like Ephesus, we have lost the passionate zeal of our first love for truth and godliness and the whole Word of God.

- Today like Smyrna, there are some who are faithful to God and God's Word and suffer much persecution.
- Today like Pergamos, there are some who have not denied the authority of God and the scriptures and yet they tolerate Nicolaitane bullying.
- Today like Thyatira, there are those who are full of good works, but in their zeal to do good to their neighbor have lost sight of their obligations to God. Do NOT mistake love of man; for love of God!

As a bride is to be faithful to her husband, our first duty is to our spiritual Husband and all good works to others are secondary. Many unconverted people are also full of good works towards humanity and do not obey God; how are we different from them if we are also full of good works for humanity and forget our LORD?

We should be filled with good works towards men; while not forgetting to put our LORD first in our lives!

What say you? If a bride put her personal charitable works ahead of her love and obedience to her husband, will the husband think that she loves her own works more than she loves him? It is a very good thing to do good works for people, but such good works should not override our zeal for our LORD!

- Today, like Sardis, the Ekklesia is largely spiritually dead, having no fire of zeal to live by every Word of God.
- Today like Philadelphia, there are some faithful who are standing on the foundation of the whole Word of God. Today they are scattered like pillars throughout the various assemblies and standing alone. In a very short time now God's two servants will call for the faithful to gather together and leave for the place which God has prepared; the faithful pillars will respond to God's call while the others will not, thus separating out the faithful from the others.
- Today like Laodicea, the Ekklesia is overwhelmingly proud, arrogant and unteachable by God. They reject large parts of God's Word and very much truth, to follow their idols of men and false traditions. They will not respond positively to God's warnings and the only way to save them from certain eternal death is to afflict the flesh to humble them so that the spirit might be saved.

## Revelation 4

When Jesus walked the earth in the flesh he said in regards to his return:

> **Matthew 24:36** But of that day and hour knoweth no man, no, not the angels of heaven, but my Father only.

Then AFTER he had died and been resurrected and ascended to heaven he was found worthy to unseal the hidden things of God the Father (Rev 4 - 5).

Now in this end time Jesus Christ is revealing these sealed hidden things to his servants in his promised surge of new knowledge and understanding for the latter days.

> **Daniel 12:4** But thou, O Daniel, **shut up the words, and seal the book, even to the time of the end: many shall run to and fro** [much travel], **and knowledge** [spiritual knowledge will be increased as the books of scripture are unsealed] **shall be increased.**

With the promised increase in spiritual knowledge we need not be taken by surprise by end time events, and as we see the biblical signs being fulfilled we can know that our redemption is at hand:

> **Luke 21:28** And when these things begin to come to pass, then look up, and lift up your heads; for your redemption draweth nigh.

**1 Thessalonians 5:4** But ye, brethren, are not in darkness, that that day should overtake you as a thief. **5:5** Ye are all the children of light, and the children of the day: we are not of the night, nor of darkness. **5:6** Therefore let us not sleep, as do others; but let us watch and be sober.

John was given a vision that he was in heaven before the throne of God the Father.

**Revelation 4:1** After this I looked, and, behold, a door was opened in heaven: and the first voice which I heard was as it were of a trumpet talking with me; which said, Come up hither, and I will shew thee things which must be hereafter. **4:2** And immediately **I was in the spirit**: and, behold, a throne was set in heaven, and one sat on the throne.

The Father is revealed as shining like a jewel, and the bow of God is around His Throne.

**4:3** And he that sat was to look upon like a jasper and a sardine stone: and there was a rainbow round about the throne, in sight like unto an emerald.

24 elders are around the throne with crowns which represent authority under God; these are the beings that work with God the Father overseeing the earth and the whole universe.

**4:4** And round about the throne were four and twenty seats: and upon the seats I saw four and twenty elders sitting, clothed in white raiment; and they had on their heads crowns of gold.

Here we have confirmed that the seven branched menorah with its flames represents the Seven Churches; for the seven lights are the seven spirits which oversee the seven churches; see Revelation 1.

**4:5** And out of the throne proceeded lightnings and thunderings and voices: and there were **seven lamps of fire burning before the throne, which are the seven Spirits of God.**

Before the throne is a vast expanse like the Courtyard in the physical temple; a place of meeting before God which is paved with clear crystal, refracting and reflecting the brilliant light of God, so that the expanse sparkled with ever color of the rainbow. John describes this in Revelation 15 as glass mingled with fire.

At the marriage of the Lamb after the resurrection, those people who were resurrected and changed to spirit will stand upon this crystal expanse before the throne of God the Father [the Most Holy Place] at the marriage of the collective bride of the faithful called out and chosen, to the Lamb!

> **Revelation 15:2** And I saw as it were a **sea of glass mingled with fire**: and them that had gotten the victory over the beast, and over his image, and over his mark, and over the number of his name, stand on the sea of glass, having the harps of God.

**Revelation 4:6** And before the throne there was a **sea of glass like unto crystal**: and in the midst of the throne, and round about the throne, were four beasts [cherubs] full of eyes before and behind.

Four angelic creatures are around the throne of God the Father; these seraphim have six wings.

**4:7** And the first beast was like a lion, and the second beast like a calf, and the third beast had a face as a man, and the fourth beast was like a flying eagle.

**4:8** And the four beasts had **each of them six wings about him; and they were full of eyes within**: and they rest not day and night, saying, Holy, holy, holy, LORD God Almighty, which was, and is, and is to come.

The Greek word Zwon [Strong's G2226] is better rendered "living creatures" due to the negative connotation of the word beasts.

These spirit seraphims are angelic spirits close to God, of the same type which Isaiah saw at the throne of God in a vision.

> **Isaiah 6:1** In the year that king Uzziah died I saw [in a vision] also the Lord sitting upon a throne, high and lifted up, and his train filled the temple.  **6:2** Above it [above the Mercy Seat or throne of God] stood the seraphims: each one had six wings; with twain he covered his face, and with twain he covered his feet, and with twain he did fly

Two of these beings cover the Throne of God in heaven, a likeness being made by Moses on the earth in the Mercy Seat.

The Father is worthy of all honor and glory!

**Revelation 4:9** And when those beasts give glory and honour and thanks to him that sat on the throne, who liveth for ever and ever, **4:10** The four and twenty elders fall down before him that sat on the throne, and worship him that liveth for ever and ever, and cast their crowns before the throne, saying,

God the Father is revealed as the Executive Authority over all things!

How can that be? Because God the Father finalized the plans and gave the command to the One who became the Son; to create all things! The Father was the executive authority, while the One who became the Son actually carried out the work of creating as the implementing authority!

**4:11** Thou art worthy, O Lord, to receive glory and honour and power: for thou hast created all things, and for thy pleasure they are and were created.

In the hands of God the Father is the Book - or key - to reveal the meaning of the prophecies of scripture which had been sealed up (Daniel 12).

No one could know or understand those things that were sealed until the Lamb qualified to open the seals by overcoming all evil and giving his life for the sins of humanity, and now Jesus Christ reveals the hidden things at the very end time as Daniel was told.

# Revelation 5

**Revelation 5:1** And I saw in the right hand of him that sat on the throne a book written within and on the backside, sealed with seven seals.

No one in heaven or on the earth was able to open and understand the sealed books of scripture (Dan 12); until the Lamb of God was found worthy to unseal the hidden things of the plan of God.

God promised in Daniel 12 that in the last days, Jesus Christ would reveal these things and that there would be a great increase of spiritual knowledge and understanding.

These things of God were sealed and kept hidden until the Appointed Time of their revealing at the very last days; which is why there has been almost no understanding of the Biblical Festivals, Biblical Calendar and most of the end time prophecies until now.

What is so very sad is that most of today's Ekklesia reject the expansion of knowledge and understanding that God has promised to reveal in this end time.

**5:2** And I saw a strong angel proclaiming with a loud voice, Who is worthy to open the book, and to loose the seals thereof? **5:3** And **no man in heaven, nor in earth, neither under the earth, was able to open the book, neither to look thereon** [to see its contents].

John wept that no one could be found worthy to open up an understanding of the prophecies.

**5:4** And I wept much, because no man was found worthy to open and to read the book, neither to look thereon.

Then the Lamb of God who overcame all sin and was resurrected at the end of the third day to rise up as the Wave Offering to be accepted for us.

He was accepted as the Redeemer of the sincerely repentant and the High Priest of God the Father for his people. He was found worthy to unseal and open up an understanding of the books: Because his sacrifice made the prophecies of the Word of God SURE!

If Jesus Christ had not been successful, there was no need to understand the prophecies because they would all have failed!

**5:5** And one of the elders saith unto me, Weep not: **behold, the Lion of the tribe of Juda, the Root of David, hath prevailed to open the book, and to loose the seven seals thereof.**

The One who became the Son, the Word of God prevailed over Satan and sin and voluntarily died as a perfect and pure sacrifice for all sincerely repented sin; and was resurrected to spirit to become the ONLY Intercessor between the people and God the Father!

It is Jesus Christ alone who is in authority over the seven churches, under God the Father, and Jesus is the ONLY High Priest and the ONLY Intercessor between God the Father and humanity forevermore: NOT any man or board of men and he has seven angelic spirits which are his eyes to keep watch on his seven churches.

The spiritually called out are espoused to Jesus Christ alone, and we are personally responsible to live by every Word of God the Father regardless of what any man claims or teaches!

The job of elders and leaders is to help keep the flock of God the Father focused on our Father in heaven; it is not to usurp the Mediator and High Priest, Jesus Christ and try to come between people and God!

Behold how Mighty and Awesome is God our Father and our espoused Husband Jesus Christ! What fools we are to compromise with their Word!

**5:6** And I beheld, and, lo, in the midst of the throne and of the four beasts, and in the midst of the elders, stood a Lamb as it had been slain, having seven horns [power over the seven churches; horns being symbols of power and strength] and seven eyes, which are the seven Spirits of God [these spirits are Christ's eyes (representatives) to see all that is done and report back to Him] sent forth into all the earth.

When Christ was found worthy; the heavenly powers bowed down before him!

**5:7** And he came and took the book out of the right hand of him that sat upon the throne. **5:8** And when he had taken the book, the four beasts and four and twenty elders fell down before the Lamb, having every one of them harps, and golden vials **full of** [pleasant] **odours** [incense], **which are the prayers of saints.**

Then the heavenly elders, cherubs and angels; sang a song about the wonderful Lamb of God

**5:9** And they sung a new song, saying, **Thou art worthy to take the book, and to open the seals thereof: for thou wast slain, and hast redeemed us to God by thy blood out of every kindred, and tongue, and people, and nation;**

The resurrected saints will be made kings and priests by God the Father there in the heavenly courtyard before the Father's throne, to replace Satan and to rule the earth to bring many others to salvation!

**5:10** And **hast made us unto our God kings and priests: and we shall reign on the earth.**

Millions and millions of angels praised the Overcoming One; who was God, and then gave up his God-hood to become flesh to die for humanity: The One who was successful and overcame Satan and sin, and was made God again in a resurrection back to spirit!

**5:11** And I beheld, and I heard the voice of many angels round about the throne and the beasts and the elders: and the number of them was ten thousand times ten thousand, and thousands of thousands [a vast number of faithful angels];

**5:12** Saying with a loud voice, Worthy is the Lamb that was slain to receive power, and riches, and wisdom, and strength, and honour, and glory, and blessing.

Prophetically, John heard every living thing give glory to God the Father and to the Lamb. This WILL happen when the plan of God for physical things is completed.

**5:13** And **every creature which is in heaven, and on the earth, and under the earth, and such as are in the sea, and all that are in them,**

**heard I saying, Blessing, and honour, and glory, and power, be unto him that sitteth upon the throne** [God the Father], **and unto the Lamb for ever and ever.**

**5:14** And the four beasts said, Amen. And the four and twenty elders fell down and worshipped him that liveth for ever and ever.

Then Jesus Christ began to open the seven seals which give understanding of the prophecies of the Word of God. John recorded these seals and the remainder of the book of Revelation as a part of the holy scriptures.

Jesus Christ the Lamb of God while unsealing the books and being given an understanding of these things by God the Father, will only give his people an understanding of these things when they need to know; that is, at the end time; to fulfill the Word of God to Daniel in Daniel 12.

> **Daniel 12:9** And he said, Go thy way, Daniel: for **the words are closed up and sealed till the time of the end.**

Brethren, that time has come!

# Revelation 6

## The Seven Seals

### The First Seal

Jesus Christ by his sinless life and willingness to die for humanity to fulfill the will of God the Father, was resurrected to spirit and had the glory that he had had before giving up his God-hood to become flesh, restored to him. He then ascended to God the Father to be accepted "for us" to be accepted as our atoning sacrifice and to be made a High Priest to intercede for us with God the Father and to reconcile us to the Father.

Being found worthy to receive eternal life and everlasting glory, Jesus Christ was also found worthy to unseal the secret things of God the Father.

**Revelation 6:1** And I saw when the Lamb opened one of the seals, and I heard, as it were the noise of thunder, one of the four beasts saying, Come and see.

The first seal is a white horse with its rider and in the grand overall scheme of things it pictures Satan the Adversary who presents himself as an angel of light to deceive the nations.

Specifically however, this refers to the end time and refers to the climax of Satan's activities and of his deceptions through human agents. This seal refers to the abomination spoken of by Daniel [Dan 12] and by Paul.

> **2 Thessalonians 2:3** Let no man deceive you by any means: for that day shall not come, except there come a falling away [a falling away from zeal for God in the brotherhood as has now happened] first, and that man of sin be revealed, the son of perdition [who is the final miracle working abomination];
>
> **2:4** Who opposeth and exalteth himself above all that is called God, or that is worshipped; so that he as God [he will be exalted by humanity as an ultimate moral authority on the earth] sitteth in the temple of God [he will falsely present himself as the head of the body of true believers, the spiritual temple] shewing himself that he is God.

This man will exalt himself above God as humanity's ultimate moral authority.

> **2:5** Remember ye not, that, when I was yet with you, I told you these things? **2:6** And now ye know what [that Christ is holding Satan back until the appointed time] withholdeth that he [the final great deceiver] might be revealed in his time.
>
> **2:7** For the mystery of iniquity doth already work [even in Paul's day men exalted other men above the Word of God]: only he who now letteth [restrains, withholds] will let [will restrain this setting up of the final great deceiver until the appointed time], until he [that is, the restraints are removed] be taken out of the way

The daily intervention of Jesus Christ will restrain the setting up of this person until the appointed time when the restraints will be removed.

> **2:8** And then shall that Wicked be revealed [From the time that he is set up doing miracles in the Vatican, he will have only 1,335 days until he is destroyed by Christ (Dan 12).], whom the Lord shall consume with the spirit of his mouth, and shall destroy with the brightness of his coming:
>
> **2:9** Even him, whose coming is after the working of Satan with all power and signs and lying wonders [doing many miracles], **2:10** And with all deceivableness of unrighteousness [deceiving men into rebellion against the Word of God] in them that

perish; because they received not the love of the truth, that they might be saved.

This miracle working deceiver will be of the earth, earthy, carnal, worldly; and will deceive most of humanity by doing amazing miracles to exalt himself above God as humanity's ultimate moral authority.

This earthy, worldly, carnal, miracle working deceiver will appear to be a man of peace and as harmless as a lamb [trying to counterfeit the true Lamb of God]; but he will speak the words of Satan the dragon, teaching all peoples to follow him instead of living by every Word of God. He will teach that HIS word is to be obeyed, because he alone can properly understand and interpret the Word of God. This same thing is being done within the Ekklesia today.

This man will do great miracles, probably in the form of trying to imitate Christ; he will call for the nations to join a new order in Europe and will be so exalted by the people that ten nations will come together in a New Federal Europe on his advice.

> **Revelation 13:11** And I beheld another beast **coming up out of the earth** [being a man of flesh]; and he had two horns [presenting himself as a meek harmless lamb] like a lamb, and he spake as a dragon.

The white horse is deceptive and shows the deceptive nature of this person who tries to appear as a shining white paragon of righteousness while he deceives men into following his own ways contrary to and in rebellion against the Word of God.

He will conquer the minds and hearts of people through his impressive miracles and smooth words.

> **Revelation 6:2** And I saw, and behold a white horse: and he that sat on him had a bow; and a crown was given unto him: and he went forth conquering, and to conquer.

This final deceiver conquers the people through deceiving them into regarding him as a great moral authority transcending all religions

### The Second Seal

The second seal reveals the terrible wars that will come upon the earth during the final 3 1/2 year period.

**6:3** And when he had opened **the second seal**, I heard the second beast [a second spirit being (seraphim) by the throne of God] say, Come and see. **6:4** And there went out another horse that was red: and **power was given to him that sat thereon to take peace from the earth, and that they should kill one another: and there was given unto him a great sword.**

The second seal is war and conflict on the earth. This begins with the occupation of Jerusalem and great bloodshed during the fall of Judea, and some two years later will come in its fullness to the rest of the world when Europe attacks the nations of Asia.

### The Third Seal

The third seal is about the terrible famine that will come because of wars, bad weather etc.

**Revelation 6:5** And when he had opened **the third seal**, I heard the third beast say, Come and see. And I beheld, and lo a black horse; and **he that sat on him had a pair of balances in his hand. 6:6 And I heard a voice in the midst of the four beasts say, A measure of wheat for a penny, and three measures of barley for a penny; and see thou hurt not the oil and the wine.**

The third seal is about great famine in America and the Anglo Saxon nations while the New Europe prospers abundantly. Starving people in America and the Anglo Saxon nations will riot and fight for food and survival, and vermin will multiply exponentially, eating up the existing food stocks and carrying disease.

### The Fourth Seal
### The great dying

**Revelation 6:7** **The fourth seal**, I heard the voice of the fourth beast [the fourth spirit being (saraphim) before God's throne] say, Come and see. **6:8** And I looked, and behold a pale horse: and his name that sat on him was Death, and Hell followed with him. And power was given unto them over the fourth part of the earth, **to kill with sword, and with hunger, and with death, and with the beasts of the earth.**

The fourth seal is about Europe attacking Asia, and with the spread of war famine and disease will also increase.

Here it is revealed that the inanimate spirits of the dead in Christ are kept in heaven under the altar of God in the Heavenly Temple of God the Father.

I did not write this; it is Holy Scripture. Yes, the spirits of the dead in Christ are kept in heaven; where they figuratively cry out for their resurrection and God's judgment on those who rebel against the Word of God and who persecute those zealous to learn and to keep the whole Word and Will of God.

Now the scriptures tell us that no conscious man has as yet ascended into heaven except Christ. This is because no flesh can pass across the vast gulf between the earth and heaven. Even Jesus while in the flesh, could not cross that gulf and visit heaven.

No flesh can travel to heaven from the earth. However SPIRIT can cross the distance between the earth and heaven, as evidenced by the angels on many occasions. Therefore it was AFTER Jesus Christ was changed to spirit at his resurrection that he was able to ascend up to heaven.

No flesh can cross the vast space between heaven and earth, however God can take the spirit in human beings who have His Holy Spirit, and keep them as inanimate spirit to be kept safe and totally secure under the heavenly altar, until the day they are returned to the earth to be placed in new bodies made of spirit in the sight of all people as a demonstration of the power and the glory of God.

Right now these disembodied spirits are inanimate and cannot function just as a disk which is not inserted into a machine cannot function; these human spirits must be plugged into new bodies to become animate and functional.

Right now the spirits of the dead in Christ are being stored in the most secure place in the universe, beneath the very altar of Almighty God in heaven; and it is their very presence that cries out to God [not any actual voice] to remember God's faithful and correct the wickedness of humanity to bring mankind to sincere repentance.

**The Fifth Seal**

The dead in Christ who lived during the past 6,000 years are judged righteous by the Ultimate Judge, but they are told that others will still join them until the Appointed Time arrives.

**Revelation 6:9** And when he had opened **the fifth seal,** I saw **under the altar the souls** [pneuma; spirits] of them that were slain for the word of God, and for the testimony which they held: **6:10** And they cried with a loud voice, saying, How long, O Lord, holy and true, dost thou not judge and avenge our blood on them that dwell on the earth? **6:11** And white robes were given unto every one of them; and it was said unto them, that they should **rest yet for a little season, until their fellowservants also and their brethren, that should be killed as they were, should be fulfilled.**

The fifth seal is a warning of a great martyrdom AFTER the son of perdition and the new Roman Empire and its ruler are set up, and occupy Judea and during the collapse of Anglo Saxon power.

When the Laodicean brethren see their false traditions destroyed by reality, the pride and self-will of very many will be crushed; then they will remember that they were warned and they will quickly and sincerely repent turning to a passionate zeal for the Eternal, with many giving up their lives in a great martyrdom.

During the tribulation, there will be a great persecution of all those who did not initially respond to God's warnings and later sincerely repented from their lack of zeal for God when they are trapped in the furnace of correction.

> **Revelation 12:17** And the dragon was wroth with the woman, and **went to make war with the remnant of her seed, which** [to persecute those who sincerely repent in great tribulation and turn to a zeal to live by every Word of God] **keep the commandments of God, and have the testimony of Jesus Christ.**

**The Sixth Seal**

The sixth seal is the appearance of Jesus Christ in his majestic glory for all people to see. After the man of sin is set up in the Vatican, after the New Europe and its leader are set up, after the defeat of Judah and the collapse of the Israelite nations, after a period of great suffering in the Israelite nations, Jesus Christ will appear in his glory in the heavens heralding the onset of the seventh seal which is the seven trumpets.

At the presence of Christ in his glory the earth shall tremble and shake [probably producing volcanic activity] and the atmospheric dust will make the moon appear red.

Consider that in the night we see the stars and during the day the brightness of the sun hides the stars and they seem to vanish from our sight. Even so, the brightness of Christ shining in his full glory, will overwhelm the sun itself which will disappear from sight in the presence of the Glorious One, while on the opposite side of the earth the moon will appear red!

**6:12** And I beheld when he had opened **the sixth seal**, and, lo, there was a great earthquake; and the sun became black as sackcloth of hair, and the moon became as blood; **6:13** And the stars [space objects in our solar system: many astral objects like meteors and boulders will fall from space doing much damage] of heaven fell unto the earth, even as a fig tree casteth her untimely figs, when she is shaken of a mighty wind. **6:14** And the heaven departed as a scroll [the sky will disappear, all else overwhelmed by the incredible brightness of the light of our Redeemer] when it is rolled together; and every mountain and island were moved out of their places.

When they see this the wicked will fear, but those that God is calling and working with, will have any self-justifying pride that is left totally crushed as they see the glory of the Holy One!

**6:15** And the kings of the earth, and the great men, and the rich men, and the chief captains, and the mighty men, and every bondman, and every free man, hid themselves in the dens and in the rocks of the mountains; **6:16** And said to the mountains and rocks, Fall on us, and hide us from the face of him that sitteth on the throne, and from the wrath of the Lamb: **6:17** For the great day of his wrath is come; and who shall be able to stand?

## Revelation 7 and 14; The 144,000

### Revelation 7

This is an explanation of the 144,000 in the prophecy of Revelation. While I believe this explanation is correct as far as it goes, I also expect this is only a partial limited understanding and that there is far more to this prophecy than what is presented here.

There are two sets of 144,000 in Revelation. The first set of 144,000 is specific to Israel and specific to those who are alive and sealed during the last 3 1/2 years before the millennium.

This 144,000 is specific to Israel and does not exclude others from also being sealed by God. This first group of 144,000 is not the same as a second group of 144,000 in Revelation 14. They are two quite different groups.

AFTER the sixth seal, the wind [the seven trumpets are held back] is held back until 144,000 people from the nations of Israel are sealed by God.

A seal represents ownership and the seal of God's ownership of a person is the gift of the Holy Spirit.

> **Ephesians 4:30** And grieve not **the holy Spirit of God, whereby ye are sealed unto the day of redemption.**

The timing of this sealing is AFTER the initial wars and great suffering of the tribulation, and immediately AFTER Jesus Christ is seen in his full glory by all nations, and before the seven trumpets blast.

The calling of God, the great suffering during the tribulation of the first five seals, the preaching of God's two servants and then the appearance of Messiah the Christ in the heavens: will bring sincere repentance and result in 12,000 of each tribe of Israel except Dan receiving the gift of being sealed [set apart to godliness] with God's holy Spirit.

They are sealed for the express purpose of setting them apart so that the trumpet plagues do not fall upon them; and they will witness to the nations of Israel during the time of the trumpet plagues and they will be resurrected to spirit along with all of the other chosen as the seven trump begins to sound as a powerful witness to the remainder of Israel.

The 12,000 from each tribe of Israel are called out to be personal witnesses to all Israel during the period of the trumpet plagues, and when they are changed to spirit in the resurrection, all Israel will be astonished and will begin to turn to God!

> **Revelation 11:11** And after three days and an half the spirit of life from God entered into them, and they stood upon their feet; and great fear fell upon them which saw them.
>
> **11:12** And they heard a great voice from heaven saying unto them, Come up hither. And **they ascended up to heaven in a cloud; and their enemies beheld them.**
>
> **11:13** And the same hour was there a great earthquake, and the tenth part of the city fell, and in the earthquake were slain of men seven thousand: and **the remnant** [those that remained behind, specifically from Israel] **were affrighted** [amazed, frightened and astonished], **and gave glory to the God of heaven.**

**Revelation 7:1** And after these things I saw four angels standing on the four corners of the earth, holding the four winds of the earth, that the wind [that the blasts of the seven trumpet plagues would be delayed] should not blow on the earth, nor on the sea, nor on any tree. **7:2** And I saw another angel ascending from the east, having the seal of the living God: and he cried with a loud voice to the four angels, to whom it was given to hurt the earth and the sea, **7:3** Saying, Hurt not the earth, neither the sea, nor the trees, till we have sealed the servants of our God in their foreheads.

144,000 are sealed, 12,000 from each of the tribes of Israel. Joseph has the double portion while Reuben and Levi are included; Dan is left out; making the tribes of the sealed an even 12.

The first point is that this first 144,000 are people during the actual end time tribulation, therefore the 144,000 does not include the ancients like David, Moses, Elijah, Able, Enoch, Noah, Daniel and so very many others including the first century apostles and the many many thousands of brethren through history; and of course it does not include any Gentiles.

This 144,000 are specifically called out, repent and are sealed with God's Holy Spirit after the tribulation and just before the Trumpet plagues. They will be a witness for God in all Israel, during the terrible time of the trumpet plagues.

**7:4** And I heard the number of them which were sealed: and **there were sealed an hundred and forty and four thousand of all the tribes of the children of Israel.**

**7:5** Of the tribe of Juda were sealed twelve thousand. Of the tribe of Reuben were sealed twelve thousand. Of the tribe of Gad were sealed twelve thousand.

**7:6** Of the tribe of Aser were sealed twelve thousand. Of the tribe of Nephthalim were sealed twelve thousand. Of the tribe of Manasses were sealed twelve thousand.

**7:7** Of the tribe of Simeon were sealed twelve thousand. Of the tribe of Levi were sealed twelve thousand. Of the tribe of Issachar were sealed twelve thousand.

**7:8** Of the tribe of Zabulon were sealed twelve thousand. Of the tribe of Joseph [Ephraim in addition to the aforementioned Manasseh] were sealed twelve thousand. Of the tribe of Benjamin were sealed twelve thousand.

Now comes the statement "AFTER THIS," meaning later; the prophecy jumps forward to the resurrection to spirit. And there before the throne of God in heaven is not merely this 144,000 but a vast multitude of all those who have been called to Christ over the entire past 6,000 years, and have endured and overcome to be chosen to be resurrected and changed to spirit.

Here stand all of the chosen overcomers who had lived and been called over six thousand years; not just the specific 144,000 from the tribes of Israel sealed immediately before the end time trumpet plagues.

This tells us that God will resurrect and change a vast multitude of His faithful to spirit, both Israel and Gentile, who lived through history; not just the 144,000 from Israel who were called out and sealed at the time of the opening of the seventh seal.

Once again as in Revelation 15 and Revelation 19; here is another prophecy of the faithful, chosen and changed, standing IN HEAVEN with the angels and the four spirit beings before the throne of God.

**7:9 After this** I beheld, and, **lo, a great multitude, which no man could number, of all nations, and kindreds, and people, and tongues, stood before the throne**, and before the Lamb, clothed with white robes, and palms in their hands; **7:10** And cried with a loud voice, saying, Salvation to our God which sitteth upon the throne, and unto the Lamb. **7:11** And all the angels stood round about the throne, and about the elders and the four beasts, and fell before the throne on their faces, and worshipped God, **7:12** Saying, Amen: Blessing, and glory, and wisdom, and thanksgiving, and honour, and power, and might, be unto our God for ever and ever. Amen.

The vast multitude before God's throne in heaven is explained as all those who have sincerely repented and been washed clean by the sacrifice of Christ; and who have faithfully endured, overcoming sin, by the power of God's Spirit; and who have internalized the nature of God through the zealous learning and keeping of the whole Word of God.

**7:13** And one of the elders answered, saying unto me, What are these which are arrayed in white robes? and whence came they?

Now we have a point of confusion as most have assumed that the term great tribulation here is in reference to the final 3 1/2 years before the resurrection to spirit. This would imply that only those who are living in the very end time would be in the resurrection of the chosen first fruits. This idea forgets God's promises to many of the ancients that they will be in this first resurrection to spirit as well.

In reference to the great multitude this does not refer to the final 3 1/2 year great tribulation. This term as used here, refers to the tribulations and trials of the called out in enduring and overcoming throughout their lives to be judged faithful: See Hebrews 11.

On the other hand 12,000 of each tribe of Israel who were sealed before the seven trumpets, will go through the end time great tribulation and will be among this great multitude!

**7:14** And I said unto him, Sir, thou knowest. And he said to me, **These are they which came out of great tribulation** [endured much suffering for godliness as per Hebrews 11]**, and have washed their robes, and made them white** [pure from sin] **in the blood of the Lamb.**

**7:15** Therefore are they [are resurrected to spirit and stand before God in heaven at the marriage of the Lamb] before the throne of God, and serve him day and night in his temple [government]: and he that sitteth on the throne shall dwell among them [referring to the Eighth Day when God the Father will come down to the earth].

**7:16** They shall hunger no more, neither thirst any more [now being spirit]; neither shall the sun light on them, nor any heat [being spirit they shall not need heat or light from physical sources]. **7:17** For the Lamb which is in the midst of the throne shall feed them [spiritual food and living waters of the Holy Spirit], and shall lead them unto living fountains of waters: and God shall wipe away all tears from their eyes.

The Second Group of 144,000 is presented in Revelation 14

## Revelation 14

The first 144,000 was explained in chapter seven.

Some would speculate that the seal of God is this or that, but we must let the scriptures explain themselves.

The seal of God is the Holy Spirit which identifies the sealed as belonging to God.

> **2 Corinthians 1:21** Now he which stablisheth us with you in Christ, and hath anointed us, is God [the Father]; **1:22** Who hath also **sealed us, and given the earnest of the Spirit in our hearts.**

In fact the Holy Spirit, if followed; empowers one to zealously keep the whole Word of God and thereby makes one godly; to be of God! It is God's Spirit that makes us godly to be God's people; and without God's Spirit we are not of God.

> **Ephesians 1:13** In whom ye also trusted, after that ye heard the word of truth, the gospel of your salvation: in whom also **after that ye believed, ye were sealed with that holy Spirit of promise, 1:14 Which is the earnest of our inheritance until the redemption** of the purchased [We are the redeemed possession,

purchased by Christ if we have the gift of God's Spirit] possession, unto the praise of his glory.

The 144,000 in chapter seven were sealed with God's Spirit immediately before the trumpet plagues, and are added to the vast multitude of those who had already been sealed with God's Spirit before that.

Throughout history thousands of Israel have been converted and sealed with God's Spirit along with thousands of Gentiles.

### The 144,000 of Revelation 7

The 144,000 of Revelation 7 is a group of Israelites exclusively, who had repented during the tribulation and are then sealed by God to protect them from the wrath of God being poured out on the earth. Why? So that they could witness to the people in the tribes of Israel during the seven trumpet plagues.

This 144,000 are a specific number from the tribes of Israel sealed at that time; this does not mean that others including many Gentiles were not also sealed with God's Spirit over the previous 6,000 years.

The Revelation 7, 144,000 will be sealed with God's Spirit and will still remain in their tribes through the trumpet plague period, witnessing to the tribes of Israel; then when God's two are resurrected along with all the other dead in Christ, the Revelation 7, 144,000 will be changed to spirit in the sight of all those who had seen them witnessing.

Their witness during the trumpet plagues, capped of by their being changed to spirit will be an awesome witness of the truth of what they had taught and of the Mighty Power of God to save! At that time Israel will begin to repent and turn to God (Rev 11:13)!

### The 144,000 of Revelation 14

The Revelation 14, 144,000 are a completely different group than those sealed before the trumpet plagues. They are those who will land on the Mount of Olives to govern the earth with Christ from the capital of the world at Jerusalem.

**Revelation 14:1** And I looked, and, lo, a Lamb stood on the mount Sion, and with him an hundred forty and four thousand, having his Father's name written in their foreheads.

John now writes about the 144,000 of Revelation 14 standing on Zion and ruling with Christ from Jerusalem.

**14:2** And I heard a voice from heaven, as the voice of many waters [much people], and as the voice of a great thunder: and I heard the voice of harpers harping with their harps:

**14:3** And they sung as it were a new song before the throne, and before the four beasts, and the elders: and no man could learn that song but the hundred and forty and four thousand, which were redeemed from the earth.

This 144,000 has been redeemed from the earth and this particular 144,000 will rule as pillars in the government of God with Christ. See the massage to Philadelphia where they will be given the very name [authority] of God's government.

**14:4** These are they which were not defiled with women [false leaders, false traditions of men and false doctrines]; for they are [spiritually chaste and absolutely loyal to the Husband of their calling] virgins. **These are they which follow the Lamb whithersoever he goeth. These were redeemed from among men, being the firstfruits unto God and to the Lamb.**

**14:5** And in their mouth was found no guile [no deceitfulness]: for **they are without fault before the throne of God.**


### The Great Multitude of Resurrected Saints

Revelation 7:9 reveals a vast multitude of resurrected saints besides the 144,000

**Revelation 7:9** After this I beheld, and, lo, a great multitude, which no man could number, of all nations, and kindreds, and people, and tongues, stood before the throne, and before the Lamb, clothed with white robes, and palms in their hands;

These are those who will rule all nations, not from Jerusalem the capital of the world, but in their own nations, under those at Jerusalem.

When the second 144,000 of Revelation 14, land on the Mount of Olives at Jerusalem with Christ, these others will be landing all over the earth and taking authority under Christ, over every nation.

The 144,000 of Revelation 7 are called and converted as examples for the nations of Israel just before the trumpet plagues.

Quite probably by the time this 144,000 is sealed, difficult access to such things as internet or even regular power would be interfering with the Israelite nations hearing the teaching of God's two witnesses.

God's calling, the witnessing of God's two and then the 144,000 and then the resurrection, will begin to bring all Israel to sincere repentance ready for the coming of Christ to deliver them!

Dearly Beloved Brethren, hopefully even some of the lax and lukewarm in today's Ekklesia will repent during the tribulation and will be among this 144,000 who are sealed with God's Spirit before the trumpet plagues!

At the resurrection a great multitude of all the dead in Christ since Abel will be changed or resurrected to spirit, including God's two servants and the Revelation 7, 144,000. At that time the Revelation 7, 144,000 will have done their job.

### God's central government at Jerusalem

As the Marriage of the Lamb takes place in heaven, millions of resurrected saints will stand before the throne of God; and God will separate out a different 144,000 from this vast multitude of resurrected saints which 144,000 pillars will rule all nations with Jesus Christ in the world central government capital at Jerusalem.

The Revelation 14, 144,000 will descend to the Mount of Olives with Christ because it is from Jerusalem that they will rule as the government of the whole earth.

The remaining vast multitude including the Revelation 7 144,000 who were proven faithful over the preceding 6,000 years will rule in their various responsibilities around the world!

**Note:** Some of the Revelation 7 144,000 might also be chosen to be in the central government of 144,000 chosen pillars who rule directly from Jerusalem.


### To Sum Up

The first (Rev 7) 144,000 are 12,000 from each tribe of Israel [except Dan] converted AFTER the six seals have been opened. They will be a witness to the tribes of Israel during the seven trumpet plagues and they will be changed to spirit when the seventh trumpet begins to sound.

Not only will these 144,000 be changed when the seventh trumpet begins to sound, but ALL the faithful dead who have lived since Abel will be resurrected and changed with them, that is the great multitude.

The first 144,000 will be a part of this great multitude and will be taken to the Heavenly Temple Courtyard before the throne of God for the marriage of the Lamb.

Then at the marriage of the Lamb, God the Father and Jesus Christ will organize their government.

A new and different 144,000 (Rev 14) will be selected from out of this great multitude to be the pillars of God's central government at Jerusalem and they will descend to the Mount of Olives with Christ as the headquarters government over the entire earth.

The remaining multitudes will be organized to serve God as rulers and teachers [kings and priests] over the various nations, cities, etc. and they will descend from heaven - not to Jerusalem - but to their various nations, cities etc to gather up Satan's demons and take local control.

## Revelation 8

### The First Trumpet

The seventh seal is the seven trumpet plagues.

**Revelation 8:1** And when he had opened **the seventh seal,** there was silence in heaven about the space of half an hour. **8:2** And I saw the seven angels which stood before God; and to them were given **seven trumpets.**

**8:3** And another angel came and stood at the altar, having a golden censer; and there was given unto him **much incense, that he should offer it with the prayers of all saints** [who are fervently praying "Your Will be done, your Kingdom come"] upon the golden altar which was before the throne. **8:4** And **the smoke of the incense, which came with the prayers of the saints, ascended up before God** [These prayers, just like the smoke of the burnt offering, picture wholehearted faithfulness and zeal to follow God and to learn and keep the whole Word and Will of God; which is a very pleasant smell like the perfume of incense to God the Father] out of the angel's hand.

**8:5** And the angel took the censer, and filled it with **fire of the altar, and cast it into the earth: and there were voices, and thunderings, and**

**lightnings, and an earthquake. 8:6** And the seven angels which had the seven trumpets prepared themselves to sound.

A great hail storm with extensive lightening will fall on much of the earth, causing many fires which burn up most of the earth's forests and grass lands.

The lightening will be accompanied by enormous awesome fear generating thundering around much of the earth, and the lightening generated fires would be expedited by the long drought and holding back of rainfall. The fires would not be limited to growing things but would also undoubtedly consume many buildings as well.

The hail and lightening would be mingled on the ground with the blood of the many people being struck by great hail and lightening, and being burned in the fires.

**8:7** The first angel sounded, and there followed hail and fire mingled with blood, and they were cast upon the earth: and the third part of trees was burnt up, and all green grass was burnt up.

This is the beginning of the wrath of a furious Jesus Christ, pouring out His anger upon a rebellious mankind; which has persecuted and tormented the godly faithful and defied the Word of God.

This means EXACTLY what it says. The hail will not be just the small pea to prune sized hail that is common; it will be a very large killer size, of many pounds in weight. The fire is doubtless lightning (Strong's 4442 pur) and the blood, is the blood of those injured, dead and dying.

**The Second Trumpet**

**8:8** And the second angel sounded, and as it were a great mountain burning with fire was cast into the sea: and the third part of the sea became blood; **8:9** And the third part of the creatures which were in the sea, and had life, died; and the third part of the ships were destroyed.

This is likely a huge meteor burning brightly as it passes through the atmosphere.

While not specifically mentioned here, it should be self-evident that such a massive and forceful displacement of water would result in a huge tsunami or tidal surge, which would be very damaging to large areas of land as well as to the sea.

The size of such a massive object, its effect multiplied by its great speed at impact, would easily create a unprecedented sloshing series of tidal waves sweeping across many coastal land masses and would certainly destroy all shipping in the affected area.

With much shipping destroyed and quite likely many oil tankers crushed, this might be the Exon Valdez disaster multiplied a thousand or more times. A vast; heavy coat of oily sludge and pollution over the sea, glinting in the sun, might just be described as looking like a sea of blood and would kill of all sea life in that area.

Whether this means just the Mediterranean Sea or all the oceans is unclear. In either case, this will still be an awesome disaster.

### The Third Trumpet

**8:10** And the third angel sounded, and there fell a great star from heaven, burning as it were a lamp, and it fell upon the third part of the rivers, and upon the fountains of waters; **8:11** And the name of the star is called Wormwood [bitter]: and the third part of the waters became wormwood [bitter, poisoned]; and many men died of the waters, because they were made bitter.

This appears to be in the nature of a comet which is made of dust and frozen gasses which would glow like a lamp on entry into the atmosphere, as opposed to the more solid nature of a meteor. This dust falling over a wide area of fresh waters, would pollute those waters and make them bitter and poisonous. A glowing comet is also much brighter over a larger area than a meteor, passing over a much longer distance in the atmosphere.

### The Fourth Trumpet

**8:12** And the fourth angel sounded, and **the third part of the sun was smitten, and the third part of the moon, and the third part of the stars;** so as the third part of them was darkened, and **the day shone not for a third part of it, and the night likewise.**

There is to be an eight hour period, half during the day and half during the night, when the natural light from the skies will be obscured on the surface of the earth.

The exact cause of this is not revealed but this darkness is to be regarded as an ominous warning of the three trumpet woes to come; the last [the seventh trumpet] is the resurrection of the chosen and includes the seven last plagues falling on the earth during the marriage of the Lamb in Heaven.  See The Marriage of the Lamb.

**8:13** And I beheld, and heard an angel flying through the midst of heaven, saying with a loud voice, Woe, woe, woe, to the inhabiters of the earth by reason of the other voices of the trumpet of the three angels, which are yet to sound!

# Revelation 9

**The Fifth Trumpet**

**The First Woe**

**Revelation 9:1** And the **fifth angel sounded**, and I saw a star [an angel] fall from heaven unto the earth: and **to him** was given the key of the bottomless pit. **9:2** And he opened the bottomless pit; and there arose a smoke out of the pit, as the smoke of a great furnace; and **the sun and the air were darkened** by reason of the smoke of the pit.

Evil spirits are released from their place of restraint to torment mankind.

**9:3** And there came out of the smoke locusts upon the earth: and unto them was given power, as the scorpions of the earth have power. **9:4** And it was commanded them that they should not hurt the grass of the earth, neither any green thing, neither any tree; but **only those men which have not the seal of God in their foreheads.**

The seal of God is the Holy Spirit.

> **Ephesians 1:13** In whom ye also trusted, after that ye heard the word of truth, the gospel of your salvation: in whom also after that ye believed, **ye were sealed with that holy Spirit of promise,**

The 144,000 were sealed with the Holy Spirit just before the first trumpet plague began to be sounded, but there have been untold multitudes of other people sealed with God's Spirit through history,

These evil spirits will have no power over the 144,000 who were sealed with God's Spirit after the tribulation, or over the many others who will also be living during that time having received the seal of God's promise [the Holy Spirit] before and during the tribulation.

**Revelation 9:5** And to them it was given that they should not kill them [the wicked], but that they should be **tormented five months: and their torment was as the torment of a scorpion**, when he striketh a man. **9:6** And in those days shall men seek death, and shall not find it; and shall desire to die, and death shall flee from them.

Keep the timeline in mind; there will be five months of torment for the wicked, from which all those sealed [not just the 144,000] with God's Spirit are protected.

**9:7** And the shapes of the locusts were like unto horses [since their appearance is like war horses the term locusts must refer to a swarm; a great mass of these beings who also had wings and flew like locusts] prepared unto battle; and on their heads were as it were crowns like gold, and their faces were as the faces of men. **9:8** And they had hair as the hair of women and their teeth were as the teeth of lions [very powerful jaws].

**9:9** And they had breastplates, as it were breastplates of iron [armoured bodies and wings to fly with]; and [there was such a vast number of them that their wings sounded like a great army of horsemen] the sound of their wings was as the sound of chariots of many horses running to battle.

In the past some have speculated that this was John's way of describing armies of men. That is not possible since these creatures cannot kill. No, these are not Apache or Cobra helicopters! They are a vast army of a specific type of demon who follows the Adversary of God, Satan the devil; and are permitted by God to torment the wicked on the earth for five months precisely.

**9:10** And they had tails like unto scorpions, and there were stings in their tails: and their power was to hurt men five months. **9:11** And they had a king over them, which is the angel of the bottomless pit, whose name in the Hebrew tongue is Abaddon [The Destroyer, utter destruction, perdition, damnation; in the sense that he leads to destruction by causing people to rebel against God.], but in the Greek tongue hath his name Apollyon [the same meaning as the Hebrew; Destroyer].

> Greek apollýōn (present participle of apollýnai to utterly destroy), equivalent to ap- **ap-**$^2$ + olly- destroy + -ōn present participle suffix.

**9:12** One woe is past; and, behold, there come two woes more hereafter.

Some have speculated that these creatures are symbols of modern war machines. There is a serious problem with that idea. War machines kill, these creatures do not (Rev 9:6).

**The Sixth Trumpet**
**The Second Woe**

**9:13** And the sixth angel sounded, and I heard a voice from the four horns of the golden altar which is before God, **9:14** Saying to the sixth angel which had the trumpet, Loose the four angels which are bound in the great river Euphrates.

Now comes the third year of the 3 1/2 years, when God begins to deliver his people.

**Revelation 9:15** And the four angels were loosed, which were prepared **for an hour, and a day, and a month, and a year, for to slay the third part of men. 9:16** And the number of the army of the horsemen were two hundred thousand thousand: and I heard the number of them.

By adding five months to the day, month and year of the Asian war, we see that the release of demons at the sounding of the fifth trumpet takes place approximately 18 months before the coming of Christ or about 24 months after the initial occupation of Jerusalem.

> The term "two hundred thousand thousand" is not an accurate translation. The literal Greek is **Revelation 9:16** and the number of the forces of the horsemen [is] two myriads of myriads, and I heard the number of them. See Young's literal translation. The actual meaning is simply "a vast unspecified number."

This is the time when Europe will become fearful at rumors from Asia and shall launch a first strike attack; after which Asia will respond with a huge attack overwhelming Europe and the Middle East, and then gather for the final battle against the false prophet and beast taking refuge in Jerusalem.

**Daniel 11:44** But tidings out of the east and out of the north shall trouble him: therefore he shall go forth with great fury to destroy, and utterly to make away many. **11:45** And he shall plant the tabernacles of his palace between the seas in the glorious holy mountain [when Europe is devastated he shall go to Jerusalem (Dan 11:40) along with the false prophet]; yet he shall come to his end [Jesus Christ will then come to destroy them, along with the attacking armies of Asia; and he will deliver Jerusalem, all Israel and all humanity and establish the Kingdom of God over all the earth.], and none shall help him.

All of these seven trumpets will take about 18 months to sound: They are NOT all sounded on the same day!

**Revelation 9:17** And thus I saw the [armies of Asia, and this time the reference is to physical armies] horses in the vision, and them that sat on them, having breastplates of fire, and of jacinth, and brimstone: and the heads of the horses were as the heads of lions; and out of their mouths issued fire and smoke and brimstone [this is a clear reference to modern military machines and the burnt cordite of gun and rocket fire].

One third of humanity will be killed in this massive thirteen month European / Asian war which will also overwhelm the Middle East.

**9:18** By these three was **the third part of men killed, by the fire, and by the smoke, and by the brimstone** [gun and rocket fire and aerial bombs], which issued out of their mouths [out of the muzzles of their weapons]. **9:19** For their power is in their mouth [Firing like modern weaponry, which can fire both to the front and to the rear.], and in their tails: for their tails were like unto serpents, and had heads, and with them they do hurt.

At this point in time neither the Gentiles nor Israel are truly repentant of their wickedness; and while Israel begins to seek deliverance from God, for the most part they are still not repentant of their wickedness just yet.

**9:20** And the rest of the men which were not killed by these plagues yet repented not of the works of their hands, that they should not worship devils, and idols of gold, and silver, and brass, and stone, and of wood: which neither can see, nor hear, nor walk: **9:21** Neither repented they of their murders, nor of their sorceries, nor of their fornication [yes physically, but also their spiritual disloyalty to God], nor of their thefts.

Five months after the restrained fallen angels are released, the New Europe attack Asia and Asia will respond to the European attack on them in the third year after the occupation of Jerusalem begins.

One third of mankind will be killed over a year, a month and a day (Rev 9:15) during this conflict; at the end of which an Asian army will mass at Har Megiddo for the final battle against the European power (Babylon Zec 14) occupying Jerusalem (Rev 11:2).

The resurrection to spirit of the dead in Christ will take place when the seventh angel begins to sound his trumpet (Rev 10). Then Christ will come to gather up his elect and take them to the Marriage of the Lamb in heaven (Rev 15, 19, Rev 7:9)

Then a few days later after the seven last plagues have been poured out, Christ will come WITH his saints to destroy the massed armies and to gather up and arrest Satan and his demons from around the earth, finally establishing God the Father's Kingdom over all the earth on the Feast of Pentecost!

Therefore the resurrection will come first and then be followed by a short time period when the armies mass at Megiddo for the final battle and the seven last plagues are poured out; while the Marriage of the Lamb takes place in heaven.

After this very short period of the heavenly marriage feast, Jesus Christ will return WITH his saints to intervene and take control; and then establish the Kingdom of God over all the earth as per Zechariah 14 and Joel 2:28; on the Feast of Pentecost!

The Kingdom will be established on Pentecost; the actual battle of Zechariah 14 may begin some days before Pentecost.

It is AFTER the resurrection [at end of the sixth day of Unleavened Bread] and during the short period up until Pentecost, that the seven last plagues will be poured out on the earth.

Since Jerusalem will be occupied for 42 months and the New Europe will have power to make war for 42 months, this "Time of Jacob's Trouble" will end when these armies are defeated, the demons gathered up to prison and the political and religious leaders are thrown into the lake of fire.

> **Revelation 19:20** And the beast [political ruler] was taken, and with him the false prophet that wrought miracles before him, with which he deceived them that had received the mark of the beast, and them

that worshipped his image. **These both were cast alive into a lake of fire burning with brimstone**.

Subtracting the 1260 days from the total 1335 days, during which the final great false prophet will deceive (Dan 12) people, means that the tribulation will begin about 75 days after the abomination is set up doing miracles.

However, Christ could easily come to defeat the armies, Satan and his demons, a few days before Pentecost; followed by a few days of waiting for Pentecost when God's Spirit will be poured out.

Then when the nations have repented and the Feast of Pentecost is fully come, God will pour out his Holy Spirit on all flesh, changing the natures of man and beast (Joel 2:28).

## Revelation 10

**Revelation 10:1** And I saw another mighty angel come down from heaven, clothed with a cloud: and a rainbow was upon his head, and his face was as it were the sun, and his feet as pillars of fire: **10:2** And he had in his hand a **little book open**: and he **set his right foot upon the sea, and his left foot on the earth**, **10:3** And cried with a loud voice, as when a lion roareth: and when he had cried, seven thunders uttered their voices.

A mighty angel descended to the earth and announced the resurrection of the chosen dead in a voice like thunder and then seven thunders also speak. These seven thunders are probably other angels thundering their message, but what they say has been sealed until the actual speaking takes place. If anyone says that he knows what the seven thunders will say; he is speaking falsely.

**10:4** And when the seven thunders had uttered their voices, I was about to write: and I heard a voice from heaven saying unto me, Seal [close up and conceal] up those things which the seven thunders uttered, and write them not.

**10:5** And the angel which I saw stand upon the sea and upon the earth lifted up his hand to heaven, **10:6** And sware by him that liveth for ever and ever, who created heaven, and the things that therein are, and the earth, and the things that therein are, and the sea, and the things which are therein, that there should be time no longer [there will be no more delay]: **10:7** But in the days of the **voice of the seventh angel, when he shall begin to sound**, the mystery of God [the early spring resurrection and the change of God's chosen to spirit] should be finished, as he hath declared to his servants the prophets.

**10:8** And the voice which I heard from heaven spake unto me again, and said, Go and take the little book which is open in the hand of the angel which standeth upon the sea and upon the earth.

John is told to take the little book of Revelation and eat it [internalize it] so that he might then write the book out for himself and send it to all of the Ekklesia of God.

The words of Revelation about the resurrection of the dead in Christ and their coming with Christ to establish a godly kingdom of peace are as sweet as honey; but the fulfillment with all the accompanying sufferings will be very bitter.

**10:9** And I went unto the angel, and said unto him, Give me the little book. And he said unto me, Take it, and eat it up; and it shall make thy belly bitter, but it shall be in thy mouth sweet as honey. **10:10** And I took the little book out of the angel's hand, and ate it up; and it was in my mouth sweet as honey: and as soon as I had eaten it, my belly was bitter.

**10:11** And he said unto me, Thou must prophesy again before many peoples, and nations, and tongues, and kings.

It is when the seventh angel **begins to sound** that the resurrection of the dead and the change of the living in Christ will take place.

> **1 Thessalonians 4:13** But I would not have you to be ignorant, brethren, concerning them which are asleep, that ye sorrow not, even as others which have no hope.
>
> **4:15** For if we believe that Jesus died and rose again, even so them also which sleep in Jesus will God bring with him.
>
> **4:15** For this we say unto you by the word of the Lord, that we which are alive and remain unto the coming of the Lord shall not prevent them which are asleep.
>
> **4:16** For **the Lord himself shall descend from heaven with a shout, with the voice of the archangel, and with the trump of God: and the dead in Christ shall rise first:**

**4:17** Then we which are alive and remain shall be caught up together with them in the clouds, to meet the Lord in the air: and so shall we ever be with the Lord.

**4:18** Wherefore comfort one another with these words.

**1 Corinthians 15:51** Behold, I shew you a mystery; We shall not all sleep, but we shall all be changed, **15:52** In a moment, in the twinkling of an eye, **at the last** [seventh] **trump**: for the trumpet shall sound, and the dead shall be raised incorruptible, and we shall be changed [into spirit]. **15:53** For this corruptible must put on incorruption, and this mortal must put on immortality.

**15:54** So when this corruptible shall have put on incorruption, and this mortal shall have put on immortality, then shall be brought to pass the saying that is written, Death is swallowed up in victory.

As our Beloved comes to take up his collective bride and take them to the Wedding Feast in heaven (Rev 15, 19 and Rev 7:9), the wicked nations will be enraged that those who they hated are being rewarded by God, and on hearing that the time of their judging has come.

Yet very many of Israel who have been warned by God's two servants and the 144,000 will see the power of the Eternal in resurrecting his chosen; and they will then sincerely repent and being totally humbled will at last be ready to accept and to follow Christ the Messiah in living by every Word of God!

After the resurrection the "Seven Last Plagues" will be poured out upon the wicked as the Wedding Feast takes place in heaven.

Then Christ will return WITH his bride to put down all rebellion and wickedness; and the nations of Israel will turn to the Messiah and will rise up to fight the enemies of God and they shall be brought back from their captivity and will yet inherit their land and dwell at peace under the mighty defense of their God.

**Revelation 11:15** And **the seventh angel sounded**; and there were great voices in heaven, saying, The kingdoms of this world are become the kingdoms of our Lord, and of his Christ; and he shall reign for ever and ever.

**11:16** And the four and twenty elders, which sat before God on their seats, fell upon their faces, and worshipped God,

**11:17** Saying, We give thee thanks, O Lord God Almighty, which art, and wast, and art to come; because thou hast taken to thee thy great power, and hast reigned.

**11:18** And **the [unrepentant wicked] nations were angry, and thy wrath is come, and the time of the dead, that they should be judged, and that thou shouldest give reward unto thy servants the prophets, and to the saints, and them that fear thy name, small and great; and shouldest destroy them which destroy the earth.**

**11:19** And the temple of God was opened in heaven, and there was seen in his temple the ark of his testament: and there were lightnings, and voices, and thunderings, and an earthquake, and great hail.

After the chosen are resurrected to spirit, they gather at the crystal paved courtyard of the heavenly Temple before the throne of God the Father for the heavenly marriage of the Lamb; during which time the last seven plagues are poured out on the wicked of the nations who would resist God.

At this point many people of the nations of Israel will be repentant and seeking deliverance from their Messiah.

The armies of Asia will mass outside Jerusalem during the seven last plagues time frame and will attack the false prophet and beast emperor who have moved into that city. The armies of Asia will take half of the city and then Messiah the Christ will come with his chosen to deliver the city Jerusalem.

### The Day of the Lord's coming

The armies of Europe and her allies of Psalm 83 will take Jerusalem at the start of the tribulation and hold it for 42 months.

**Zechariah 14:1** Behold, the day of the Lord cometh, and thy spoil shall be divided in the midst of thee.

**14:2** For I will gather all nations against Jerusalem to battle; and the city [the whole city of Jerusalem shall be trodden down of the Gentiles [the New Federal Europe and the nations of Psalm 83] for 42 months Rev. 11:2] shall be taken, and the houses rifled, and the women ravished; and **half of the city** [half of the Jewish population will be removed from Jerusalem] **shall go forth into captivity, and the residue of the people shall not be cut off from the city.**

Then the armies of Asia will gather outside the city at the end of 42 months and Christ will come with his resurrected chosen and deliver Jerusalem, Judah and Israel!

**14:3 Then shall the Lord go forth, and fight against those nations, as when he fought in the day of battle.**

Christ will come WITH his resurrected chosen (Jude 1:14) and 144,000 of them will stand on the Mount of Olives. Then a great earthquake will split the Mount, and the people, the women and children, will flee the battle.

**14:4** And **his feet shall stand in that day upon the mount of Olives,** which is before Jerusalem on the east, and the mount of Olives shall cleave in the midst thereof toward the east and toward the west, and there shall be a very great valley; and half of the mountain shall remove toward the north, and half of it toward the south.

**14:5** And ye shall flee to the valley of the mountains; for the valley of the mountains shall reach unto Azal [The king's (Uzziah) garden at the base of the southernmost point of the Mount of Olives *Nahal Atzal* (נחל אצל).]: yea, ye shall flee, like as ye fled from before the earthquake in the days of Uzziah king of Judah: and the LORD my God shall come, and all the saints with thee.

This day will be one of dark cloud and the gloominess of battle, and the light of the Eternal shall brighten that night and the day.

**14:6** And it shall come to pass in that day, that the light shall not be clear, nor dark: **14:7** But it shall be one day which shall be known to the LORD, not day, nor night: but it shall come to pass, **that at evening time it shall be light.**

**14:8** And it shall be in that day, that **living waters shall go out from Jerusalem**; half of them toward the former sea, and half of them toward the hinder sea: in summer and in winter shall it be.

These physical waters are a picture of the flowing of the Living Waters of the Holy Spirit from the throne of God in the heavenly Temple down upon all flesh (Joel 2:28).

**Ezekiel 47** Afterward he brought me again unto the door of the house [the Ezekiel Temple]; and, behold, waters issued out from under the threshold of the house eastward: for the forefront of the house stood toward the east, and the waters came down from under from the right side of the house, at the south side of the altar. **Read the whole chapter.**

**Zechariah 14:9** And **the LORD shall be king over all the earth**: in that day shall there be one LORD [all humanity will worship YHVH (the Father and the Son) and there will be no other God worshiped by man in all the earth], and his name one.

**14:10** All the land shall be turned as a plain from Geba to Rimmon south of Jerusalem: and it shall be lifted up [Jerusalem will be lifted up and surrounded by a flat plateau, so that Jerusalem will be exalted above the surrounding land], and inhabited in her place, from Benjamin's gate unto the place of the first gate, unto the corner gate, and from the tower of Hananeel unto the king's winepresses.

**14:11** And **men shall dwell in it, and there shall be no more utter destruction; but Jerusalem shall be safely inhabited.**

The armies of Asia which come up against the army of the New Federal Europe based at Jerusalem will join with the European army to resist Christ (Rev 16:14), and they will both be consumed by Christ at his coming.

**Revelation 14:19** And the angel thrust in his sickle into the earth, and gathered the vine of the earth, and cast it into the great winepress of the wrath of God. **14:20** And the winepress was trodden without [the Asian army will be destroyed outside the city] the city, and blood came out of the winepress, even unto the horse bridles [in pools 3 to 4 feet deep], by the space of a thousand and six hundred furlongs [200 miles].

**Zechariah 14:12** And this shall be the plague wherewith the LORD will smite all the people that have fought against Jerusalem; **Their flesh shall consume away while they stand upon their feet, and their eyes shall consume away in their holes, and their tongue shall consume away in their mouth.**

**14:13** And it shall come to pass in that day, that a great tumult [overwhelming panic and terror] from the LORD shall be among them; and **they shall lay hold every one on the hand of his neighbour, and his hand shall rise up against the hand of his neighbour.**

When God has destroyed the armies of the wicked outside the city, the men of Judah will rise up to fight.

> **14:14** And **Judah also shall fight at Jerusalem;** and the wealth of all the heathen round about shall be gathered together, gold, and silver, and apparel, in great abundance.

Even the animals of the invaders will be destroyed.

> **14:15** And so shall be the plague of the horse, of the mule, of the camel, and of the ass, and of all the beasts that shall be in these tents, as this plague.

Then ALL nations will repent and they will know the Eternal (Joel 2:28).

> **14:16** And it shall come to pass, that **every one that is left of all the nations which came against Jerusalem shall even go up from year to year to worship the King, the LORD of hosts,** and to keep the feast of tabernacles.

All flesh shall observe God's seventh day [Friday sunset to Saturday sunset] Sabbaths and the New Moons.

> **Isaiah 66:23** And it shall come to pass, that **from one new moon to another, and from one sabbath to another, shall all flesh come to worship before me, saith the Lord.**

> **Zechariah 14:17** And it shall be, that whoso will not come up of all the families of the earth unto Jerusalem to worship the King, the LORD of hosts, even upon them shall be no rain.

> **14:18** And if the family of Egypt go not up, and come not, that have no rain; there shall be the plague, wherewith the LORD will smite the heathen that come not up to keep the feast of tabernacles.

Keeping the Sabbath and the New Moons is reckoned with keeping the Feast of Tabernacles! Jesus Christ the King of kings, will require these three things and to live by every Word of God, after he comes!

Why do supposedly converted leaders and brethren reject the sanctity of the Sabbath and High Days buying in restaurants and otherwise polluting God's Holy Sabbath and High Days, and reject the new moons today? Why do they condemn those who are zealous in these things which God obviously wants us to do? Because they are NOT godly men! They make the Word of God of no effect by the false traditions of men!

**14:19** This shall be the punishment of Egypt, and the punishment of all nations that come not up to keep the feast of tabernacles.

**14:20** In that day shall there be upon the bells of the horses, HOLINESS UNTO THE LORD; and the pots in the LORD's house shall be like the bowls before the altar.

The pots shall be holy so that the sacrifice of the peace offerings may be cooked in them, and there shall be peace between mankind and the Eternal God!

**14:21** Yea, every pot in Jerusalem and in Judah shall be holiness unto the LORD of hosts: and all they **that sacrifice shall come and take of them, and seethe therein**: and in that day there shall be no more the Canaanite [The Canaanite was a allegorical type of sin, therefor spiritually this means that no more sin will be tolerated!] in the house of the LORD of hosts.

## Revelation 11; God's Two Witnesses

Revelation 11 is an inset prophecy about God's two witnesses, placed here because they will be resurrected when the seventh trumpet begins to sound. The seventh trumpet is the third woe for humanity because immediately after the resurrection - while the faithful are at the wedding feast in heaven - the seven last plagues will be poured out as part of the seventh trumpet on the earth.

In 31 A.D. God officially moved the Shikinah or Holy Spirit from the physical temple to the spiritual temple of his called out faithful.

John is told to measure the temple including the courtyard of the priests where the altar or holy place was, and thereby figuratively measure out and set apart the true faithful called out zealous servants of God.

**Revelation 11:1** And there was given me a reed like unto a rod: and the angel stood, saying, Rise, and measure the temple of God, and the altar, and them that worship [worship God in truth, living by every Word of God] therein.

The city of Jerusalem is not to be measured out or set apart, because it is given over to captivity by the Gentiles for 42 months (Rev 11:2).

There is no physical temple today, therefore separating the temple from the city of Jerusalem is speaking metaphorically about dividing and separating the zealous who live by every Word of God from the wicked in the nation including the lukewarm spiritually lax Laodiceans.

Measuring out the courtyard obviously refers to measuring out the people who are called to be priest and stand in the courtyard closest to God and are therefore the closest to God.

In this instance, the temple is separated from the city and is also divided into its courtyards; the Most Holy Place and the Inner Court where only the faithful priests are allowed are called the Temple and they are separated from the Outer Court where those further form God but still calling themselves the people of God congregate.

Those who are close to God and zealously living by every Word of God will be spared and will not be given over to correction by the Gentiles like the wicked and the lukewarm spiritually lax represented by the Outer Court and the city.

The Outer Court of the Temple and the whole city of Jerusalem is to go into great tribulation for 42 months. Since God told Daniel that Prince Titus would stop the daily - which he did by demolishing the temple, and that the temple would remain desolate until Messiah comes; this measuring of the temple is obviously a metaphor for setting apart the spiritually faithful, while the city is occupied for 42 months in our time.

The spiritually lax in today's Ekklesia who do not believe the warnings [Laodicea (Rev 3:16); the people will be judged] will also be severely corrected during that 42 months, so that by afflicting the flesh the spirit might be saved.

Both the city of Jerusalem AND the people who call themselves the people of God today but who are really very far from God (Rev 3:16), will be sternly corrected for a period of 42 months.

**11:2** But the **court which is without the temple** [the outer courtyard of the temple] leave out, and measure it not; for it is given unto the Gentiles: and **the holy city shall they tread under foot forty and two months**.

### The complimentary prophecy is Ezekiel 9

> **Ezekiel 9:1** He cried also in mine ears with a loud voice, saying, Cause them that have charge over the city to draw near, even every man with his destroying weapon in his hand.

**9:2** And, behold, six men came from the way of the higher gate, which lieth toward the north, and every man a slaughter weapon in his hand; and **one man among them was clothed with linen, with a writer's inkhorn by his side**: and they went in, and stood beside the brasen altar.

**9:3** And the glory of the God of Israel was gone up from the cherub, whereupon he was, to the threshold of the house. And **he [God] called to the man clothed with linen, which had the writer's inkhorn by his side;**

**9:4 And the LORD [YHVH] said unto him, Go through the midst of the city, through the midst of Jerusalem, and set a mark upon the foreheads of the men that sigh and that cry** [mourn over all the evil] **for all the abominations that be done in the midst thereof.**

Those who love the righteousness of God and are vexed by the lack of zeal for godliness and the evil in today's Spiritual Ekklesia are Marked Out and Separated Out from the spiritually lax and Spared; while the spiritually lax and sinful are strongly corrected and physically afflicted.

**9:5** And to the others he said in mine hearing **go ye after him through the city, and smite: let not your eye spare, neither have ye pity:**

**9:6 Slay utterly old and young, both maids, and little children, and women: but come not near any man upon whom is the mark; and begin at my sanctuary. Then they began at, Go the ancient men** [The strong correction will begin with the leaders and elders who think themselves wise] **which were before the house.**

**9:7** And he said unto them, Defile the house, and fill the courts with the slain: go ye forth. And they went forth, and slew in the city.

The wicked of this world today, think that God is gone far away and does not see or care what they do. Despite denials, deep down this same attitude is prevalent in today's Ekklesia, who declare that God has placed them in charge to do as they think right. This vile evil attitude is the root cause of their apostasy.

**9:8** And it came to pass, while they were slaying them, and I was left, that I fell upon my face, and cried, and said, Ah Lord GOD! wilt thou destroy all the residue of Israel in thy pouring out of thy fury upon Jerusalem?

**9:9** Then said he unto me, The iniquity of the house of Israel and Judah is exceeding great, and the land is full of blood, and the city full of perverseness: for they say, **The LORD hath forsaken the earth, and the LORD seeth not.**

This is the LORD of Moses speaking, and we know that this was the very Being who became Jesus Christ [Hebrew: Yeshua Mashiach]. All of the false teachers who claim that Jesus will tolerate sin, will be made to eat their wicked words in the furnace of correction.

**9:10** And as for me [Jesus Christ speaking] also, **mine eye shall not spare, neither will I have pity, but I will recompense their way upon their head.**

The writer did as he was commanded and marked out those who loved the righteousness of God and were full of zeal for the Word of God, and who were sorrowed by all the evil in the world and in today's Spiritual Ekklesia; marking them so that they could be spared when correction comes to the earth over the last 42 months before Christ comes.

**9:11** And, behold, the man clothed with linen, which had the inkhorn by his side, reported the matter, saying, I have done as thou hast commanded me.

God will send his two Servants who will witness that the Eternal is God and beside Him there is NO other (Deu 4:35, 4:39); teaching zeal for the whole Word of God against all of the evil in the world and in today's Ekklesia.

Clothed in sackcloth refers to an attitude of humility before God and mourning over all the evils in the world, just as others were marked out for mourning over all the evils in the world and in the Ekklesia today.

**God's Two Witnesses**

**Revelation 11:3** And I will give power unto my two witnesses, and they shall prophesy a thousand two hundred and threescore days, clothed in sackcloth.

The olive tree produces olive oil which is then burned in the menorah lamp stand, giving light. This is analogous of the Holy Spirit bringing a burning zeal for godliness in a person, thereby producing the works of faith and godly righteousness that make that person a Shining Light of example to others.

Today the Holy Spirit has been quenched by most brethren in the assemblies of the called out, and their light is flickering out.

God is sending his Two Servants to revive the dying Ekklesia and fill them with the oil of God's Spirit by calling the brethren to sincere repentance.

**11:4** These are the two olive trees, and the two candlesticks standing before the God of the earth.

This is a reference to:

**Zechariah 4:11**

> **4:11** Then answered I, and said unto him, What are these two olive trees upon the right side of the candlestick and upon the left side thereof?
>
> **4:12** And I answered again, and said unto him, What be these two olive branches which through the two golden pipes empty the golden oil out of themselves [into the seven branched lamp stand of the Ekklesia]?
>
> **4:13** And he answered me and said, Knowest thou not what these be? And I said, No, my lord.
>
> **4:14** Then said he, These are the two anointed ones, that stand by the LORD of the whole earth.

**Revelation 11:5** And if any man will hurt them, **fire proceedeth out of their mouth, and devoureth their enemies: and if any man will hurt them, he must in this manner be killed.**

This means that they can command fire in self-defense, it does not mean that they literally breath fire. They will have great power, but of course they like Moses and Elijah, would not think of exercising such power on their own whims; rather like Moses and Elijah they will do as God commands them to do.

**11:6** These have power to shut heaven, that it rain not in the days of their prophecy: and have power over waters to turn them to blood, and to smite the earth with all plagues, as often as they will.

**11:7** And when they shall have finished their testimony, the beast that ascendeth out of the bottomless pit [regardless of the person who kills them, the deed is ultimately done by Satan] shall make war against them, and shall overcome them, and kill them.

**11:8** And their dead bodies shall lie in the street of the great city, which spiritually is called Sodom and Egypt [Jerusalem], where also our Lord was crucified.

Humanity, not believing their message and seeing them as tormentors, will greatly rejoice over their death; and by the apparent victory of the false prophet over these two the nations will see the false prophet as the true man of God and think these two to be false prophets.

**11:9** And they of the people and kindreds and tongues and nations shall see their dead bodies three days and an half, and shall not suffer their dead bodies to be put in graves.

**11:10** And they that dwell upon the earth shall rejoice over them, and make merry, and shall send gifts one to another; because these two prophets tormented them that dwelt on the earth.

These two would have proclaimed that they would die and after 3 1/2 days they would be resurrected and ascend into heaven. Perhaps it is because of that prediction that the people will not let them be buried, desiring to see if their prediction comes to pass.

**11:11** And after three days and an half [as the seventh trumpet begins to sound, the faithful chosen dead - including these two - will be resurrected to spirit] the spirit of life from God entered into them, and they stood upon their feet; and great fear fell upon them which saw them.

**11:12** And **they heard a great voice from heaven saying unto them, Come up hither. And they ascended up to heaven in a cloud; and their enemies beheld them.**

At this amazing sign many people of Judah in Jerusalem and many others across the world especially in the nations of Israel who see the 144,000 and many others changed to spirit and rising up to heaven; will sincerely repent and glorify God.

Then over the following days the armies of Asia and the European beast emperor may decide to join forces against Christ (Rev 16:14), who Satan knows will come with his resurrected bride just a few days later, after the wedding feast in heaven.

**11:13** And the same hour was there a great earthquake, and the tenth part of the city fell, and in the earthquake were slain of men seven thousand: and **the remnant** [of Judah and Israel in particular, since the armies of the wicked will still fight Christ at his coming to rule] **were affrighted, and gave glory to the God of heaven.**

**11:14** The second woe is past; and, behold, the third woe cometh quickly.

The resurrection of the chosen at the beginning of the sounding of the seventh trumpet which ushers in the seven last plagues is the third great woe.

The resurrection of the chosen at sounding of the seventh trumpet which ushers in the seven last plagues is the third great woe for the forces of evil among humanity.

The resurrection of the chosen at sounding of the seventh trumpet which ushers in the seven last plagues is the third great woe for the forces of evil among humanity.

As the seventh angel begins to blast his trumpet and the resurrection takes place, it is Judah/Israel who begins to repent and turn to God.

Because of the calling of God, the sign of Christ in the heavens, the preaching of God's two servants and the personal witness of the 144,000 during the Trumpet Plagues, Israel will turn to God when they see the reality of the resurrection to spirit and the Power of God to deliver His faithful!

Nevertheless, the wicked leaders of the nations will be angry because they finally see that are in grave jeopardy of losing their authority over the nations, and they will turn and prepare to fight Christ and his chosen when they return.

This has very much to do with the rulers of the nations at that time not wanting to give their offices and positions up; just as in the first century it was the rulers who saw Jesus as a personal threat to their power and crucified him.

**11:15** And the seventh angel sounded; and there were great voices in heaven, saying, The kingdoms of this world are become the kingdoms of our Lord, and of his Christ; and he shall reign for ever and ever.

**11:16** And the four and twenty elders, which sat before God on their seats, fell upon their faces, and worshipped God,

**11:17** Saying, We give thee thanks, O LORD God Almighty, which art, and wast, and art to come; because thou hast taken to thee thy great power, and hast reigned.

**11:18** And **the nations were angry, and thy wrath is come, and the time of the dead, that they should be judged, and that thou shouldest give reward unto thy servants the prophets, and to the saints, and them**

that fear thy name, small and great; and shouldest destroy them which destroy the earth.

At the resurrection of the chosen, the Temple of God is heaven is opened and the saints stand on the crystal pavement of the Inner Courtyard before the Most Holy Throne of God the Father for the Marriage of the Lamb.

**11:19** And the temple of God was opened in heaven, and there was seen in his temple the ark of his testament: and there were lightnings, and voices, and thunderings, and an earthquake, and great hail.


## Sackcloth

**Revelation 11:3** And I will give power unto my two witnesses, and they shall prophesy a thousand two hundred and threescore days, clothed in sackcloth.

### Strong's Exhaustive Concordance
sackcloth - sakkos (Strong's # 4526). Of Hebrew origin (saq); "sack"-cloth, i.e. Mohair (the material or garments made of it, worn as a sign of grief) – sackcloth. see HEBREW saq

Sackcloth, saq (Strong's # 8242) From shaqaq; properly, a mesh (as allowing a liquid to run through), i.e. Coarse loose cloth or sacking (used in mourning and for bagging); hence, a bag (for grain, etc.) -- sack(-cloth, -clothes).

### Thayer's Greek Lexicon
STRONGS NT 4526: σάκκος (Attic σάκος), σάκκου, ὁ, Hebrew שַׂק (cf. Fremdwörter, under the word), a sack (Latinsaccus) i. e.
a. a receptacle made for holding or carrying various things, as money, food, etc. (Leviticus 11:32).
b. a coarse cloth (Latincilicium), a dark coarse stuff made especially of the hair of animals (A. V. sackcloth): Revelation 6:12; a garment of the like material, and clinging to the person like a sack, which was usually worn (or drawn on over the tunic instead of the cloak or mantle) by mourners, penitents, suppliants, Matthew 11:21; Luke 10:13, and also by those who, like the Hebrew prophets, led an austere life, Revelation 11:3 (cf. what is said of the dress of John the Baptist, Matthew 3:4; of Elijah, 2 Kings 1:8). More fully in Winers RWB under the word Sack; Roskoff in Schenkel 5:134; (under the word in B. D.; also in McClintock and Strong. (From Herodotus down.))

**Jewish Encyclopedia SACKCLOTH (Hebrew, "saḳ") definition**
By: Joseph Jacobs, Wilhelm Nowack

A term originally denoting a coarsely woven fabric, usually made of goat's hair. It afterward came to mean also a garment made from such cloth, which was chiefly worn as a token of mourning by the Israelites. It was furthermore a sign of submission (I Kings xx. 30 et seq.), and was occasionally worn by the Prophets.

Sackcloth and ashes were used in Old Testament times as a symbol of humility, mourning, and/or repentance. Someone expressing deep repentance and mourning over his sins would often wear sackcloth, sit in ashes and put ashes on the head.

When someone died, the act of putting on sackcloth showed heartfelt sorrow for the loss of that person. We see an example of this when David mourned the death of Abner, the commander of Saul's army (2 Samuel 3:31). Jacob also demonstrated his grief by wearing sackcloth when he thought his son, Joseph, has been killed (Genesis 37:34). These instances of mourning for the dead mention sackcloth but not ashes.

Ashes accompanied sackcloth in times of national disaster or repenting from sin. Esther 4:1, for instance, describes Mordecai tearing his clothes, putting on sackcloth and ashes, and walking out into the city "wailing loudly and bitterly." This was Mordecai's reaction to King Xerxes' declaration giving the wicked Haman authority to destroy the Jews (Esther 3:8–15). Mordecai was not the only one who grieved. "In every province to which the edict and order of the king came, there was great mourning among the Jews, with fasting, weeping, and wailing. Many lay in sackcloth and ashes" (Esther 4:3). The Jews responded to the devastating news concerning their race with sackcloth and ashes, showing their intense grief and distress, but even more their repentance before God and calling on God, relying on God's deliverance.

Sackcloth and ashes were used as a public sign of repentance and humility before God.

When Jonah declared to the people of Nineveh that God was going to destroy them for their wickedness, everyone from the king on down responded with repentance, fasting, and sackcloth and ashes (Jonah 3:5–7). They even put sackcloth on their animals (verse 8). Their reasoning was, "Who knows? God may yet relent and with compassion turn from his fierce anger so that we will not perish" (verse 9). It is clear that the Ninevites' donning of sackcloth and ashes was not a meaningless show.

God saw genuine change—a humble change of heart represented by the sackcloth and ashes—and it caused Him to "relent" and not bring about His plan to destroy them (Jonah 3:10).

Other people in the Bible mentioned as wearing sackcloth include King Hezekiah (Isaiah 37:1), Eliakim (2 Kings 19:2), King Ahab (1 Kings 21:27), the elders of Jerusalem (Lamentations 2:10), Daniel (Daniel 9:3), and the two witness in Revelation 11:3.

Very simply, sackcloth and ashes were used as an outward sign of one's inward condition of humility before God and mourning over sin in deep repentance.

Such a symbol reflected the innermost feelings and thoughts. It was not the act of putting on sackcloth and ashes itself that moved God to intervene, but the humility that such an action demonstrated (see 1 Samuel 16:7). God's forgiveness in response to genuine repentance is celebrated by David's words: "You removed my sackcloth and clothed me with joy" (Psalm 30:11).

### KJV Dictionary Definition: mourn

MOURN, v.i. L. maereo.
1. To express grief or sorrow; to grieve; to be sorrowful. Mourning may be expressed by weeping or audible sounds, or by sobs, sighs or inward silent grief.
Abraham came to mourn for Sarah and to weep (Gen.23).
Blessed are they that mourn, for they shall be comforted (Mat.5).

MOURN, v.t. To grieve for; to lament over.

### KJV Dictionary Definition: humility

HUMILITY, n. L. humilitas.
1. In ethics, freedom from pride and arrogance; humbleness of mind; a modest estimate of one's own worth.

In theology, humility consists in lowliness of mind; a deep sense of one's own unworthiness in the sight of God, self-abasement, penitence for sin, and submission to the divine will.
Before honor is humility (Prov.15).

Serving the Lord with all humility of mind (Acts.20).

**KJV Dictionary Definition: repent**

RE'PENT, to creep, fall down before, submit to.

REPENTANCE, n.
1. Sorrow for any thing done or said; the pain or grief which a person experiences in consequence of the injury or inconvenience produced by his own conduct.
2. The pain, regret or affliction which a person feels on account of his past conduct. This sorrow proceeding merely from the fear of punishment, is called legal repentance, as being excited by the terrors of legal penalties, and it may exist without an amendment of life.
3. Theologically real penitence; sorrow or deep contrition for sin, as an offense and dishonor to God, a violation of his holy law. This is genuine repentance, and is accompanied and followed by a lifelong change of conduct.

Repentance is a change of mind resulting in a change of conduct, or a conversion from sin to godliness.

Godly sorrow worketh repentance to salvation. (2 Cor 7, Mat 3). Repentance is the relinquishment of any practice, that is offensive to God and a genuine change of attitude and conduct towards living more godly life.

The reference to God's Two Witnesses being clothed in sackcloth is a metaphor for being clothed in humility and submissiveness to God, while mourning over the wickedness and sin in the Ekklesia and in the world.

## Revelation 12

The 70 Weeks Prophecy answers the vital questions: Will there be 42 months from a Mideast peace deal until the great tribulation begins? Will a temple or tabernacle be built in Jerusalem? Will the daily sacrifice start again only to be stopped?

The great tribulation is at the door, it could come as soon as late 2020 or within a few years after that; the books of the prophets are being unsealed as God promised Daniel (Dan 12).

Very important decisions are approaching and it is imperative that we know the answers to these key questions!

Revelation 12 is the explanation of Daniel's Seventy Week Prophecy

**Revelation 12:1** And there appeared a great wonder in heaven; a woman clothed with the sun, and the moon under her feet, and upon her head a crown of twelve stars:

**12:2** And she being with child cried, travailing in birth, and pained to be delivered.

This speaks of the mother of Christ, as a type of the called out faithful Ekklesia.

**12:3** And there appeared another wonder in heaven; and behold **a great red dragon, having seven heads and ten horns, and seven crowns upon his heads.**

This is Satan, and the later satanic system on the earth is described as the scarlet beast; Scarlet being the color of the blood of the saints that have been shed by this beast.

**12:4** And **his tail drew the third part of the stars** [when Satan rebelled against God one third of the angels followed him] **of heaven, and did cast them to the earth**: and the dragon stood before the woman which was ready to be delivered, for to devour her child [Jesus Christ] as soon as it was born.

Satan at his original fall, led a third of the angels with him in rebellion against God, and as Jesus [Hebrew: Yeshua] was about to be born, Satan stood up to destroy him.

**12:5** And she brought forth **a man child, who was to rule all nations with a rod of iron**: and her **child** [died for the sins of humanity and was then resurrected and has risen to God the Father in heaven] **was caught up unto God, and to his throne**.

The child being spoken of, is identified as Christ the Messiah; for ONLY Jesus Christ has been resurrected to spirit and has so far been "caught up to God, ascending to God the Father's throne.

Now we come to the first half of the 70th week; the first 3 1/2 year flight of the faithful, which was to Pella; NOT Petra!

**12:6** And the woman fled into the wilderness, where she hath a place prepared of God, that they should feed her there a **thousand two hundred and threescore days** [1,260 days, or 42 months].

This was the first one half of the 70th Week, for 1,260 days, is 42 months or one half of seven years, the 70th Week, being 7 years, or 2520 days.

This was fulfilled when the saints fled from Jerusalem to Pella in Moab when the Romans besieged the Jerusalem c 66-70 AD.

NOTICE that at an unspecified time AFTER that; there was war in heaven. This is clearly at the end time, for it begins at the point immediately preceding the tribulation.

**12:7** And **there was war in heaven: Michael and his angels fought against the dragon; and the dragon fought and his angels,**

This is after the first half of the week has passed, and much later just before the second half of the 70th week begins.

**12:8** And prevailed not; neither was their place found any more in heaven.

**12:9** And the great dragon was cast out, that old serpent, called the Devil, and Satan, which deceiveth the whole world: he was cast out into the earth, and his angels were cast out with him.

Daniel 12:1 tells us that Michael will stand up to fight against Satan - when Satan rises up to attack God - and Michael casts Satan and his demons down to the earth, which will be right before the beginning of the tribulation.

> **Daniel 12:1** And at that time shall Michael stand up, the great prince which standeth for the children of thy people: and **there shall be a time of trouble, such as never was since there was a nation even to that same time: and at that time thy people shall be delivered, every one that shall be found written in the book.**

Knowing that his imprisonment is near at hand, Satan rises up to attack God one more time and is defeated and thrown down again.

**Revelation 12:10** And I heard a loud voice saying in heaven, Now is come salvation, and strength, and the kingdom of our God, and the power of his Christ: for the accuser of our brethren is cast down, which accused them before our God day and night.

**12:11** And they overcame him by the blood of the Lamb, and by the word of their testimony; and they loved not their lives unto the death.

**12:12** Therefore rejoice, ye heavens, and ye that dwell in them. **Woe to the inhabiters of the earth and of the sea! for the devil is come down unto you, having great wrath, because he knoweth that he hath but a short time** [there will be only 3 1/2 years remaining].

All converted faithful believers are to rejoice and to hold their heads up, as they see the imminence of the resurrection to eternal life and the Marriage to the Lamb of God!

> **Luke 21:28** And when these things begin to come to pass, then look up, and lift up your heads; for your redemption draweth nigh.

**Revelation 12:13** And when the dragon saw that he was cast unto the earth, he persecuted the woman which brought forth the man child.

Obviously Mary could not have lived into the end time; therefore the woman is the Spiritual Ekklesia, the body of faithful believers and doers of the Word and Will of God.

Satan through his human instruments, works to destroy all who will not bow to him.

To enforce his will, Satan will fully empower the abomination, setting up the miracle working false prophet in the Vatican, who will then call for the nations to join a New Federal Europe, who's leader is also called a "beast."

This abomination [false prophet, son of perdition] will then go to the Holy Place to trigger the war, close to or before 75 days AFTER he is set up doing miracles in Rome. Then the woman [the Faithful Ekklesia] will flee to Pella for the SECOND time!

**12:14** And to the woman were given two wings of a great eagle, that she might fly into the wilderness, into her place [for the SECOND time, this time immediately BEFORE the second half of the 70th Week], where she is **nourished for a time, and times, and half a time**, from the face of the serpent.

The time, times and half a time of the Times of the Gentiles is equal to 3 1/2 years, or 1,260 days, or 42 months, or the second half of the 70th Week!

The "Great Eagle" is God, to whom the zealous saints are faithful; and the two wings that are given to the saints which take them to the place prepared [probably the same place as the first time: Pella]: Are the Two Prophets sent by God! These two servants will see that the faithful to the place that God has prepared and will then prepare the world for the coming of Christ.

**12:15** And the serpent cast out of his mouth water as a flood after the woman, that he might cause her to be carried away of the flood. **12:16** And the earth helped the woman, and the earth opened her mouth, and swallowed up the flood which the dragon cast out of his mouth.

When the faithful arrive in Moab [Jordan], Satan will inspire the Jordanians to chase and attack them since Jordan will ally with the New Europe (Psalm 83).

The flood is the pursuing army, and God will cause an earthquake to destroy them.

Then Satan will turn back to attack the majority of the Ekklesia who have initially not believed the warnings; many of whom, after this tribulation begins, will then remember and believe and sincerely repent.

**12:17** And the dragon was wroth with the woman, and went to make war with the remnant of her seed, which keep the commandments [at least make a pretense of keeping] of God, and have the testimony of Jesus Christ.

At the moment that the faithful escape, Satan will turn to attack Jerusalem and Judea, and he will attack those who repent of making a mere show of keeping the commandments while being lukewarm for the things of God and idolizing men above the sovereignty of God.

While Judea will be occupied, attacks on the other Israelite nations could be in other forms like cyber or economic attacks and might not involve occupation at all.

Jesus Christ will protect and nourish his people who are faithful to God in the place which God has prepared for them! He did this for the first 1/2 week after his resurrection; and he will do this for the SECOND 1/2 week at this end time!

**The two halves complete one full week; the 70th week of the prophecy!**

Where in the scripture is the nourishment, protection and caring for those who zealously live by every Word of God mentioned, in the context of two halves of a week?

Remember that one half of a week is three and one half days, which is three and one half years, or forty two months, or 1260 days.

The explanation of the 70th Week of Daniel is found in the twelfth chapter of Revelation!

A woman clothed with the sun (the brightness of the LIGHT), and the moon under her feet (the darkness of spiritual ignorance underneath her feet) and wearing a crown of twelve stars (a Queen) brought forth a man child who was to rule all nations (Jesus Christ).

She - the faithful Ekklesia - fled into the wilderness where she was fed (nourished) by God for 1260 days [1/2 week = 3 1/2 days = 3 1/2 years = 1,260 days].

Later there will be war in heaven and Satan will be cast out triggering a great time of trouble in the later days (Dan 12:1) and Satan will go to persecute that same woman [the faithful Ekklesia], who will again be taken

"INTO HER PLACE", where she will again be nourished for a time, times and half a time; the times of the Gentiles (Dan 12:7), or 1260 days.

The woman is the faithful Ekklesia who KEEP THE COMMANDMENTS of God, HAVING THE LAW OF GOD WRITTEN IN THEIR HEARTS (Heb 8:10). And the nourishing for these two halves of the week; is the confirming of the Husband's part of the New Covenant by Jesus Christ!

In history, the saints fled from Jerusalem and Judea to Pella in modern Jordan about 66 - 67 A.D. after receiving a supernatural warning. This began the first half of the week, as Jesus Christ preserved His people, His bride.

This was just before the city of Jerusalem was besieged and destroyed in the Jewish-Roman wars. See: Josephus, Wars of the Jews, the fall of Jerusalem. The city was surrounded in 66 A.D. and then Vespasian was recalled to Rome after the suicide of Nero. the siege was slightly relaxed and a voice was heard in the temple declaring: "let us remove hence". The saints then fled to Pella in what is now Jordan.

The saints of God are now about to once again be taken to their place of nourishment before the fall of Jerusalem and the collapse of the nations of Israel.

The Daily Sacrifice ended with the destruction of Jerusalem and the temple by Prince Titus at the end of the first half of the week after a 42 month siege, during which God's faithful were preserved for the first half of the 70th week in Pella. After that destruction in 70 A.D. the temple and Daily Sacrifice were to remain desolate until Messiah comes to build the Ezekiel Temple.

During this time, those of God's people who respond to the warning and live by every Word of God; will be cared for in the place which God has prepared on the earth. No, there will not be some "Rapture" to heaven!

Our Lord WILL NOT destroy the righteous along with the guilty. He WILL NOT destroy those who LOVE HIM and zealously KEEP HIS WORD along with those who reject any zeal to live by every Word of God.

Just as God delivered Lot from the destruction of Sodom and as He delivered Noah from death, so will He deliver His beloved faithful from the evil to come.

Exalt the sovereignty of Almighty God above ALL else; Seek the LORD your God with all your hearts, and he will deliver you.

The God who later gave up his God-hood to become flesh as Jesus Christ is a RIGHTEOUS GOD, who KEEPS HIS COVENANTS; He will fulfill His role as a loving Husband to a faithful wife.

Yes, Jesus Christ loves his bride as only He can LOVE; therefore, fear not and hold your head up, you who live by every Word of God for your redemption draws nigh (Luk 21:28) .

Be strong and have courage, be zealous for our Mighty God: Both the Father and the Son!

Be filled with faith and courage, deliverance is at hand! This world is ready to give birth to a New Age of Righteousness!

And finally: What place? The phrase; "her place" (Rev 12:14) appears to indicate that she will return to the same special place that she went to the first time. It is quite probably in Moab (Isaiah 16:4, Dan 11:41).

God will reveal this in due time, when He sends the two eagles wings (empowers His two prophets) to deliver His zealously faithful people into their place (Rev 12:14, Rev 11:3-13). As the faithful were spared and protected by their espoused Husband Jesus Christ during the fall of Jerusalem in the first century A.D. they shall be preserved a second time in the 21st century.

**These two periods of 3 1/2 years each, total the full seven years of the last 70th week of the prophecy.**

Yes; He, Jesus Christ will confirm His New Marriage Covenant with His loyal espoused Bride for a full week!

The first 42 month half of the week have ALREADY been fulfilled; and the second 42 month half of the week which begins with the taking of Jerusalem in the latter days (Rev 13:5, Rev 11:2, Luk 21:24 and Rev 12:6,) will also be fulfilled!

When ALL the Biblical signs are present; and when the final false prophet goes to the Holy Mount and Peace and Safety are being declared: sudden destruction will come upon a stubborn and rebellious people (1 Thess 5:3).

Many lukewarm people in the faith who have lost their zeal for living by every Word of God and have fallen into a lukewarm complacency, will lack the oil of God's Spirit to respond to the warnings; and will become the victims of strong delusion.

Preferring to lean on their false traditions instead of standing on the Word of God; they will fall into the correction of great tribulation.

### Daniel 9:24-27  The 70th Week Prophecy

There are those who believe that the full 70th week of Daniel 9 is still to come with a period of 3 1/2 years after a peace deal in the Middle East before the tribulation begins.

There are a variety of explanations concerning the Seventieth or Last Week, of the Seventy Weeks Prophecy. Most of which have been around for a long time and were first put forth as a part of the Protestant Reformation. We know that these explanations cannot be true because the understanding of these things has been sealed until the last days.

**Daniel 12:9**  And he said, Go thy way, Daniel: for **the words are closed up and sealed till the time of the end.**

A common explanation of the seventieth week put out by certain folks, is that the False Prophet will make a peace deal with Judah, possibly allowing them to build a temple or set up a tabernacle and start sacrifices.

Then after 3 1/2 years that peace covenant will be broken, the sacrifices stopped and the tribulation will begin and last for a second 3 1/2 years. This explanation gives rise to the theory that a temple, or at least some kind of tabernacle must be built and physical sacrifices must start.

We KNOW that this explanation CANNOT BE TRUE for the scripture says that when "Peace and Safety" is declared; SUDDEN, IMMEDIATE, AT THAT TIME; destruction will come: 1 Thes 5:3. There will be NO 3 1/2 years of peace!

Jesus Christ said that when the abomination spoken of by Daniel goes to the Holy Place; sudden, immediate great tribulation will begin (Mat 24:15).

Daniel tells us that his prophetic words are SEALED UNTIL THE END (Dan 12:9). This means that explanations written many years ago: CANNOT BE CORRECT.

### The seventieth week of the prophecy is found in Daniel 9:24-27.

Each week is seven days; so seven weeks is forty nine days and sixty two weeks is four hundred and thirty four days.

Each day representing one year, therefore the city would be built in forty nine years, then Messiah would come after another four hundred and thirty four years. Indicating that Messiah would come four hundred and eighty three years after the commandment to rebuild the city was issued.

Then at an unspecified point after the four hundred and eighty three years, Messiah would be cut off, but not for Himself: and then after Christ's death, resurrection and ascension, came the fist half of the 70th week when the Ekklesia fled to Pella and the first century destruction of Jerusalem and the temple by Titus stopped the daily sacrifice after a 42 month siege and BEFORE the second 42 months of tribulation.

**Daniel 9:24** Seventy weeks are determined upon thy people and upon thy holy city, to finish the transgression, and to make an end of sins, and to make reconciliation for iniquity, and to bring in everlasting righteousness, and to seal up the vision and prophecy, and to anoint the most Holy.

In the first century reconciliation was offered to only a very few and transgressions have not yet been finished on this earth, nor yet in Judah, nor has sin been ended. It is when He shall return that Messiah shall be Anointed King over all the earth and will put an end to all wickedness.


**Titus and the first Roman destruction of Jerusalem ending the Daily**

**Daniel 9:25** And the people of the prince that shall come shall destroy the city and the sanctuary: and the end thereof shall be with a flood, and unto the end of the war desolations are determined.

And He [Messiah] shall CONFIRM A COVENANT [the New Covenant] for one week [seven years]:

The prophecy now addresses the siege of Jerusalem by Prince Titus

. . . and in the midst of the week [at the end of the first 3 1/2 years, after a 42 month siege during which the Ekklesia had fled to Pella]; He [The Roman Prince Titus besieged Jerusalem and after 42 months the city fell and the temple was burned stopping the daily sacrifice.] shall cause the sacrifice and oblation to cease and for the overspreading of abominations He shall make it desolate [This was fulfilled at the end of the first half of the week when God allowed Prince Titus to destroy the temple.], even until the consummation [The temple would remain destroyed and the daily sacrifice stopped until the end of the age and the completion of the seventy weeks, when Christ comes to build the Ezekiel Temple!], and that determined shall be poured upon the desolator [the final abomination will be destroyed at the coming of Messiah, Daniel 9:27].

At that time, the New Covenant of espousal between Jesus Christ and the called out was confirmed for the first half of the 70th week when the Ekklesia fled to Pella about c 66 A.D., to be preserved from the destruction of the Roman war against Jerusalem! This fulfilled the first 3 1/2 years or the first half of the 70th week, as I shall presently show!

Once the Romans had destroyed the temple and ended the Daily Sacrifice; at the END of three and a half years of war [in the midst of the week of seven years]; it is prophesied that **the temple will not be rebuilt, and that the Daily Sacrifice will not be renewed and not resume; until the end of the second half of the week and the coming of Messiah:** Until the consummation, or end, of the 70 weeks!

**The time line of The Seventy Weeks Prophecy**

1) The decree goes out to build the city; Messiah appears and begins his ministry in autumn 27 A.D. 483 years after the command to rebuild the city,

He is cut off 3 1/2 years later and resurrected; only then does the New Covenant officially begin, and verse 27,

2) Jesus Christ confirms the New Covenant with many by taking them and preserving them in Pella during the 42 month siege of Jerusalem for the first half of the 70th week or 3 1/2 years, fulled in years for days!

3) Then after a 3 1/2 year siege, at the end of the first half of the seventieth week and before the second half of the seventieth week, God caused the sacrifice and oblation to cease by allowing Prince Titus to conquer Jerusalem and destroy the city and the temple; stopping the daily sacrifice!

Brethren, the physical daily sacrifice has already been stopped! and it is to remain stopped until the consummation of the end of the 70th week and the coming of Christ!

NOTICE: The seventieth week does NOT BEGIN until after the resurrection of Jesus Christ. It is not until c 66 A.D. that the first half of the seventieth week is confirmed for three and one half years by the protection of the faithful in Pella during the siege of Jerusalem by the

Romans; and it is not until our day that the second half of the 70th week will come, as per Daniel 9.

## What covenant is being talked about?

Why, the New Covenant; which was not made sure until after the sacrifice of Christ was accepted by God the Father on Wave Offering Sunday. The MARRIAGE Covenant of Espousal, of Betrothal; between Jesus Christ and His called out first fruits, His bride; was then made official at Pentecost 31 A.D.

Jesus Christ the espoused Husband, promised to cherish and nurture the bride; and the espoused bride [the sincerely repentant person as part of the collective bride] promises to love, to follow and to faithfully obey Him.

The New Covenant like the Mosaic Covenant is a Marriage Covenant!

Jesus Christ would then confirm His New Covenant with His espoused bride when the city (Jerusalem) was under siege and destroyed after 42 months in circa 70 A.D. (Dan 9:26-27).

In the first century, the faithful fled to Pella in Jordan and remained there for the first 1/2 week (a day for a year; 3 1/2 years) preserved by Jesus Christ from the Roman armies, in a first century fore-type of the final 42 month great tribulation.

This refuge in Pella for 1,260 days, fulfilled the first half of the 70th week

The people of the prince that shall come shall destroy the city and the sanctuary; and the end thereof shall be with a flood, and unto the end of the war desolations are determined (Dan 9:26).

Messiah had no sin and did not die for His own sin, but died for the sins of mankind. AFTER His death and resurrection, Judah rebelled against Rome and was destroyed, Jerusalem falling in c 70 AD. This was a precursor of or a fore-type of; the final great tribulation.

And He [Christ] shall CONFIRM A COVENANT for one week: and in the midst of the week He [Christ] shall cause the sacrifice and oblation to cease and for the overspreading of abominations [Christ shall give the city over to a desolator, the Roman prince Titus; and this will be repeated in the last days with the second half of the week (3 1/2 years)].

The Roman Prince Titus made the temple and the Daily Sacrifice desolate, and it will remain desolate, even until the consummation [the end of the 70th week and the coming of Messiah, and that determined [When the

King of kings comes he will destroy the desolating political leader and his false prophet with their armies.] shall be poured upon the desolator (Dan 9:27).

Notice the time-line. The seventieth week, of seven years; does not begin until after the death and resurrection of Jesus Christ!

Jesus Christ was to appear at the end of the seven plus sixty-two weeks (69 weeks) Dan 9:26, which was in 27 A.D.

There is no way that the ministry of Christ could have fulfilled the first half of the 70th week since this could ONLY be fulfilled AFTER he was "Cut Off," AFTER he was killed and resurrected!

The first half or the 70th week was fulfilled when the faithful fled Jerusalem for Pella in c 66 A.D.

According to the time line and the flow of events, the 70th week could not begin until Messiah had been "Cut Off" and resurrected, rising to be accepted by God the Father on Wave Offering Sunday for us.

ONLY when Christ was accepted as our sacrifice and High Priest, could there be a Covenant to confirm; for the Mosaic Covenant was ended by his death as Husband of Israel, and the New Covenant did not officially begin until Christ was accepted by the Father.

Then He, Jesus Christ, PERSONALLY; not some apostle or disciple, shall confirm a covenant for seven years, or one prophetic week after His resurrection.

The New Covenant could NOT OFFICIALLY BEGIN until Jesus Christ fulfilled His mission and died to pay the penalty for the sins of men. Therefore only after Messiah had died and been resurrected could the New Covenant be confirmed.

ONLY AFTER THE DEATH AND SACRIFICE OF JESUS CHRIST COULD THE NEW COVENANT BE CONFIRMED; the first half of the last seventieth week could not begin until after the death and resurrection of Christ!

Therefore Messiah could not have been confirming a part of the 70th week covenant during His physical earthly ministry; as some wrongly teach.

In the midst of the week, after three and one half years of siege and before the final three and one half years; God caused the daily sacrifice to be stopped by allowing Prince Titus to destroy the temple in c 70 A.D.

As Jerusalem will once again be given over to her enemies (Rev 11:2, Rev 12:6), Jesus Christ will protect the faithful bride once again, for 1/2 week (3 1/2 years) thus confirming the New Covenant of ESPOUSAL with His Bride for the second half of the 70th week.

What covenant is being confirmed? The ONLY covenant mentioned in scripture to exist after the resurrection of Christ; THE NEW COVENANT, between Christ and those called out of season as a kind of first fruits of the NEW COVENANT of Jeremiah 31:31!

What does confirmed mean? To fulfill, to make sure. What is this covenant? A marriage agreement to PROTECT, NOURISH and CARE FOR His espoused bride, those who KEEP HIS COMMANDMENTS!

The true explanation of the whole 70th Week is found in Revelation 12 and Daniel 9.

## Revelation 13

The word "sea" can be a symbol for many peoples; here the meaning is symbolic of a human government system [Babylon the Great] and its political leaders rising up out of many people.

This beast will be discussed at length in Revelation 17. However it is identified as the Holy Roman Empire which began with Justinian and it would have a total of seven revivals. The ten crowns are the final ten kings which will come together in the seventh revival. The name of blasphemy lies in its calling itself "Holy."

This beast is the Holy Roman Empire [Babylonian Mysteries church state system] and its leaders.

**Revelation 13:1** And I stood upon the sand of the sea, and saw a beast rise up out of the sea, having seven heads and ten horns, and upon his horns ten crowns, and upon his heads the name of blasphemy.

The Babylonian Empire was replaced by the Persian Empire which was replaced by the Greek Empire which was replaced by Rome. Rome then developed ito te Holy Roman Empire.

**13:2** And the beast [the whole statue of Daniel 2 system] which I saw was like unto a leopard [Greece], and his feet were as the feet of a bear [Persia], and his mouth as the mouth of a lion [Babylon]: and the dragon [Satan] gave him his power, and his seat, and great authority [power].

**13:3** And I saw one of his heads as it were wounded to death; and his deadly wound was healed: and all the world wondered after the beast.

The sixth revival of the system by Mussolini [he became Holy Roman Emperor with his concordat with the Vatican] was totally destroyed in World War 2, and now in the next few years a miracle working pope will call for another revival of the church state Holy Roman Empire system, and bring it back to life.

The whole world will be amazed at this revival of a New Federal Europe and at its great power; especially after it occupies Judea and Egypt and replaces the Anglo Saxon peoples as the world's great power.

Once America is eclipsed [not necessarily occupied] by this New Europe; the whole world will be awed into exalting it as the world's preeminent power.

**13:4** And they worshipped the dragon which gave power unto the beast: and they worshipped the beast, saying, Who is like unto the beast? who is able to make war with him?

This prophecy of a Holy Roman Empire type government of a now rising New Federal Europe then drifts into speaking of its leader, identified by the usage of the word "him."

This leader will make grand claims as he leads people away from God in the name of peace. This political leader [by whatever title he is given] and the seventh revival of this system, which is the feet of Babylon of Daniel 2 will be destroyed by the huge rock of Jesus Christ at his coming.

**13:5** And there was given unto him a mouth speaking great things and blasphemies; and **power was given unto him to continue** [or to occupy Jerusalem and to make war] **forty and two months.**

This ruler blasphemes God by telling people to obey the religious leader as having the authority of God, in the same way that the leaders of today's Spiritual Ekklesia blaspheme by making the same claim that they have the authority of God, even when they teach and act contrary to scripture.

The power of this Babylonian Mysteries style Holy Roman Empire system will enforce the religious leader as man's ultimate moral authority, and the religion will, in return, use its persuasive powers to enforce the authority of the state.

**13:6** And he opened his mouth in blasphemy against God, to blaspheme his name, and his tabernacle, and them that dwell in heaven.

This system will persecute anyone within its boundaries who does not accept the complete moral authority of the associated religious leader, including anyone who seeks to live by the Word of God: for example those wanting to observe God's Biblical Sabbath rather than the unbiblical Sunday.

**13:7** And it was given unto him to make war with the saints, and to overcome them: and power was given him over all kindreds, and tongues, and nations [for about two years until Europe falls out with Asia].

**13:8** And all that dwell upon the earth shall worship [the word "worship" means to fear and obey, or not to try to resist] him, whose names are not written in the book of life of the Lamb slain from the foundation of the world.

**13:9** If any man have an ear, let him hear.

**13:10** He that leadeth into captivity shall go into captivity: he that killeth with the sword must be killed with the sword. Here is the patience and the faith of the saints

The sincerely repentant who are faithful to God must endure this persecution patiently until Christ comes to deliver them.

The scripture now proceeds from the section on the political beast of the Holy Roman Empire; to the religious leader.

### The Final Miracle Working Man of Sin

A final miracle working religious leader who exalts himself above all that is called God by claiming ultimate moral authority over all religions, will arise very soon now. This is the abomination spoken of by Daniel in Daniel 12 and by Jesus in Matthew 24:15, and by Paul in 2 Thessalonians.

**13:11** And I beheld another beast coming up out of the earth [earthy, worldly, carnal, rebellious against godliness]; and he had two horns like a lamb [he presents himself and appears as an angel of light, a wise man of peace], and he spake as a dragon.

This deceiver teaches his own words and ways contrary to God's Word and God's ways, just like most leaders of today's Spiritual Ekklesia, which is satanic rebellion against God; However this man of sin works miracles and is supported by the power of the political system once he manages its rise.

**13:12** And he exerciseth all the power of the first beast [he will have the full support and power of the political aspect of the Holy Roman Empire system] before him, and causeth the earth and them which dwell therein to worship the first beast, whose deadly wound was healed.

This miracle working pope will endorse the revival of the Holy Roman Empire church state system, and convince the peoples of ten European nations to join that system, which will then be allied with the Roman Catholic and Islamic nations, Psalm 83, of the earth.

**13:13** And he doeth great wonders, so that he maketh fire come down from heaven on the earth in the sight of men,

Even the majority of the Jews and Americans will be deceived that this is a great man of peace and ultimate moral authority. In Judea only the settler movement extremists will be against him and provoke war when this man goes to the Holy Place within 75 days after he is set up doing miracles in the Vatican.

This miracle working man of sin will impress people into reviving the Holy Roman Empire Babylonian Mysteries church state government system in Europe.

**13:14** And deceiveth them that dwell on the earth by the means of those miracles which he had power to do in the sight of the beast; saying to them that dwell on the earth, that they should make an image [likeness] to the beast, which had the wound by a sword, and did live.

**13:15** And he had power to give life unto the image [a likeness or revival of the Holy Roman Empire system] of the beast, that the image of the beast should [so that the likeness of this system should cone into existence as the now rising New Federal Europe] both speak, and cause that as many as would not worship the image of the beast should be killed.

Most people will exalt this miracle working pope as the ultimate man of peace and ultimate moral authority, regardless of their own religious traditions. They will also be in awe of this church state political system which will become extremely prosperous for a short time, but after two years the political leader of the New Europe will hear rumors out of Asia and will attack them; bringing retaliation and destruction upon Europe and the Middle East (Dan 11:42 on.).

## The Mark of the Beast

People will be deceived into believing and doing what this false religious leader says, contrary to believing and living by every Word of God.

All humanity except for a few overcoming called out ones, has been deceived in their foreheads [beliefs of their minds] to follow Satan in their deeds [of their hands] since Adam and Eve. During this final end time that deception will climax.

Right now this deception and mark of the beast has already overwhelmed the Spiritual Ekklesia who prefer to follow idols of men in place of any zeal to keep the Word of God.

Following idols of men in the assemblies is exactly the same thing as following this final man of sin; the only difference is the name of the person being followed to believe and act contrary to the Word of God.

**13:16** And he causeth all, both small and great, rich and poor, free and bond, to receive a mark in their right hand [referring to actions and deeds], or in their foreheads [referring to what is believed in the mind]:

Just as in today's church of God groups; you must accept the system for the system to accept you. To function in this church state system people will have to accept it, or be rejected by it.

**13:17** And that no man might buy or sell, save he that had the mark, or the name of the beast, or the number of his name.

The mark of the Beast is the mark of Satan; it is compromising with and rebellion against God and any part of God's Word; it is a rejecting of any zeal to live by every Word of God.

It is what Satan taught Eve in the garden; it is to decide for ourselves what is right and wrong, instead of standing on God's Word.

The Mark of God is to obey and follow God in all things! Which mark only comes by sincere repentance and being sealed with the Holy Spirit! One can only do that through the indwelling presence of God's Holy Spirit which is given to those who have committed to Obey him in all things (Acts 5:32).

When we have been called by God the Father in heaven to have a part in the collective bride for the son, and we respond positively to that call washing away past sin and committing to remain sinless through the power of God at our baptism, then the atoning sacrifice of Jesus Christ the Lamb of God is applied to us and God the Father pours out his Holy Spirit upon us.

God's Spirit is in complete unity with God the Father in heaven and with the son, and will bring us into complete unity with God the Father in heaven if we follow its lead when we are sealed with that Spirit of Promise.

> **Ephesians 1:12** That we should be to the praise of his glory, who first trusted in Christ. **1:13** In whom ye also trusted, after that ye heard the word of truth, the gospel of your salvation: in whom also after that ye believed, **ye were sealed with that holy Spirit of promise,**

Those sealed with God's Spirit will learn to understand the things of God and will grow into a full unity of mind, spirit and deeds with God; IF they endure and follow the lead of the Spirit of God.

God's elect will become like God in all things, and will diligently work to internalize the very nature of God the Father in heaven through a passionate love for him and his will and commandments; loving God the Father as Jesus loves the Father.

For if we are of God we will have Jesus Christ dwelling within us through God's Spirit, and we will love those things that Christ loved, and we will do those things that Christ did and does.

> **1 John 2:3** And hereby we do know that we know him, if we keep his commandments.
>
> **2:4** He that saith, I know him, and keepeth not his commandments, is a liar, and the truth is not in him.
>
> **2:5** But whoso keepeth his word, in him verily is the love of God perfected: hereby know we that we are in him.
>
> **2:6** He that saith he abideth in him ought himself also so to walk [live], even as he walked [lived].

The sign of God's people is that they are filled with love for God and they diligently live by every Word of God, and they will keep all of God's Word without compromise or tolerance for any sin.

The Mark of God is zealous faithfulness to God our heavenly Father, being sealed by the Holy Spirit and being diligent to live by every Word of God; and the Mark of Satan [The Mark of the Beast] is to follow Satan into his spiritual rebellion against and compromise with the nature and Word of Almighty God!

For those who think that this mark is only Sunday observance; what about the billions who do not observe Sunday and are still rejecting the practical application of God's Word in many other things? For those who claim that this mark of the beast is polluting God's seventh day Sabbath; what about those who do keep God's seventh day Sabbath and rebel against other parts of God's Word?

Remember that breaking any one point of the law is breaking the whole law, no matter which point we have broken. Breaking ANY law is rebellion against God and is just as sinful as breaking the Sabbath which is universal in the Ekklesia today. Today the Ekklesia call the Sabbath holy as they shamelessly pollute it!

Many are even rejecting the ONLY Mediator between man and God the Father; our High Priest and ONLY Intercessor, Jesus Christ.

> **1 Timothy 2:5** For there is one God, and **one mediator between God and men, the man** [lexicon G444 1b2 God] **Christ Jesus**; **2:6** Who gave himself a ransom for all, to be testified in due time.

There is ONLY ONE Intercessor, ONLY ONE Mediator between men and God the heavenly Father, Jesus Christ ALONE! NOT ANY other!

There is ONLY one sacrifice for sin, and ONLY one High Priest that mediates for the sincerely repentant before God the Father!

For Jesus Christ ascended to God the Father as our Wave Sheaf to be accepted as a sacrifice for us and to be made a High Priest for our salvation.

> **Hebrews 4:14** Seeing then that we have a great high priest, that is passed into the heavens, Jesus the Son of God, let us hold fast our profession.
>
> **4:15** For we have not an high priest which cannot be touched with the feeling of our infirmities; but was in all points tempted like as we are, yet without sin.
>
> **4:16** Let us therefore come boldly unto the throne of grace, that we may obtain mercy, and find grace to help in time of need.

The Mark of Satan [Mark of the Beast]; is to decide for ourselves what is right and wrong instead of relying on and obeying God our Father in heaven.

The "Primacy of Peter" heresy is the mark of the beast and the Mark of Satan, for it exalts men above God as judges of the Word and Will of Almighty God!

This mark of the beast applies to ALL of mankind who are doing their own thing and not enthusiastically living by every Word of God in its fullness; and that includes the Ekklesia.

Brethren, this applies to the church of God today: it applies to all those who are lukewarm for the practical application of any part of God's Word.

Nearly all people in the world today and throughout history have had or have the mark of the beast, as they do what they think is right, instead of zealously doing what God says is right!

Do not be deceived into thinking that you have the mark of God and do not have the mark of the beast, just because you have been baptized and follow the teachings of some man! All of the major corporate COG leaders and brethren have the mark of the beast, as is self-evident by their rejection of much truth and large parts of the Word of God.

**The Number of the final Babylon the Great, the Beast**

The mark of the beast and the number of his name are two entirely different things. The mark of the beast identifies those who rebel against God. The NUMBER of the name identifies this system and the religious leader himself.

**Revelation 13:16** And he causes all, both small, great, rich and poor, free and bond to receive a **mark** in their right hand or in their foreheads. **13:17** And that no man might buy or sell, save he that had the mark**, OR the number of his name**. **13:18** Here is wisdom. Let him that has understanding count the number of the beast. For it is **the number of a man; and his number is six hundred sixty and six.**

This is the number of a MAN, and this number is also the number of Babylon the Great, and the final legs, feet and ten toes Rome of Daniel 2.

NOTICE CLEARLY that these are two DIFFERENT THINGS; yet very closely related, for the number is the letter number of the man who deceives; while the MARK identifies the people who follow the deceiver.

## The Number of the Beast

**Revelation 13:18** Here is wisdom. Let him that hath understanding count the number of the beast: for it is the number of a man; and his number is Six hundred threescore and six.

The number of his name, refers to the numerical value name of this beast in the Koine Greek that the book of Revelation was written in.

The number of his name is 666 and this has been indelibly written on the Roman pontiffs and the Holy Roman Empire from their beginnings; because in the Koine Greek that Revelation was written in; the English word Rome is "Latinos."

Here is wisdom. Let him that hath understanding count the number of the beast: for it is the number of a man; and his number is six hundred, three score and six (666) Rev 13:18. Yes, the number of this end time Babylon and the great deceiver is 666.

To understand this number, we need to be reminded that this was written in Koine Greek, the Greek of the common man.

In the Greek, as it was written here, the name for Rome was LATEINOS.

In the Greek letters the prophecy number can be numerically rendered as:
L 30 A 1 T 300 E 5 I 10 N 50 O 70 S 200

**TOTAL: 666**

This number is indelibly stamped on Rome!

| | | | | | | | | |
|---|---|---|---|---|---|---|---|---|
| A, | α´, | 1. | I, | ι´, | 10. | P, | ρ´, | 100. |
| B, | β´, | 2. | K, | κ´, | 20. | Σ, | σ´, | 200. |
| Γ, | γ´, | 3. | Λ, | λ´, | 30. | T, | τ´, | 300. |
| Δ, | δ´, | 4. | M, | μ´, | 40. | Y, | υ´, | 400. |
| E, | ε´, | 5. | N, | ν´, | 50. | Φ, | φ´, | 500. |
| | ϛ´, | 6. | Ξ, | ξ´, | 60. | X, | χ´, | 600. |
| Z, | ζ´, | 7. | O, | ο´, | 70. | Ψ, | ψ´, | 700. |
| H, | η´, | 8. | Π, | π´, | 80. | Ω, | ω´, | 800. |
| Θ, | ϑ´, | 9. | Ϟ, | ϟ´, | 90. | | ϡ´, | 900. |

Greek Letter Numbers

| | |
|---|---|
| Λ | 30 |
| α | 1 |
| τ | 300 |
| ε | 5 |
| ι | 10 |
| ν | 50 |
| ο | 70 |
| ς | 200 |
| | 666 |

Lateinos [Rome]

## Revelation 15

An introduction to the seven last plagues which will be poured out AFTER the resurrection at the beginning of the seventh trump, and BEFORE the later return to the earth of Messiah with God's chosen.

The resurrected chosen stand in the heavenly temple courtyard before the Throne of God.

**Revelation 15:1** And I saw another sign in heaven, great and marvellous, **seven angels having the seven last plagues; for in them is filled up the wrath of God.**

**15:2** And I saw as it were [like a] a sea of glass mingled with fire: [this is the vast court before the throne of God the Father; paved with something that reflects and refracts the light from God into many shimmering colors; either thinly beaten gold or a kind of crystal] and them that had gotten the victory over the beast, and over his image, and over his mark, and over the number of his name, [The resurrected chosen, stand in the courtyard of the temple before the throne of God in heaven.] **stand on the sea of glass,** having the harps of God.

The first few lines of this Song of Moses are stated to differentiate it from the other Songs of Moses.

**15:3** And they sing the song of Moses the servant of God, and the song of the Lamb, saying, Great and marvellous are thy works, Lord God Almighty; just and true are thy ways, thou King of saints.

**15:4** Who shall not fear thee, O Lord, and glorify thy name? for thou only art holy: for all nations shall come and worship before thee; for thy judgments are made manifest.

If you have prepared yourself and have been passionately zealous for our Beloved and every Word of God to become LIKE HIM and to overcome all worldliness; then you too shall stand before the throne of God the Father and sing this song of rejoicing at the Marriage of the Lamb!

In the spiritual context of the resurrection to eternal life and the marriage of the Lamb, this song refers to complete victory over Satan, sin and death by our Husband Jesus Christ, for those who follow HIM!

This is about the chosen called out, rising from the grave like Israel rose up from the Red Sea, and the nations of the world quaking and trembling at the mighty deeds of Messiah the Christ as he resurrects his chosen, pours out these terrible plagues and then comes to destroy all resistance and rule all nations.

**The Song of Moses**

If you have prepared yourself and have been passionately zealous for our Beloved and every Word of God and overcome all worldliness; then you too will stand before the throne of God the Father and Link: sing this song of rejoicing at the Marriage of the Lamb!

> **Exodus 15:1** Then sang Moses and the children of Israel this song unto the LORD, and spake, saying,
>
> I will sing unto the LORD, for he hath triumphed gloriously: the horse and his rider hath he thrown into the sea.

Just as God defeated pharaoh, our Lord has defeated the armies of Satan, the god-king of this world!

> **15:2** The LORD is my strength and song, and he is become my salvation: he is my God, and I will prepare him an habitation; my father's God, and I will exalt him.

We must trust ONLY in our God who is Mighty to Deliver, and he will build us into a Temple [a dwelling place] for our God through the gift of God's Spirit dwelling in us!

**15:3** The LORD [Who later gave up his God-hood to be made flesh as Jesus Christ] is a man of war: the LORD [YHVH, the Eternal] is his name.

The Eternal is our defense and our Deliverer, NO ONE can stand before him!

**15:4** Pharaoh's chariots and his host hath he cast into the sea: his chosen captains also are drowned in the Red sea. **15:5** The depths have covered them: they sank into the bottom as a stone. **15:6** Thy right hand, O LORD, is become glorious in power: thy right hand, O LORD, hath dashed in pieces the enemy. **15:7** And in the greatness of thine excellency thou hast overthrown them that rose up against thee: thou sentest forth thy wrath, which consumed them as stubble. **15:8** And with the blast of thy nostrils the waters were gathered together, the floods stood upright as an heap, and the depths were congealed in the heart of the sea.

**15:9** The enemy said, I will pursue, I will overtake, I will divide the spoil; my lust shall be satisfied upon them; I will draw my sword, my hand shall destroy them.

**15:10** Thou didst blow with thy wind, the sea covered them: they sank as lead in the mighty waters.

Who is like God the Father and Jesus Christ?

**15:11** Who is like unto thee, O LORD, among the gods? who is like thee, glorious in holiness, fearful in praises, doing wonders? **15:12** Thou stretchedst out thy right hand, the earth swallowed them.

**15:13** Thou in thy mercy hast led forth the people which thou hast redeemed: thou hast guided them in thy strength unto thy holy habitation.

**15:14** The people shall hear, and be afraid: sorrow shall take hold on the inhabitants of Palestina.

**15:15** Then the dukes of Edom shall be amazed; the mighty men of Moab, trembling shall take hold upon them; all the inhabitants of Canaan shall melt away.

The Canaanites were types of wickedness and rebellion against God!

**15:16** Fear and dread shall fall upon them; by the greatness of thine arm they shall be as still as a stone; till thy people pass over, O LORD, till the people pass over, which thou hast purchased.

The sincerely repentant spiritual people which Christ has purchased with his blood; will pass through the Sea of Death [the grave] into eternal life, and they will be given an inheritance as kings and priests over all the earth!

> **15:17** Thou shalt bring them in, and plant them in the mountain of thine inheritance, in the place, O LORD, which thou hast made for thee to dwell in, in the Sanctuary, O LORD, which thy hands have established.
>
> **15:18** The LORD shall reign for ever and ever.

Oh, what a great rejoicing in Israel on that High Holy Day of the Seventh Day of Unleavened Bread!

Oh, what a fantastic millennium of rejoicing the resurrected chosen saints will have as they bring the millennial harvest of first fruits into the family of God, in the very presence of the Creator himself!

Then Miriam led all Israel in a Song of Rejoicing at the deliverance and power of the Eternal from physical Egypt; and the resurrected chosen will also sing a Song of Rejoicing at the deliverance and power of the Eternal to deliver from bondage to Satan, sin and death!

> **15:20** And Miriam the prophetess, the sister of Aaron, took a timbrel in her hand; and all the women went out after her with timbrels and with dances. **15:21** And Miriam answered them, Sing ye to the LORD, for he hath triumphed gloriously; the horse and his rider hath he thrown into the sea.

**Revelation 15:5** And after that I looked, and, behold, the temple of the tabernacle of the testimony in heaven was opened:

**15:6** And the **seven angels came out of the temple, having the** [last] **seven plagues**, clothed in pure and white linen, and having their breasts girded with golden girdles.

**15:7** And one of the four beasts gave unto the seven angels seven golden vials full of the wrath of God, who liveth for ever and ever.

**15:8** And the temple was filled with smoke from the glory of God, and from his power; and no man was able to enter into the temple, till the seven plagues of the seven angels were fulfilled.

# Revelation 16

## The Seven Last Plagues

While the multitudes of saints making up the collective bride of Christ stand on the vast expanse of glittering crystal before the temple of God in heaven (Rev 7:9, Rev 19); seven angels are given the seven bowls of God's wrath to be poured out on the earth.

**Revelation 16:1** And I heard a great voice out of the temple saying to the seven angels, Go your ways, and pour out the vials of the wrath of God upon the earth.

The first viol or bowl was poured out on the earth and men were afflicted with grievous sores.

After witnessing the resurrection and change to spirit of the faithful, many in Israel will begin to repent and seek God's deliverance; at the same time most of humanity will still follow their leaders, who fearing the loss of their positions continue to resist God.

This affliction was poured out on those who remain in rebellion against God and refuse to live by every Word of God.

**16:2** And the first went, and poured out his vial upon the earth; and there fell **a noisome and grievous sore** upon the men which had the mark of the beast [all those who refuse to live by every Word of God], and **upon them which worshipped his image**.

The word "noisome" means disgusting, fetid, putrid, rotten, stinking; and is usually a reference to weeping sores which ooze pus and noxious material. The word grievous refers to extreme pain.

**16:3** And the second angel poured out his vial **upon the sea**; and it became as the blood of a dead man: and every living soul [creature] died in the sea.

The second viol will follow quickly after the second, and the "sea" will be turned into a coagulated mess. This could refer to all seas or to just the Mediterranean Sea.

**16:4** And **the third angel** poured out his vial upon the rivers and fountains of waters; and they became blood. **16:5** And I heard the angel of the waters say, Thou art righteous, O Lord, which art, and wast, and shalt be, because thou hast judged thus. **16:6** For they have shed the blood of saints and prophets, and thou hast given them blood to drink; for they are worthy. **16:7** And I heard another out of the altar say, Even so, Lord God Almighty, true and righteous are thy judgments.

The third angel poured out his viol and the open bodies of fresh water are polluted. People will need to dig wells for water as the Egyptians did when the Nile was turned to the same kind of bloody mess.

**16:8** And **the fourth angel** poured out his vial upon the sun; and power was given unto him to scorch men with fire. **16:9** And men were scorched with great heat, and blasphemed the name of God, which hath power over these plagues: and they repented not to give him glory.

The fourth angel will cause the sun to flare with great heat upon the earth. This would affect the entire earth.

**16:10** And **the fifth angel** poured out his vial upon the seat of the beast; and his kingdom was full of darkness; and they gnawed their tongues for pain, **16:11** And blasphemed the God of heaven because of their pains and their sores, and repented not of their deeds.

Then the fifth angel obscured the light in the kingdom of the beast, so that his place will be plunged into complete darkness. This seems to be some kind of particulate like smoke or dense dust which prevents even artificial light from being seen.

After the beast [the New Europe, the seventh revival of the scarlet beast and its ruler] is counter attacked after he attacks Asia in the third year, he will move to Jerusalem as his last redoubt; and the armies of Asia will pursue him there.

> **Daniel 11:42** He shall stretch forth his hand also upon the countries: and the land of Egypt shall not escape. **11:43** But he shall have power over the treasures of gold and of silver, and over all the precious things of Egypt: and the Libyans and the Ethiopians shall be at his steps.
>
> **11:44** But **tidings out of the east and out of the north shall trouble him: therefore he shall go forth with great fury to destroy, and utterly to make away many.**
>
> **11:45** And **he shall plant the tabernacles of his palace between the seas in the glorious holy mountain; yet he shall come to his end, and none shall help him.**

The Asian armies will counter attack Europe and will turn south towards Jerusalem in hot pursuit of the beast and false prophet, and the sixth angel will open the way for them by drying up the river Euphrates.

Remember all of these things are being poured out during the Marriage Banquet Feast of the Lamb, given by God the Father in heaven to celebrate the resurrection of the early harvest and their complete unity with the Father and the Son!

Along with the rejoicing, duties and responsibilities of the many offices will be assigned and the kingdom will be organized before they return to the earth.

**Revelation 16:12** And **the sixth angel** poured out his vial upon the great river Euphrates; and the water thereof was dried up, that the way of the kings of the east might be prepared.

As the Euphrates dries up and these armies gather before Jerusalem, demons will go forth to deceive all of these nations to agree together to resist the coming of Christ with his saints.

**16:13** And I saw three unclean spirits like frogs come out of the mouth of the dragon, and out of the mouth of the beast, and out of the mouth of the false prophet. **16:14** For they are the spirits of devils, working miracles, which go forth unto the kings of the earth and of the whole world, to gather them to the battle of that great day of God Almighty.

Then Jesus Christ will come to take and rule the Kingdom WITH his resurrected saints (Jude) and he will destroy wickedness and rule the earth in righteousness. This is not referring to the resurrection of the bride which already happened as the seventh trump began to sound.

These viols of plagues will be poured out while the wedding feast is taking place in heaven; after the resurrection and before Christ comes with them to rule the earth.

Blessed is the one who is watching and keeping himself from joining the rebellious!

**16:15** Behold, I come [to rule, coming suddenly and surprising the wicked] as a thief. Blessed is he that watcheth, and keepeth his garments [is clothed with righteousness, referring to those repenting during this time], lest he walk naked [of righteousness], and they see his shame [the shame of our wickedness is revealed].

**16:16** And he gathered them together into a place called in the Hebrew tongue Armageddon [the armies outside Jerusalem will mass on a plateau north of Jerusalem].

Now the seventh angel pours out his viol and Jesus Christ will come from the Marriage of the Lamb in heaven, back to the earth WITH his saints.

> **Zechariah 14:2** For I will gather all nations against Jerusalem to battle; and the city shall be taken, and the houses rifled, and the women ravished; and half of the city shall go forth into captivity, and the residue of the people shall not be cut off from the city.

Jesus Christ will come with the resurrected faithful and destroy te armies of teh wicked.

> **14:3** Then shall the LORD go forth, and fight against those nations, as when he fought in the day of battle. **14:4** And his feet shall stand in that day upon the mount of Olives, which is before Jerusalem on the east, and the mount of Olives shall cleave in the midst thereof toward the east and toward the west, and there shall be a very great valley; and half of the mountain shall remove toward the north, and half of it toward the south.
>
> **14:5** And ye shall flee to the valley of the mountains; for the valley of the mountains shall reach unto Azal: yea, ye shall flee, like as ye fled from before the earthquake in the days of Uzziah king of Judah: and the LORD my God shall come, and all the saints with thee.
>
> **14:6** And it shall come to pass in that day, that the light shall not be clear, nor dark: **14:7** But it shall be one day which shall be known to

the LORD, not day, nor night: but it shall come to pass, that at evening time it shall be light.

**Revelation 16:17** And the seventh angel poured out his vial into the air; and there came a great voice out of the temple of heaven, from the throne, saying, It is done.

The seventh vial represents the coming of Christ with his chosen second 144,000 to the Mount of Olives and their entry into Jerusalem to set up a world government, while vast numbers of other resurrected chosen will arrive in the various nations around the earth to take over local administration.

**16:18** And there were voices, and thunders, and lightnings; and there was a great earthquake, such as was not since men were upon the earth, so mighty an earthquake, and so great.

Revelation 16:19 refers to the great earthquake spoken of in Zechariah 14:4-5. This is the Zechariah earthquake which splits the Mount of Olives and shakes the whole earth as Messiah the Christ arrives with the resurrected faithful.

**16:19** And the great city was divided into three parts, and the cities of the nations fell: and great Babylon came in remembrance before God, to give unto her the cup of the wine of the fierceness of his wrath.

**16:20** And every island fled away, and the mountains were not found.

**16:21** And there fell upon men a great hail out of heaven, every stone about the weight of a talent: and men blasphemed God because of the plague of the hail; for the plague thereof was exceeding great.

Consider that all these events including the movement of mighty armies could not take place in the one day of the resurrection of the bride as the seventh trump began to sound. These plagues were poured out while the saints stood before the Temple of God in heaven over approximately 45 days.

The key to understanding this is the difference between the 1,290 days and the 1,335 days of Daniel 12. The resurrection is at the end of 1,290 days AFTER the man of sin is set up doing miracles, and the final plagues take some days to be poured out.

Be careful here, the 1,335 days could mark the setting up of God's kingdom on Pentecost, or it could refer to Christ's coming to destroy the wicked and arrest Satan and his demons; and then wait for a few days until

Pentecost for God's Spirit to be poured out (Joel 2:28) and begin the Kingdom of God over all the earth.

Remember that after Israel arrived at Sinai they waited several days before God appeared on Mt Sinai, and the disciples waited for ten days after Christ's ascension before Pentecost came.

# Revelation 17

## The King of the North

Daniel chapter 8 and Daniel chapter 11, both concern the rivalry between the Kings of the North and South. To understand the end time application of these prophecies, it is necessary to know who these kings represent.

The explanation of the King of the North is found in Daniel 2, where king Nebuchadnezzar was given a special dream and God gave Daniel the understanding. Daniel states in verse 29 that the dream was given by God, to reveal what shall come to pass.

The dream consisted of an image of a man with a head of gold, a breast and arms of silver, a belly and thighs of brass and legs of iron with feet of mixed iron and clay (Dan 2:31-33). This image was destroyed by a stone cut out without hands, smiting the image on it's feet and breaking them to pieces. This stone then became a great mountain that filled the whole earth (Dan 2:34-35).

God gave Daniel the interpretation, which he revealed to the king. The head of gold is Nebuchadnezzar, King of Babylon verse 38. The other body parts are other kingdoms which shall come being different peoples but maintaining the same Babylonian church state mystery religion system verse 39.

Historically we know that the Empire of Babylon gave way to the Empire of the Persians, which passed on to the Greeks and was finally inherited by Rome and finally the Holy Roman Empire.

This final Holy Roman Empire will be partly strong and partly brittle verse 42 as the toes were part of iron and part of clay. And in the days of these kings shall the God of Heaven set up a kingdom, which shall break in pieces all of these kingdoms verse 44.

This image represents a system which started in Babylon and continued through these succeeding empires. As each one supplanted the previous empire, they adopted the same system. A different race of people ruled, but the system of government and the religion remained.

As the head contains the brain and mind and controls the body, so this image was dominated by it's head; Babylon. Each of these successive empires was essentially a continuation of the Babylonian Empire System by different peoples.

This is why the whole statue and the systems it represents is called Babylon, and why the Holy Roman Empire of the ten toes of the coming New Europe, which is to be destroyed by the God of Heaven through Christ at his coming, is called Babylon the Great (Rev 18:2).

An angel from God came to Daniel in response to his prayer, revealing what would become of Daniel's people in the LATTER DAYS (Dan 10:1-14).

This angel revealed to Daniel that the Kingdom of Persia which followed the Empire of Babylon would be replaced by the Greeks (Dan 11:2-4). The first king of Greece would be broken and his kingdom would be divided into four parts. One of these parts was to be called the king of the north in the prophecies; and one part, Egypt, to be called the king of the south. Daniel 11 is chiefly concerned with the rivalry between these two divisions through history.

Historically, King Philip of Macedon prepared plans to unite the Greeks and conquer the Persians, but died before carrying them out. His son Alexander became the first king of a united Greece, and conquered the Medo-Persian Empire.

Alexander died of fever in 323 B.C. and then after much infighting, the kingdom was eventually divided between numerous of Alexander's officers. (To see how there eventually came to be four parts, see the 2300 Days Prophecy in the Daniel article).

Ptolemy became ruler of Egypt which also included Judea, ans this Egypt Judea kingdom was called the kingdom of the SOUTH.

During a dip in Ptolemy's fortunes, one of his generals, Seleucus Nicator seized the province of Babylon NORTH of Jerusalem. Daniel 11 concerns itself with the rivalry that developed between the two kingdoms.

This Kingdom of the NORTH was eventually swallowed up by Rome even as the Greeks swallowed up the Empire of Persia, which had, in its turn replaced Babylon!

ALL these Kingdoms were part of the Babylonian system, which will be destroyed by Jesus Christ at his coming. The original King of the North was Nicator whose kingdom was called Babylon! Its final remnant the kingdom of Pergamos was absorbed by Rome with the death of Atallus 3 in 133 B.C.

The modern, rising New Europe is a revival of the Babylonian System, and the final revival of the Holy Roman Empire, is today's King of the North.

### The King of the South

At the time of the end shall the King of the South [Egypt and Palestine in ancient times, or Egypt and the Jewish state today] push at him [will provoke the New Europe] and the King of the North will come against them (Dan 11:40-43). Who will the North enter? Why those who provoked him of course.

Who is that? EGYPT and JUDEA; and the Anglo Saxon nations will fall into economic collapse.

Who is the King of the South? EGYPT allied with Judah is and has always been the King of the South! When Ptolemy became king of EGYPT, the King of the South, he also ruled JUDEA! JUDEA was a part of Egypt at that time.

> The King of the South refers to that area which was [is] SOUTH of Jerusalem.
>
> The King of the North, Babylon the Great, today's rising New Europe; will enter JUDEA and EGYPT.

All the Israelite peoples will fall with them (Hos 5:5). It is very interesting to see that EGYPT, the JEWISH STATE, the USA and the BRITISH are ALL closely allied together at this time, and they are ALL specifically mentioned as falling together, to Babylon the coming New Europe!

The king if the south in Daniel chapter eleven is about EGYPT, why would Egypt suddenly NOT BE the King of the South at the end of the chapter? This just makes NO SENSE.

Egypt, along with her allies has been the King of the South for about 2,300 years and remain the King of the South.

In summary; The King of the South is and has always been EGYPT and Judea together, and will fall with their allies at the start of the final forty two months.

The King of the North was Babylon and is still Babylon, the feet of Babylon; the now rising New Europe.

This final revival of the Holy Roman Empire [the feet of Babylon] will occupy Jerusalem and Judea for forty two months (Rev 13:5).

The scriptures tell us that Jerusalem, and Judea will be occupied for 42 months, but nothing is said about occupying America, the British countries or Scandinavia; it is only said that they will fall in a process lasting 42 months.

> **Daniel 12:7** And I heard the man clothed in linen, which was upon the waters of the river, when he held up his right hand and his left hand unto heaven, and sware by him that liveth for ever that it shall be for a time, times, and an half [42 months, i.e. 3 !/2 years] ; and **when he shall have accomplished to scatter the power of the holy people, all these things shall be finished.**

### The Woman and the Scarlet Beast

The scarlet beast had seven heads and ten horns.

The seven heads are the seven revivals of the Holy Roman Empire; which was and is dominated or ridden by a woman which is the great religious entity known as the Babylonian Mysteries.

This system is explained in Revelation 13 as the system of Satan.

This scarlet beast system began to be ridden by the woman during the empire of Justinian when Justinian authorized the woman to become the authority in the Roman empire because of the breakdown of the civil system due to the collapse of Imperial Rome.

> **Revelation 12:3** And there appeared another wonder in heaven; and behold a great red dragon, having seven heads and ten horns,

and seven crowns upon his heads. **12:4** And his tail drew the third part of the stars of heaven, and did cast them to the earth:

The ten horns are the ten kings of the last and soon coming final seventh revival of the scarlet beast Holy Roman Empire system, ridden by the woman or religion. By whatever name this new Europe is called, it will be brought into being by a final miracle working religious leader (Rev 13).

**Revelation 17:3** So he carried me away in the spirit into the wilderness: and I saw a woman **sit upon a scarlet coloured beast, full of names of blasphemy** [the unholy "Holy" Roman Empire], having **seven heads** [seven revivals] **and ten horns** [the seventh and last revival consisting of ten rulers [nations] under a central federal leader].

**17:4** And **the woman** was arrayed in purple and scarlet colour, and decked with gold and precious stones and pearls, having a golden cup in her hand full of abominations and filthiness of her fornication:

**17:5** And **upon her forehead was a name written, MYSTERY, BABYLON THE GREAT, THE MOTHER OF HARLOTS AND ABOMINATIONS OF THE EARTH.**

**17:6** And I saw **the woman** [the religion which dominates the scarlet beast political system] **drunken** with the blood of the saints, and with the blood of the martyrs of Jesus: and when I saw her, I wondered with great admiration [awe].

**17:7** And the angel said unto me, Wherefore didst thou marvel? I **will tell thee the mystery of the woman, and of the** [scarlet] **beast that carrieth her** [that she rides upon], which hath the seven heads and ten horns.

**The woman who rides the scarlet beast**

The woman is the Babylonian Mystery religion now disguising itself as "Christian" rides the Scarlet Beast [the Holy Roman Empire system] which is the feet of the Statue of Babylon in Daniel 2, further explained in Daniel 7. The woman began to ride this scarlet beast [the Holy Roman Empire] during the reign of Justinian.

**17:8** The [eighth] beast [the religion] that thou sawest was, and is not [is no longer]; and shall ascend out of the bottomless pit, and go into perdition [will go to complete destruction]: and they that dwell on the earth shall wonder, whose names were not written in the book of life from the foundation of the world, when they behold the beast that was, and is not, and yet is.

**17:9** And here is the mind which hath wisdom. The seven heads are seven mountains [they are the seven political revivals of the scarlet beast (which is the Holy Roman Empire) which this religion dominates], on which the woman sitteth.

The interpretation of the seven mountains is the seven hills of Rome, and the seven dynasties or political revivals of the scarlet beast [Holy Roman Empire] system as revealed in the next verse.

**17:10** And **there are seven kings**: five are fallen, and one is [the sixth, Mussolini existed at the time of this vision], and the other is not yet come; and when he cometh, he must continue a short space [time].

The sixth beast, Mussolini, fell in WW 2, just like all of the other revivals of this system also fell before him!

At some point after the Mussolini [sixth] version of the scarlet beast ended, another [seventh] and final version will be brought to life and will have power to make war for 42 months.

Today a seventh revival of the Holy Roman Empire is at hand!

Besides the seven revivals of the scarlet beast, there is an eighth beast [the religion and its leader] which will also be destroyed.

**17:11** And **the beast that was, and is not** [is no longer, the Holy Roman Empire religious leader who will be destroyed at Christ's coming], **even he is** [will be associated with and rides the seven revivals of the Holy Roman Empire] **the eighth,** and is [He dominates but is not one of the seven political revivals of the Holy Roman Empire beast; the eighth beast being the woman [religion] which rides (controls) the Holy Roman Empire system.] of the seven, and **goeth into perdition.**

The eighth beast which was and is not, will no longer exists after Christ comes and destroys him and this whole system.

The eighth beast is the religious system which rides the seven revivals of the Holy Roman Empire, and this eighth beast who looks like a lamb will be totally destroyed along with the New European political system and its political leader at the coming of Christ (Dan 2)!

The beast "which was and is not," is NOT one of the seven; but is an eighth, and the eighth is the religion which rides the seven successive political empires!

The expression "was and is not" refers to the fact that in this vision John saw that this religion would cease to exist and would go into perdition

[Gehenna fire] in the vision, yet in our day it still exists and will remain for a short time longer.

The prophecy of the total destruction of this eighth beast [a false religion] is sure and is presented as an accomplished fact. Now look at Revelation 17:16 where it is these very ten latter day kings who will turn on this false religion and destroy it once the deception has been removed at the coming of Christ!

This eighth beast is revealed in:

> **Revelation 13:11** And I beheld another beast coming up out of the earth; and he had two horns like a lamb, and he spake as a dragon [this is a false religion disguised as being godly].

This religious beast rides the Holy Roman Empire and the final false prophet is the climax of that deceptive religious system; appearing innocent and godly while teaching people to obey and follow him as their ultimate moral authority in place of God, acting as if he were God.

This religious leader will have the power to do miracles from Satan; he will revive the Holy Roman Empire political system and he will exercise the power of the state; that is the government will support him.

> **13:12** And he exerciseth all the power of the first beast before him, and causeth the earth and them which dwell therein to worship the first beast, whose deadly wound was healed. **13:13** And he doeth great wonders, so that he maketh fire come down from heaven on the earth in the sight of men,
>
> **13:14** And deceiveth them that dwell on the earth by the means of those miracles which he had power to do in the sight of the beast; saying to them that dwell on the earth, that they should make an image [a replica, a likeness of the Holy Roman Empire system] to the beast, which had the wound by a sword, and did live.
>
> **13:15** And **he had power to give life unto the image of the beast, that the image of the beast should both speak, and cause that as many as would not worship the image of the beast should be killed.**

The ten horns are ten rulers of nations which are a part of the seventh revival of the Holy Roman Empire. Each of these ten will be leaders of their own nations and will give authority to a central federal authority; and an overall leader will be chosen who will have the collective power of the whole federal [American style state federal system].

**Revelation 17:12** And the ten horns which thou sawest **are ten kings, which have received no kingdom as yet; but receive power as kings one hour** [will be joined together for a short time] with the [political] beast. **17:13** These have one mind, and shall give their power and strength unto the beast [the political leader of the seventh revival].

At the end of this seventh revival, Jesus Christ will come with his chosen and destroy this Babylonian Holy Roman Empire church state mystery system as well as the eighth beast religious system.

**17:14** These shall make war with the Lamb, and the Lamb shall overcome them: for he is Lord of lords, and King of kings: and they that are with him are called, and chosen, and faithful.

**17:15** And he saith unto me, **The waters which thou sawest**, where the whore sitteth, **are peoples, and multitudes, and nations, and tongues** [which this religion dominates].

When the political and religious leaders are destroyed and the deception is lifted, the ten rulers will repent and turn on and destroy this political system and the religious system of exalting men above the Word of God.

**17:16** And the ten horns [kings, rulers] which thou sawest upon the beast, **these shall hate the whore, and shall make her desolate and naked, and shall eat her flesh, and burn her with fire.**

The ten rulers and nations will realize how they have been deceived into ruin and they will turn on this religious system and destroy it. After Christ comes, all people will sincerely repent and turn to live by every Word of God.

**17:17** For **God hath put in their hearts to fulfil his will, and to agree, and give their kingdom unto the beast, until the words of God shall be fulfilled.**

**17:18** And the woman which thou sawest is that great city [the Vatican, ROME; the eighth beast], which reigneth over the kings of the earth.

The list of seven Holy Roman Empire revivals includes: Justinian, Otto the Great, Charlemagne, Napoleon, The Hapsburg's and Mussolini; with one more to come.

Historians regard Charlemagne as the first Holy Roman Emperor, however the church state scarlet beast system that is ridden by the papacy is what I am referring to, not some historian's label. In fact it was Justinian who elevated the Catholic Church above the state to maintain order because of the fall of Rome to the barbarians.

## Conclusion

### The Woman

In Revelation 17:1 a certain woman is identified as a great whore "that sitteth upon many waters". This is explained in Revelation 17:15; where the many waters are explained as a great multitude of many peoples, nations and languages. So this woman [religion] sits upon or dominates many nations and very many peoples; she is a very large influential church organization having relationships with governments.

> **17: 2** the kings or rulers have committed fornication with her.

She has close and intimate relationships with the rulers of this world, and the nations are intoxicated by their relationships with her.

> **17:3** In spirit (in a vision); **17:4** I saw her arrayed in purple and scarlet and decked with precious stones and holding a cup filled with abominations and fornications (Having relationships with the nations, rather than a relationship with God.).

In Revelation 17:5 she is called Babylon the Great, Mother of Harlots. V6; she was drunk with the blood of the saints; the godly people she has persecuted through the ages.

> **Revelation 17:9** the seven heads are seven mountains [the seven hills of Rome are symbolic of seven governments], on which the woman sitteth.

In scripture, a virgin is symbolic of purity, perfect loyalty and true godliness; symbolic of the Called of God (2 Corinthians 11:2).

Therefore a whore or harlot, symbolizes a fallen or unfaithful woman or religious organization which is not faithful to live by every Word of God.

This whore is the religious part of the Babylonian church state system and she rides the Roman beast of Daniel 7.

This false religion which is the Babylonian Mysteries now calling herself "Christian," rides the seven revivals of the political scarlet beast.

This fallen church is not faithful to God, rather she stands on her own traditions instead of the Word of God. She exalts her leaders ABOVE GOD'S WORD through the Primacy of Peter heresy.

Rather than being faithful to the Word of God, she thinks to change times and laws; changing the Sabbath from the Seventh Day to Sunday, the first day of the week, and changing from God's Scriptural Calendar to other calendar systems.

Today's Spiritual Ekklesia does EXACTLY the same thing, exalting their human traditions above the Word of God and changing times and laws with their apostate High Day Calendar and their rejection of the sanctity of God's Sabbath!

Yet, there is only one woman or church which organized the crusades, most of which were against dissenters within Europe; who organized inquisitions against truth seekers and who slaughtered the saints of God.

Only one centered in a city of seven hills (mountains) both literally and which has dominated six historic "holy" empires with one more remaining. Only one who adorns it's leaders with scarlet and purple and jewels; and maintains relationships with the governments and rulers of this earth.

Only one who has many daughters (other churches coming out of her in protest, yet still clinging to many of her false teachings).

Only one church who was the very first one to adopt the Primacy of Peter heresy to exalt herself above God's Word: And together with all these things dominates many multitudes and nations. She is the ultimate one who claims to be Christian, who uses the name of Christ while substituting her own traditions for the Word of God.

**The Scarlet Beast**

Revelation 17:3; The woman sits upon, rides, dominates and controls; a scarlet colored political beast, full of the names of blasphemy (made scarlet with the blood of the saints), having seven heads and ten horns.

The final miracle working pope is the EIGHTH beast and rides the Scarlet Beast's seven revivals. This eighth beast is of the seven, associated with the seven but not one of the seven political revivals: Riding on the seven political empires, dominating them through religious influence on the masses of people and teaching all people to follow itself as their ultimate moral authority instead of being zealous for the Word of God.

**The Seven Heads**

Verse 3; the beast has seven heads. Verse 9; the seven heads are seven mountains (mountains symbolize governments). Verse 10; and there are seven kings: five are fallen, and one is [sixth], and the other is not yet come; and when he [the seventh] cometh, he must continue a short space.

There were six Holy Roman Church State Empires: Justinian, Otto the Great, Charlemagne, Napoleon. The Hapsburg's and Mussolini; with one more to come.

We are now about to see the seventh and last revival of the scarlet beast; rise from the death of the sixth Holy Roman Empire, to become the climax of the Babylon system; rising up to torment all within its influence who will not submit to it.

**The Ten Horns of the last head or the final revival of the Scarlet Beast system**

Verse 3; this final beast has ten horns

> **Revelation 17:12** And the ten horns which thou sawest are ten kings, which have received no kingdom as yet; but receive power as kings one hour with the beast. **17:13** these have one mind, and shall give their power and strength unto the beast [the seventh revival of the scarlet beast satanic system]. **17:14** These shall make war with the Lamb, and the Lamb shall overcome them.

Finally these kings shall realize that they have been had, they have been deceived and they shall turn against and destroy this False Religion that has ridden on them by deceiving them.

> **17:16** And the ten horns [kings, rulers] which thou sawest upon the beast, **these shall hate the whore, and shall make her desolate and naked, and shall eat her flesh, and burn her with fire.**

Six revivals of scarlet beast church state Babylonian Mystery system have come and gone in Rome, all ridden by the same church; with is the Babylonian Mystery religion disguised as "Christian."

In these last days; ten kings [rulers] will set up a new seventh revival of the same system, as the seventh and last revival of the political scarlet beast, giving their authority to one president or emperor; approved by the final papal false prophet.

This will be a government structure based on the "Babylonian church state" model of the Babylonian Mysteries church state system.

They will rule for one hour (a short time) and will make war for 42 months (Rev 11:2). Their empire will end with the return of the Lamb of God, Jesus Christ.

At that time the ten nations, freed from the chains of deception; will turn against the False Church, the great whore and destroy her (Rev 17:16-17).

The prophecy covers much more than the years immediately preceding the coming of Christ; it covers the whole period of the seven revivals of the Holy Roman Empire.

The "one that is" is the sixth mentioned; Mussolini was the sixth Church/State Holy Roman Empire. Mussolini by the Vatican Concordat did revive the sixth Holy Roman Empire.

The seventh and last revival of the scarlet beast system by whatever name it is called, is about to come and will exist only a "short time" [a little more than 42 months or 1.260 days].

The final system now coming, is the Seventh revival of the Roman church state Babylonian Mysteries Holy Roman Empire system, by whatever name it will be called.

## Revelation 18

### Babylon is Fallen!

The empire of Babylon was established as the HEAD of the statue of Daniel 2, and as the head controls the body, the subsequent empires of Persia, Greece, Rome and the holy Roman Empire are all the same system being different people but following the same Babylonian Mysteries system.

The statue refers to the political empire's of the Babylonian system while false religion began in the garden of Eden with Satan and after the flood this system began anew at Babel with the tower or pyramid of Babel and God confused the races and languages to separate the people.

The people then spread on the earth carrying with them their false religion in new languages with new names for their gods, Then the Babylonian empire was established as a great empire which was controlled by the Babylonian Mysteries priesthood riding the political system of the Babylonian empire and its successive political empire systems; leading mankind into following themselves and their own ways instead of living by every Word of God.

Sound familiar? Satan's methods of deception have not changed and it is the same in the Ekklesia today.

The head of the statue of Babylon symbolizes the whole system of successive empires making up the Babylonian church state system since the days of this dream.

The refusal of the three men to bow before this statue of Babylon is symbolic of the courage and faith of people throughout the millennia who have refused to bow before this system of Satan

> **Daniel 2:36** This is the dream; and we will tell the interpretation thereof before the king.
>
> **2:37** Thou, O king, art a king of kings: for the God of heaven hath given thee a kingdom, power, and strength, and glory. **2:38** And wheresoever the children of men dwell, the beasts of the field and the fowls of the heaven hath he given into thine hand, and hath made thee ruler over them all. Thou art this head of gold.

The Babylonian system of religion, which is rebellion against God's commandments and doing whatever we decide for ourselves is right; rules over all men except those liberated by the call of God the Father who fully commit to live by his every Word.

This dream is about the political systems that will continue to perpetuate this false religious system, from the Babylonian Empire to the coming of Christ to rule the nations.

> **2:39** And after thee shall arise another kingdom inferior to thee, and another third kingdom of brass, which **shall bear rule over all the earth.** [Meaning to dominate not necessarily to rule directly.]

Historically the Babylonian Empire was supplanted by the Medo-Persian Empire who took over the same religion and the same governmental system.

The Persian Empire was exactly the same as the Babylonian system in religion and governance; only ruled by a different people.

The Persian Empire was then supplanted by the Hellenic Greeks of Alexander, who continued with the exact same system of governance and religion of Babylon'

Finally a fourth kingdom of the Romans took over world dominance from the Greeks.

Remember that this prophecy is in generalities

**2:40** And the fourth kingdom shall be strong as iron: forasmuch as iron breaketh in pieces and subdueth all things: and as iron that breaketh all these, shall it break in pieces and bruise.

**2:41** And whereas thou sawest the feet and toes , part of potters' clay, and part of iron, the kingdom shall be divided; but there shall be in it of the strength of the iron, forasmuch as thou sawest the iron mixed with miry clay.

We see that the Roman Empire was to be a mixture of peoples some brittle and inflexible yet strong, and some malleable and weak like clay.

The final Roman kingdom of the toes shall be partly strong and partly weak, including many peoples. Today we see the European races being mixed even further with a far greater number of peoples through immigration. Islamic immigration alone is a major influence on Europe.

**2:42** And as the toes of the feet were part of iron, and part of clay, so the kingdom shall be partly strong, and partly broken. **2:43** And whereas thou sawest iron mixed with miry clay, they shall mingle themselves with the seed of men: but they shall not cleave one to another, even as iron is not mixed with clay.

Below Daniel alludes to the ten toes as being kings, in a double meaning of the empires of the statue and the ten toes of Rome.

**2:44** And in **the days of these** [ten kings Rev 17:12] **kings** shall the God of heaven set up a kingdom, which shall never be destroyed: and the kingdom shall not be left to other people, but it shall break in pieces and consume all these kingdoms, and it shall stand for ever.

**2:45** Forasmuch as thou sawest that the stone was cut out of the mountain without hands, and that it brake in pieces the iron, the brass, the clay, the silver, and the gold [The entire statue and system of rebellion against God by doing what is right in the eyes of men and rejecting what God declares is right]; the great God hath made known to the king what shall come to pass hereafter: and the dream is certain, and the interpretation thereof sure.

## Revelation 18

An angel prophesies of the imminent destruction of Babylon [the now rising New Federal Europe] during the Marriage of the Lamb in heaven, as the Seven Last Plagues are poured out

**Revelation 18:1** And after these things I saw another angel come down from heaven, having great power; and the earth was lightened with his glory.

**18:2** And he cried mightily with a strong voice, saying, **Babylon the great is fallen, is fallen,** and is become the habitation of devils, and the hold of every foul spirit, and a cage of every unclean and hateful bird.

**18:3** For all nations have drunk of the wine of the wrath of her fornication [disloyalty to the Creator], and **the kings of the earth have committed fornication with her** [bonding and becoming one with her, instead of becoming one with God], and the merchants of the earth are waxed rich through the abundance of her delicacies.

**18:4** And I heard another voice from heaven, saying, Come out of her, my people, that ye be not partakers of her sins, and that ye receive not of her plagues.

Brethren, this shows that God's people are partaking of the Babylonian Mysteries in this latter day! How? By following the Babylonian Mysteries idolatrous system of exalting men as idols above any zeal for keeping and living by every Word of God!

In today's Ekklesia we are committing the same sin and we are following the same false doctrine of the Babylonian Mysteries; we are following that doctrine of demons which teaches that we must follow someone other than the Husband of our baptismal espousal! That some man has ultimate moral authority on the earth!

**18:5** For her sins have reached unto heaven, and God hath remembered her iniquities. **18:6** Reward her even as she rewarded you, and double unto her double according to her works: in the cup which she hath filled fill to her double.

**18:7** How much she hath glorified herself, and lived deliciously, so much torment and sorrow give her: for she saith in her heart, I sit a queen, and am no widow, and shall see no sorrow.

**18:8** Therefore shall her plagues come in one day, death, and mourning, and famine; and she shall be utterly burned with fire: for strong is the Lord God who judgeth her.

The soon coming New European revival of Babylon is to become fabulously wealthy during the first part of the tribulation, and they shall mourn greatly when the Asian nations destroy her and then Christ [The Rock of Daniel 2] comes to totally destroy all that remains of her.

**18:9** And the kings of the earth, who have committed fornication and lived deliciously with her, shall bewail her, and lament for her, when they shall see the smoke of her burning, **18:10** Standing afar off for the fear of her torment, saying, Alas, alas that great city Babylon, that mighty city! for in one hour is thy judgment come.

**18:11** And the merchants of the earth shall weep and mourn over her; for no man buyeth their merchandise any more: **18:12** The merchandise of gold, and silver, and precious stones, and of pearls, and fine linen, and purple, and silk, and scarlet, and all thyine wood, and all manner vessels of ivory, and all manner vessels of most precious wood, and of brass, and iron, and marble,

**18:13** And cinnamon, and odours, and ointments, and frankincense, and wine, and oil, and fine flour, and wheat, and beasts, and sheep, and horses, and chariots, and slaves, and souls of men. **18:14** And the fruits that thy soul lusted after are departed from thee, and all things which were dainty and goodly are departed from thee, and thou shalt find them no more at all.

**18:15** The merchants of these things, which were made rich by her, shall stand afar off for the fear of her torment, weeping and wailing, **18:16** And saying, Alas, alas that great city, that was clothed in fine linen, and purple, and scarlet, and decked with gold, and precious stones, and pearls!

**18:17** For in one hour so great riches is come to nought. And every shipmaster, and all the company in ships, and sailors, and as many as trade by sea, stood afar off, **18:18** And cried when they saw the smoke of her burning, saying, What city is like unto this great city!

**18:19** And they cast dust on their heads, and cried, weeping and wailing, saying, Alas, alas that great city, wherein were made rich all that had ships in the sea by reason of her costliness! for in one hour is she made desolate.

**18:20 Rejoice over her, thou heaven, and ye holy apostles and prophets; for God hath avenged you on her.**

**18:21** And a mighty angel took up a stone like a great millstone, and cast it into the sea, saying, Thus with violence shall that great city Babylon be thrown down, and shall be found no more at all.

**18:22** And the voice of harpers, and musicians, and of pipers, and trumpeters, shall be heard no more at all in thee; and no craftsman, of whatsoever craft he be, shall be found any more in thee; and the sound of a millstone shall be heard no more at all in thee;

**18:23** And the light of a candle shall shine no more at all in thee; and the voice of the bridegroom and of the bride shall be heard no more at all in thee: for thy merchants were the great men of the earth; for by thy sorceries were all nations deceived.

**18:24** And in her was found the blood of prophets, and of saints, and of all that were slain upon the earth.

Then the chosen resurrected saints at the Father's banquet and their marriage feast in heaven will rejoice at the fall of the Babylonian Mysteries System, at the coming of the Kingdom of God and at the inheritance given to them to destroy and replace Babylon the Great!

# Revelation 19

**Revelation 19:1** And after these things I heard a great voice of **much people in heaven** [the resurrected chosen will go to heaven for the marriage feast before coming back to the earth (Rev 15, Rev 7:9)], saying, Alleluia; Salvation, and glory, and honour, and power, unto the Lord our God:

**19:2** For true and righteous are his judgments: for he hath judged the great whore, which did corrupt the earth with her fornication, and hath avenged the blood of his servants at her hand.

**19:3** And again they said, Alleluia And her smoke rose up for ever and ever.

**19:4** And the four and twenty elders and the four beasts [living beings] fell down and worshipped God that sat on the throne, saying, Amen; Alleluia.

**19:5** And a voice came out of the throne, saying, Praise our God, all ye his servants, and ye that fear him, both small and great.

**19:6** And I heard as it were the voice of a great multitude, and as the voice of many waters, and as the voice of mighty thunderings, saying, Alleluia: for the Lord God omnipotent reigneth.

After the resurrection of the chosen, Jesus Christ will take them to the Heavenly Temple for the Marriage of the Lamb, while the seven last plagues are poured out on the earth. Then after the wedding feast and the distribution of offices they will return to the earth for the final destruction of wickedness and the beginning of the Kingdom of God over all the earth.

**19:7** Let us be glad and rejoice, and give honour to him: **for the marriage of the Lamb is come, and his wife hath made herself ready.**

**19:8** And to her was granted that she should be arrayed in fine linen, clean and white: for the **fine linen is** [represents] **the righteousness of saints**.

**19:9** And he saith unto me, Write, Blessed are they which are called unto the marriage supper of the Lamb. And he saith unto me, These are the true sayings of God.

The angel then told John that the testimony of Jesus Christ [the proof that he dwells in us] is the Spirit of prophecy, the Spirit of the prophets [the indwelling of God's Holy Spirit which enables us to live by every Word of God]; which is the Holy Spirit of God.

**19:10** And I fell at his feet to worship him. And he said unto me, See thou do it not: I am thy fellowservant, and of thy brethren that have the testimony of Jesus [those who have the Spirit of God the Father and Jesus Christ in them]: worship God: for the testimony of Jesus is the spirit of prophecy.

Then Jesus Christ, the Husband of the collective spiritual bride, is revealed with his armies of resurrected saints as he makes ready to come to the earth to destroy Babylon the Great and to rule all nations.

**19:11 And I saw heaven opened, and behold a white horse; and he that sat upon him was called Faithful and True, and in righteousness he doth judge and make war.**

**19:12 His eyes were as a flame of fire, and on his head were many crowns; and he had a name written, that no man knew, but he himself.**

So much for the mainstream tolerant of sin, false Jesus, now being adopted by some in today's Ekklesia!

**19:13 And he was clothed with a vesture dipped in blood: and his name is called The Word of God.**

**19:14 And the armies** [**Jude 1:14** And Enoch also, the seventh from Adam, prophesied of these, saying, Behold, **the Lord cometh with ten thousands of his saints,**] **which were in heaven followed him upon white horses, clothed in fine linen, white and clean.**

**19:15** And out of his mouth goeth a sharp sword, that with it he should smite the nations: and he shall rule them with a rod of iron: and he treadeth the winepress of the fierceness and wrath of Almighty God [Zech 14].

**19:16** And he hath on his vesture and on his thigh a name written, KING OF KINGS, AND LORD OF LORDS.

Those who resist Christ in the massive armies gathered and fighting at Jerusalem will perish and become carrion for scavenger birds and animals.

**19:17** And I saw an angel standing in the sun; and he cried with a loud voice, saying to all the fowls that fly in the midst of heaven, Come and gather yourselves together unto the supper of the great God;

**19:18** That ye may eat the flesh of kings, and the flesh of captains, and the flesh of mighty men, and the flesh of horses, and of them that sit on them, and the flesh of all men, both free and bond, both small and great.

It would appear that when Christ comes, both the armies of Asia and the army of the New Europe will turn to fight Messiah the Christ as he sets foot on the Mount of Olives.

**19:19** And I saw **the beast** [the New Europe]**,** and **the kings of the earth, a**nd their armies [the Asian armies], gathered together to make war against him that sat on the horse, and against his army [of the resurrected chosen].

**19:20** And **the beast** [the political leader of the New Europe] **was taken, and with him the false prophet** [the eighth beast] that wrought miracles before him, with which he deceived them that had received the mark of the beast, and them that worshipped his image. **These both were cast alive into a lake of fire burning with brimstone.**

**19:21** And the remnant [of the armies gathered at Jerusalem] were slain with the sword of him that sat upon the horse, which sword proceeded out of his mouth [the command of Christ to destroy them]: and all the fowls were filled with their flesh.

## Revelation 20

Immediately after Christ and the resurrected chosen return to the earth, they will round up Satan and his demons, defeat the opposing armies and they will cast the political and religious leaders of the Babylonian Mysteries Holy Roman Empire system into the fire, burning them alive as a graphic example for all peoples concerning the end of those who refuse to sincerely repent and refuse to live by every Word of God.

The false teaching of a wimpy Jesus who winks at and tolerates willful sin: Is a Ridiculous Doctrine of Demons!

At that same time, just as the kingdom of God is ready to be established, Satan the Adversary and his spirits are to be bound up for a thousand years; and the earth will enjoy a millennial Sabbath of rest from his deceptions and wickedness! This millennial Sabbath of rest is represented by the seventh and High Holy Day of the Feast of Unleavened Bread.

**Revelation 20:1** And I saw an angel come down from heaven, having the key of the bottomless pit and a great chain in his hand. **20:2** And he laid hold on the dragon, that old serpent, which is the Devil, and Satan, and **bound him a thousand years,**

**20:3** And cast him into the bottomless pit, and shut him up, and set a seal [locked up the door of his detention] upon him, that **he should deceive the**

**nations no more, till the thousand years should be fulfilled: and after that he must be loosed a little season.**

For the details of Satan's release and see: 101: From Pentecost to Trumpets and Satan's Release

**20:4** And I saw thrones, and they [the resurrected chosen] sat upon them, and judgment [authority to teach and enforce the Word of God as kings and priests] was given unto them: and I saw the souls of them that were **beheaded** [martyred] **for the witness of Jesus, and for the word of God,** and which had not worshipped the beast, neither his image, neither had received his mark upon their foreheads, or in their hands; and **they lived and reigned with Christ a thousand years.**

Those who rule well during the millennium will also reign with Christ in positions of leadership forever.

There will be no other resurrections of the dead during the millennium, from the resurrection of the chosen as the seventh trump begins to sound, until after the end of the millennium when the main fall harvest of Tabernacles resurrections come.

Those living into the millennium could be changed to spirit or destroyed when they reach 100 years old; the same as those resurrected to flesh during the main harvest.

> **Isaiah 65:19** And I will rejoice in Jerusalem, and joy in my people: and the voice of weeping shall be no more heard in her, nor the voice of crying.
>
> **65:20** There shall be no more thence an infant of days, nor an old man that hath not filled his days: for **the child shall die an hundred years old; but the sinner being an hundred years old shall be accursed.**

**Revelation 20:5** But **the rest of the dead lived not again until the thousand years were finished.** This is the first resurrection.

**20:6** Blessed and holy is he that hath part in the first resurrection: on such the second death hath no power, but **they shall be priests of God and of Christ, and shall reign with him a thousand years.**

Satan will be released after the thousand year millennial Sabbath of rest from his deceptions and given one last chance to repent. Instead he will again deceive millions into following him away from God.

**20:7** And when the thousand years are expired, Satan shall be loosed out of his prison,

Ezekiel 38-39 will be partially fulfilled when the nations of Asia come up against Jerusalem the first time just at the coming of Messiah the Christ; and after the millennium Ezekiel 38 - 39 will be fulfilled in its fullness.

**20:8** And shall go out to deceive the nations which are in the four quarters of the earth, Gog, and Magog [the nations of Asia], to gather them together to battle: the number of whom is as the sand of the sea.

**20:9** And they went up on the breadth of the earth, and compassed the camp of the saints about, and the beloved city: and fire came down from God out of heaven, and devoured them.

In King James time torture was a common practice in deciding a judgment, therefore the word "judged" is here rendered "tormented." The sense of the meaning is that Satan has been judged finally and eternally forever, and shall be destroyed never to rise up again.

This is a reference to Satan having been previously restrained and then released, and refers to the seven revivals of the Holy Roman Empire of Satan; God is reassuring us that Satan has been eternally judged and will never return again.

**20:10** And the devil that deceived them was cast into the lake of fire and brimstone, where the beast and the false prophet are [the word "are" was added by the translators according to their bias, and should have been rendered "were"], and shall be tormented [judged and condemned to eternal destruction, never to rise again] day and night for ever and ever.

Brethren, I have absolutely no doubt that the vast majority of people and religious people sincerely think that they are pleasing God and doing God a service in all that they do. Satan has deceived the whole world and once he is removed this world will be a far better place.

Then after the millennium comes the main harvest of the dead during the seven thousand years represented by the Feast of the Ingathering of Nations [the Feast of Tabernacles].

**20:11** And I saw a great white throne, and him that sat on it, from whose face the earth and the heaven fled away; and there was found no place for them.

**20:12** And I saw the dead, small and great, stand before God; and the books were opened: and another book was opened, which is the book of life: and **the dead were judged out of those things which were written in the books, according to their works.**

**20:13** And the sea gave up the dead which were in it; and death and hell delivered up the dead which were in them: and **they were judged every man according to their works.**

Do not believe the lies being spread in the Ekklesia today!

Jesus is NOT some weak "tolerate anything" being; he is the Mighty One who destroyed the whole earth for the wickedness of men during the life of Noah!

The Son is zealous to live by EVERY WORD of God the Father! All those who refuse to live by EVERY WORD of God; all who say that Jesus is love and will wink at our willful self justified sins: Shall be burned alive in the fire.

**20:14** And death and hell were cast into the lake of fire. This is the second death.

**20:15** And whosoever was not found written in the book of life was cast into the lake of fire.

## Revelation 21

After the millennial Sabbath of rest, and after the Feast of Tabernacles main harvest of humanity; the earth is to be destroyed by fire.

> **2 Peter 3:7** But **the heavens and the earth, which are now, by the same word are kept in store, reserved unto fire against the day of judgment and perdition of ungodly men**.
>
> **3:8** But, beloved, be not ignorant of this one thing, that **one day is with the Lord as a thousand years, and a thousand years as one day.**
>
> **3:9** The Lord is not slack concerning his promise, as some men count slackness; but is longsuffering to us-ward, not willing that any should perish, but [God wants all to come to sincere repentance and be brought into the Family of God after which all wickedness will be destroyed along with the earth and its atmosphere.] that all should come to repentance.

Here, Peter uses the term "Day of the Lord" in reference to the complete destruction of the earth and all wickedness, after the fist resurrection to spirit and the millennium and after the main harvest of humanity.

**3:10** But the day of the Lord will come as a thief in the night; **in the which the heavens shall pass away with a great noise, and the elements shall melt with fervent heat, the earth also and the works that are therein shall be burned up.**

If God will destroy all wicked men who will not live by EVERY WORD of God, and will destroy the whole earth, its seas and its atmosphere: WHY should we then live by our own ways? or will we turn to live by EVERY WORD of God; wherein is life eternal?

**3:11** Seeing then that all these things shall be dissolved, what manner of persons ought ye to be in all holy conversation [conduct] and godliness,

**3:12** Looking for and hasting unto **the coming of the day of God, wherein the heavens being on fire shall be dissolved, and the elements shall melt with fervent heat?**

**3:13** Nevertheless we, according to his promise, **look for new heavens and a new earth, wherein dwelleth righteousness.**

**3:14** Wherefore, beloved, seeing that ye look for such things, be diligent that ye may be found of him in peace [that we may be at peace with God and reconciled to God and living by every Word of God], without spot [with no spot of sin], and blameless [without any sin].

**The Feast of the Eighth Day**

A New Beginning with all wickedness including Satan himself with his spirits and every person who does not live by EVERY WORD of God; DESTROYED by fire!

God the Father himself coming down to live with his redeemed children on a new planet now cleansed by fire and recreated pure from all evil; and God and humanity going forward into eternity in the peace and prosperity that living by Every Word of God brings!

**Revelation 21:1** And I saw **a new heaven and a new earth: for the first heaven and the first earth were passed away;** and there was no more sea.

**21:2** And I John saw **the holy city, new Jerusalem, coming down from God out of heaven**, prepared as a bride adorned for her husband.

**21:3** And I heard a great voice out of heaven saying, **Behold, the tabernacle of God is with men, and he will dwell with them, and they**

shall be his people, and God himself shall be with them, and be their God.

**The Wondrous Meaning of the Feast of the Eighth Day!**

No more suffering or tears of pain. All people at peace with and united with God and therefore at peace with and united with all others who are united with God!

The way to peace, is for the ultimate deceiver to be removed and the truth and the true way to peace made available to all.

The longing of humanity is for a peace that people cannot achieve without the wisdom of God. Real peace is not imaginary; IT IS COMING!

**21:4** And **God shall wipe away all tears from their eyes; and there shall be no more death, neither sorrow, nor crying, neither shall there be any more pain: for the former things are passed away.**

**21:5** And he that sat upon the throne said, **Behold, I make all things new**. And he said unto me, Write: for these words are true and faithful.

**21:6** And he said unto me, It is done. I am Alpha and Omega, the beginning and the end. **I will give unto him that is athirst of the fountain of the water of life** [the Holy Spirit of God] **freely.**

**21:7** He that overcometh [through learning and living by Every Word of God] shall inherit all things [the entire universe is included in the term "All Things"]; and I **will be his God, and he shall be my son.**

Those who think they can sin with impunity will be destroyed for the good of the whole; so that they do not damage the peace of others. It is an ignorant and foolish person who claims to be godly and justifies his sins claiming that God is love and will overlook our willful sins.

It is because God is love that he will NOT overlook our sins! Because our sins hurt ourselves and they hurt others; and God loves ALL people! Almighty God will not permit any self-justifying willful sinner who harms his other children to enter his eternal spiritual family!

**21:8** But the fearful [those who are too afraid of men to follow and obey God], and unbelieving [those who will not believe that we must stop sinning], and the abominable [the self-justifying willful perpetrators of any sin are an abomination to God], and murderers, and whoremongers [spiritually those who follow other gods and are not loyal to the Eternal], and sorcerers [consorters with evil spirits], and idolaters [as in making idols of men and corporate organizations to exalt their words above the

Word of God], and all liars [including those who tell partial truths to deceive], shall have their part in the lake which burneth with fire and brimstone: which is the second death.

Those who say that we should not expose and condemn sin: Hear the Word of the Lord:

> **Isaiah 58:1** Cry aloud, spare not, lift up thy voice like a trumpet, and shew my people their transgression, and the house of Jacob their sins.
>
> **Leviticus 19:17** Thou shalt not hate thy brother in thine heart: thou shalt in any wise rebuke thy neighbour, and not suffer sin upon him.

The resurrected chosen will be the collective bride of the Lamb and they are faithful to God and Jesus Christ who will rule the universe from the New Jerusalem. The New Jerusalem where God dwells, is a type of the bride who dwells with her Husband and His Father.

**Revelation 21:9** And there came unto me one of the seven angels which had the seven vials full of the seven last plagues, and talked with me, saying, Come hither, I will shew thee the bride, the Lamb's wife.

**21:10** And he carried me away in the spirit to a great and high mountain, and shewed me that great city, the holy Jerusalem, descending out of heaven from God,

**21:11** Having the glory of God: and her light was like unto a stone most precious, even like a jasper stone, clear as crystal;

**21:12** And had a wall great and high, and had **twelve gates**, and at the gates twelve angels, and names written thereon, which are **the names of the twelve tribes of the children of Israel:**

**21:13** On the east three gates; on the north three gates; on the south three gates; and on the west three gates.

**21:14** And the wall of the city had **twelve foundations, and in them the names of the twelve apostles of the Lamb.**

**21:15** And he that talked with me had a golden reed to measure the city, and the gates thereof, and the wall thereof.

A furlong being 1/8 of a mile making the city a 1,500 mile cube.

**21:16** And the city lieth foursquare, and the length is as large as the breadth: and he measured the city with the reed, twelve thousand furlongs. The length and the breadth and the height of it are equal.

**21:17** And he measured the wall thereof, an hundred and forty and four cubits, according to the measure of a man, that is, of the angel. **21:18** And the building of **the wall of it was of jasper**: and **the city was pure gold, like unto clear glass.**

The foundations of the walls are made of the gems representing each tribe of Israel.

**21:19** And the foundations of **the wall** of the city were garnished with all manner of precious stones. The first foundation was jasper; the second, sapphire; the third, a chalcedony; the fourth, an emerald;

**21:20** The fifth, sardonyx; the sixth, sardius; the seventh, chrysolyte; the eighth, beryl; the ninth, a topaz; the tenth, a chrysoprasus; the eleventh, a jacinth; the twelfth, an amethyst.

**21:21** And the twelve gates were twelve pearls: every several gate was of one pearl: and **the street of the city was pure gold, as it were transparent glass.**

**21:22** And I saw no temple therein: for the Lord God Almighty and the Lamb are the temple of it.

**21:23** And the city had **no need** of the sun, neither of the moon, to shine in it: for the glory of God did lighten it, and the Lamb is the light thereof.

This does not mean that there will no longer be a sun and moon, only that the light of God will fill the earth so that there will be no need for light from the sun and moon.

**21:24** And the nations of them which are saved shall walk in the light of it: and the kings of the earth do bring their glory and honour into it.

> **1 John 1:5** This then is the message which we have heard of him, and declare unto you, that **God is light, and in him is no darkness at all.**

**Revelation 21:25** And the gates of it shall not be shut at all by day: for there shall be no night there.

**21:26** And they shall bring the glory and honour of the nations into it.

No one who justifies willful sin shall ever enter into eternal life and the City of God.

**21:27** And **there shall in no wise enter into it any thing that defileth, neither whatsoever worketh abomination, or maketh a lie**: but they which are written in the Lamb's book of life.

## Revelation 22

The river of water of life coming out from the throne of God is a picture of the Holy Spirit of life eternal, flowing out from God.

**Revelation 22:1** And he shewed me a pure river of **water of life**, clear as crystal, proceeding out of the throne of God and of the Lamb.

The tree of life nourished by the water; as a type of eternal life coming from the Holy Spirit and the keeping of the whole Word of God bringing forth the tree of life bearing the fruits of the Spirit of God. The leaves which give life to a tree are represented as giving spiritual healing [eternal salvation] to the nations.

**22:2** In the **midst of the street** of it, and on either side of the river, was there the tree of life [overspreading to both sides is the tree of eternal life], which bare twelve manner of fruits [figurative of the fruits of the Holy Spirit], and yielded her fruit every month [the trees bore a new kind of fruit each month]: and the leaves of the tree were for the [spiritual] healing of the nations.

A natural tree has a trunk representing Jesus Christ and branches representing the faithful who are in Christ. It would also have leaves which turn the light of the sun into energy giving strength and life to the whole tree. The leaves would therefore represent the Holy Spirit which takes in the LIGHT [every Word of God] of God and turns it into spiritual energy, pouring spiritual health and life through the branches and producing the fruits of the Holy Spirit and healing the nations. See The Tree of Life article.

**22:3** And there shall be no more curse [sin or the decay and death that sin brings]: but the throne of God and of the Lamb shall be in it; and his servants shall serve him:

**22:4** And they [the people now changed to spirit] shall see his face; and his name shall be in their foreheads [the nature of God will dwell in the minds of all people who are changed to spirit; absolutely no sin allowed].

**22:5** And there shall be no night there; and they need no candle, neither light of the sun; for the Lord God giveth them light: and **they** [the chosen and changed] **shall reign for ever and ever.**

**22:6** And he said unto me, These sayings are faithful and true: and the Lord God of the holy prophets sent his angel to shew unto his servants the things which must shortly be done.

The saying "I come quickly" is addressed to those in the later day, when knowledge and understanding shall be increased, and the wise shall receive an understanding of these things (Dan 12). The blessing on those who "keep the sayings of the book" is a blessing on those who keep the instructions to "Live by EVERY WORD of God."

**22:7** Behold, I come quickly: **blessed is he that keepeth the sayings of the prophecy of this book.**

**22:8** And I John saw these things, and heard them. And when I had heard and seen, I fell down to worship before the feet of the angel which shewed me these things.

We are to worship [exalt and obey in moral matters] no man, no not an angel from heaven; we are to worship [exalt and obey] God alone.

**22:9** Then saith he unto me, See thou do it not: for I am thy fellowservant, and of thy brethren the prophets, and of them which keep the sayings of this book: **worship God**.

Today, at this latter day; these things are being unsealed because the time is at hand.

**22:10** And he saith unto me, Seal not the sayings of the prophecy of this book: for the time is at hand.

This does not mean that God does not want the wicked and unjust to repent, rather it means that after having been given every opportunity the time for judgment is at hand.

**22:11** He that is unjust, let him be unjust still: and he which is filthy, let him be filthy still: and he that is righteous, let him be righteous still: and he that is holy, let him be holy still.

Those who live by every Word of God shall have a good reward and those who justify sin shall receive strong and bitter correction, and if they still will not sincerely repent they shall be cast into the fire of eternal destruction.

**22:12** And, behold, I come quickly; and **my reward is with me, to give every man according as his work shall be.**

**22:13** I am Alpha and Omega, the beginning and the end, the first and the last.

Jesus Christ existed at the beginning before the creation of men; and he will exist forever!

**22:14 Blessed are they that do his commandments, that they may have right to the tree of life, and may enter in through the gates into the city** [enter into eternal life].

**22:15** For without are dogs [dogs follow other dogs in packs, picturing men with a group instinct following the crowd and exalting idols of men], and sorcerers, and whoremongers, and murderers, and idolaters [today the Ekklesia has had a great falling away into idolatry of men], and whosoever loveth and maketh a lie.

**22:16** I Jesus have sent mine angel to testify unto you these things in the churches. I am the root [the beginning of, the Father of, by virtue of creating] and the offspring of David, and the bright and morning star.

A call to sincerely repent and come to live by every Word of God.

**22:17** And the Spirit and the bride say, Come. And let him that heareth say, Come. And let him that is athirst come. And whosoever will, let him take the water of life freely.

**22:18** For I testify unto every man that heareth the words of the prophecy of this book, If any man shall add unto these things, God shall add unto him the plagues that are written in this book:

**22:19** And if any man shall take away from the words of the book of this prophecy, God shall take away his part out of the book of life, and out of the holy city, and from the things which are written in this book.

**22:20** He which testifieth these things saith, Surely I come quickly. Amen. Even so, come, Lord Jesus.

**22:21** The grace of our Lord Jesus Christ be with you all. Amen.

### Visit Our Website
theshininglight.info

www.ingramcontent.com/pod-product-compliance
Lightning Source LLC
Chambersburg PA
CBHW081210230426
43666CB00015B/2698